ex
with love from
Stephen
4. xii. 97

The Faith of the Managers

WHEN MANAGEMENT BECOMES RELIGION

STEPHEN PATTISON

CASSELL

London and Washington

In memory of
Kieron Walsh

Cassell
Wellington House
125 Strand
London WC2R 0BB

PO Box 605
Herndon, VA 20172

First published 1997

British Library Cataloguing-in-Publication Data
A catalogue record for this book is available from the British Library.

ISBN 0–304–70144–0

Typeset by York House Typographic Limited, London.
Printed and bound in Great Britain by Redwood Books,
Trowbridge, Wiltshire.

Contents

Preface

A number of people have helped in the production of this book. Andrew Wall and James Woodward both patiently read drafts and the book is sharper as a result of their incisive criticism. One of my collaborators, Rob Paton, encouraged me to develop my work and make it more widely available, while Michael Walsh at Cassell offered me an opportunity to do this. Clearly, I am responsible for the final result, but I hope each of the above will feel that their considerable efforts have been worthwhile. I thank them all for their help.

This book is dedicated to the memory of Kieron Walsh who was Professor of Public Service Management at the University of Birmingham until his tragically early death at the age of 46 in 1995. Kieron started life as a Catholic seminarian and, though robustly agnostic by the time I became his student in 1989, he encouraged me to take a sideways look at management as religion. That is really where this book started, and Kieron and I continued to have fragmentary conversations about this approach until the time he died. Indeed, just a week before his death I received his draft of the joint paper that we had always been meaning to write together on this topic. I have incorporated some of the shrewd insights from that paper (which, sadly, was not anywhere near being ready for publication) into this book. It is a very inadequate tribute to a man who was not only a fine thinker with a polymathic range of interests (including refuse collection and medieval mystical theology!) but a truly great, encouraging teacher and a good friend.

One of Kieron's close colleagues, Vivien Lowndes, has written: 'As well as being a natural intellectual and a natural teacher, Kieron was a natural leader – and it is for these qualities that we miss him, every day.' I remember with gratitude the stimulus he gave me.

Grateful acknowledgement is made to the following journals and publishers for permission to use material written by the author and first published in earlier versions by them:

Contact: The Interdisciplinary Journal of Pastoral Studies
Crucible
Health Care Analysis (published by John Wiley and Sons)
The Health Service Journal (published by Macmillan)
Iconoclastic Papers
Local Government Studies (published by Frank Cass)
Modern Believing

Introduction: Mystical management

The church of San Clemente, near the Colosseum in Rome, looks unremarkable from the sunny street outside. Once you go inside, however, this impression changes. At street level, you find yourself standing inside a beautiful but modest twelfth-century basilica. This in turn is built upon the foundations of a fourth-century church that can be visited by going down some stairs. And beneath this fourth-century Christian structure, 60 feet below street level and far removed from the glaring sunlight of the outside world, is a gloomy room that served as a Mithraic temple. Here those who had passed through seven stages of initiation into the mystery cult of Mithras, mostly soldiers, sacrificed bulls and practised their religion. Even now, not much is known about the content of this cult, or the men who belonged to it. It is and was a mystery.

In some ways, *The Faith of the Managers* is like a visit to San Clemente. The book argues that within and beneath the everyday practice of management lie hidden religio-ethical assumptions that mostly go unnoticed by the casual observer. Just because they are unnoticed does not mean that they are not important or influential – indeed, some of the foundations of management may rest upon them. Critical approaches and perspectives from many disciplines have been fruitfully applied to the understanding of management. In this volume, readers are invited to apply the lens of religio-ethical understanding and critique to this activity in the hope that this will be illuminating.

There are some superficial similarities between Mithraism and modern management such as a penchant for men meeting in little rooms, being secretive and giving much emphasis to the virtues of loyalty, obedience and fidelity. In the present context, however, management may be thought of as mystical in two main senses. In the first place, it is mysterious and surrounds itself with a certain mystique. Although the practices and language of management are all around us, very few members of the public actually understand what management is or

1

does. It has the qualities of another world, somewhat secretive, esoteric and enclosed, understood only by initiates, and suspected, perhaps even feared, by those who feel themselves to be outside it.

Related to the idea of management as mystique is the sense of management as a kind of religion – a set of ideas, rituals, practices and words, not necessarily internally consistent, empirically verifiable or rationally based, that provide a total world view and way of life that binds existence and organizations together and shapes people, purposes and actions in a fundamental way. It is this twofold perception of management as mystical that provides the broad framework for this book. *The Faith of the Managers* is a critical archaeology of management as, in some ways, a religious movement.

The aim of this book

Although management is of growing importance in most spheres of life, and books about it proliferate, it is not well understood or popular amongst the general population. *The Faith of the Managers* aims to dispel some of the lack of understanding and indifference towards management. It will encourage managers and all those whose lives are affected by management to take a critical look at an activity which is increasingly central to all organizations and societies. This will be done by subjecting some of the theories and practices of management to a critique that particularly emphasizes the religio-ethical aspects of management. The critique is conducted from a 'worm's eye' perspective.

Management often tries to present itself as a solid, scientific, rational activity that is concerned with such unquestionable realities as the economic bottom line. Here, however, I want to suggest that management can usefully and credibly be seen as a kind of implicit religion with particular doctrines, rituals, practices and ethics that form a real faith system. Although management has no official deity of a traditional, metaphysical kind, it is laden with the kinds of faith presuppositions, irrationalities, paradoxes and symbols that are often directly associated with religions. Like Christianity, management may be regarded as a set of principles, faith assumptions and theories enacted in practice. Indeed, it is possible to argue that modern management has many of the characteristics and assumptions of a radical Christian sect. It could even be seen as a kind of Christian heresy in its beliefs and assumptions about the world. Identifying and examining some of the religious features and elements implicit in management will bring new critical light to bear upon it. This should be illuminating and empowering for managers and critics alike.

Drawing out the moral dimensions and assumptions of some aspects of managerial theory and practice also casts management in a new light. Like most religions or religious movements, management provides a powerful moral and value perspective on life and work. Furthermore, management techniques and theories have important effects, for good and for ill, upon people, organizations and societies. If management can be seen as having substantial moral roots and effects, it is important that these are recognized so they can be oriented towards human well-being as far as possible. To maximize the possibilities of doing this, a perspective that allows critical distance is required. This should help managers and those who are managed to use appropriate theories and practices rather than the theories and practices using them.

The Faith of the Managers takes a sideways look at some aspects of managerial theory and practice from the perspective of an author who has been more managed than managing. As in most religions, the perspective of those who do not run the cult is often not attended to or taken notice of; the 'worm's eye' view is missing. Having studied management in its literary purity and personally experienced its messy practical outworkings, it seems appropriate to introduce this missing vantage point here.

Managers and those who are managed need to have a grip on management as a tool, rather than simply inhabiting a set of beliefs and practices that cannot be questioned. By seeing much of modern management as in some ways a profoundly religious and ethical activity that looks different to those who are managed rather than managing, I hope to place it in a new light. Management is deified by some and demonized by others. Subjecting it to a partial critique that emphasizes religious and ethical features should help both protagonists and detractors to see management for what it is – a human activity with strengths, weaknesses, possibilities and pitfalls.

In writing this book, I hope to encourage managers themselves to become more realistic, critical and articulate about some of the potential, limits and implications of their activity. Those who are not managers or who are contemplating introducing management into their organizations should also gain a critical perspective on an activity that can be harmful as well as helpful. Management is far too significant to be left only to its self-proclaimed defenders and practitioners. We need good, effective managers whose role is understood and respected by their fellow workers and citizens. Insofar as this book aids understanding and dispels fogs of mystical gloom it may be seen as a contribution towards responsible debate and dialogue about the nature of management in society today. It may help to promote responsive, self-critical management that promotes human well-being and lives up to its own best ideals and principles.

The background to this book

At my primary school one day, about 30 years ago, the teacher asked each member of the class what our fathers did for a living. In those days of (relatively) full male employment, my schoolfellows proudly volunteered that their fathers were doctors, builders, decorators, salesmen, council officials or policemen. As far as I can remember, I was the only person in the class who had to say that his father was a manager. Even I did not really understand what a manager was or did, though I knew that it had something to do with business – basically, my father ran a shop.

Being a manager of any kind in Britain in the 1960s was relatively rare and lacked social influence or cachet. Professionals and trained craftspeople occupied the heights of the occupational ladder. It seemed inconceivable at that time that managers and management would ever have the prominence that they have in most social institutions today. Managers and management have proliferated in organizations of all kinds, not only in the private sector, but also in voluntary organizations and charities, and in public-sector institutions such as universities, local authorities and the National Health Service (NHS). There seems to have been some sort of revolution that has turned managers into the rather improbable cultural heroes of our times.

I first realized the size and extent of this revolution when, in 1990, as an NHS employee, I noticed that one of the very few men's toilets had been removed from the entrance of our local children's hospital. This allowed one of the burgeoning cadre of new managers to have a tiny office. In a building that was desperately short of space for clinical activity, this really was radical change, and a symbolic as well as physical statement about priorities.

In the 30 years between shamefacedly admitting to having a father who was a manager and seeing the change of use of the toilet space in the hospital, a lot happened to me. I went to university and studied theology and religion. I did research in ethics and practical theology and was a hospital chaplain. In due course, I taught theology at a university, then became an administrator for an organization called a Community Health Council which tried to represent the views and interests of patients in the NHS. This was in 1988, some years after general management had been introduced into the NHS. The implications of this change were just working their way through, receiving a powerful boost in 1990 when quasi-markets and business methods were used to restructure health and community care services in government reforms. In 1989, I enrolled on a public-sector management degree to try and understand the environment in which I was working and the changes that were coming about. The next year I was made redundant from the health service due to changes in the boundaries between local health authorities. At this point I joined the Open University which, in common with other universities, was just introducing management reforms and mechanisms such as staff appraisal, five-year planning and change management. It is from this very mixed personal background and experience, academic and other, that this book arises.

The Faith of the Managers emerges from three basic personal perceptions acquired from my interaction with the theory and practice of management.

As a theologian I was trained to recognize and analyse systems of belief. It was not long after I initially encountered management that I began to realize that this activity had many of the features of symbolism, ritual, irrationality and faith that traditionally accompany religious activity. This led me to the first critical perception that underlies this book: management is a kind of religion, or at least has very substantial religious analogies and connotations.

As an ethicist, I realized that management theory and practice is laden with basic moral values and practices which shape a vision of the world and what it is to be human. Furthermore, the exercise of management has substantial moral and ethical effects, both intended and unintended, within and outside organizations. This led to the perception that management is a profoundly moral and ethical activity at a level much more basic than that of simply asking questions about how it is expedient to act which has characterized much of business ethics.

As an organizational member, I have had managerial responsibilities from time to time, but I have mostly experienced management from 'below'. Most of the people who talk and theorize about management are themselves either managers or consultants who see the world from a managerial perspective. This brings me to my final undergirding perception, namely that there is a distinct absence of writing and thinking about management from the viewpoint of those who are managed rather than managers. For some reason, even managers who have been managed (i.e. most managers) do not tend to discuss this experience or see it as an important source of knowledge and learning. Management theory is, therefore, very one-sided. It largely ignores the views and perceptions of most of the people who actually have to live with managerial practices.

The need to reflect upon management as in some ways a significantly religious and moral activity which may look different to those who are managed from the way it looks to those who manage or theorize about management has led me to construct what might be described as a religio-ethical critique of management from a worm's eye perspective.

Perhaps this will sound more intelligible if I paraphrase it by describing
the book as 'what a theologian and ethicist who is not a senior manager
notices and worries about upon encountering management theory and
practice'. In the pages that follow, I will construct a critical evaluation of
management as I have experienced or learned about it which rests
particularly, but not exclusively, upon these important but often
ignored perceptions.

The nature of this book

The Faith of the Managers is a set of reflections that are intended to raise
questions about the fundamental nature and practice of management.
The approach adopted is at all times partial and selective. Readers will
not find all the topics and approaches that could usefully be considered
or discussed in a critical book about management herein, much less a
management textbook.

Because my interest has been mainly in the public and voluntary
sectors, most of the concerns and examples used come from that
context. Although the systematic adoption of managerial practices has
come only relatively recently into the non-profit sector, it is a good
vantage point from which to assay the character, strengths and weaknesses of management in general. It is, perhaps, easier to see the main
characteristics of a particular set of theories and practices when they are
introduced into a new context in which people have consciously to
adopt and adapt them.

The book is not a theological work written for people who are
religious believers or thinkers. Management can be regarded as a kind
of religion. It may be in some ways heavily influenced in its practice and
theories by Christianity. Because this appears to be the case, it seems
valid and useful to use some critical Christian theological categories
and insights for analytic purposes. However, this does not demand of
readers any knowledge of, or sympathy with, Christian theology or
religious practice. All that is required is provisional assent to the notion
that theological and religious analytical categories might be as illuminating in looking at managerial ideas and activities as categories drawn
from other kinds of discourse such as anthropology, economics, politics
or sociology. 'Theology' is often used as a euphemism for words that
are idealistic, unreal or fanciful. Theology can, however, be a critical,
questioning, academic discipline that clarifies the nature of belief and
clears up misunderstandings, half-truths and deceptions.[1] In due
course, it will be possible for each reader to evaluate the usefulness of a
loosely theological perspective.

The Faith of the Managers is not a narrowly academic book in terms of its style, coverage or anticipated audience. It is designed to reach and stimulate all those who are affected by management. In the text which follows, I will occasionally show myself to be partial, polemical, select-ive and opinionated – cardinal sins within the academic world. Following in the steps of many managerial theorists, I shall be un-ashamedly anecdotal at times, brazenly extrapolating from my own experiences and making no attempt to present these as scientifically collected data. In this context, I would argue that even one person's individual experience or observation is evidence of a kind – even if it is not typical or universal. None of which means that matters of truth, fact, evidence, universality and argument are unimportant. In the interests of generating interest and debate, a partial, polemical approach may elicit more active thought and clarity about issues than would the more moderate approach usually associated with the word 'academic'.

I hope this will not be perceived as 'another manager-bashing book'. Managers often have a bad press, particularly in the public and volun-tary sectors.[2] They are more likely to be ridiculed or vilified than praised and admired. When government, for example, wants to make itself popular as anti-bureaucratic in its thrust, it often turns on the managers who have actually been appointed and fostered by govern-ment policy as the butt of its discontents – 'Too many men in grey suits in the Health Service' is a popular gambit when elections come round and resources for providing health care seem inadequate. Academics, too, are prone to denigrating or lampooning managers, forgetting that academic life has follies of its own.

Management is an important and necessary function in the modern world. No organization that is in any sense organized can do without some kind of management function, and it is unhelpful and unrealistic to hope that management will go away or can be dispensed with. Rather, management needs to be improved and made more effective. This might be expedited in part by helping both managers and the managed to become more self-consciously aware and articulate about the nature of this activity and the assumptions upon which it rests. It is to this end that this particular work aims to contribute.

Recognizing the inevitability and desirability of management does not, however, require a strategy of unalloyed, uncritical admiration. While trying to be fair and evaluative in my approach to management and managers, I do not assume that management is basically an uncontroversial good that is simply a set of 'innocent' techniques. There are quite enough paid apologists for management for it to seem legit-imate for me to point up the sometimes baleful, unhelpful implications of this activity.

The shape and contents of the book

The main, but not exclusive, framing analytic perspectives for this book are those of religion, ethics and values, and the view from below. None of these perspectives will be slavishly pursued at all points, however. Sometimes one will be more apparent than another. Often they will be combined together. Some of the time, they may not be present at all in any overt way. Each chapter has a good deal of critical material constructed from a wide variety of sources and perspectives.

The first three chapters of the book provide introductory material of different kinds. They can easily be omitted or returned to by readers who would prefer to move more directly into the issue-focused critique that starts in Chapter 4. Indeed, this might be as good a way of reading the book as starting from the beginning and working straight through to the end.

Chapter 1 provides background for the whole book. It outlines the history, context and tasks of management. Because the main example to be used to assay the nature of management in the rest of the book is that of the British public sector, the introduction of management, its implementation, practice and problems in that sector are then considered. This opens up the way for a discussion of management as a religious-type phenomenon in the next two chapters. After examining the nature and definition of religion generally, Chapter 2 advances the hypothesis that management can be seen as a religion, indeed in many ways a charismatic, fundamentalist kind of religious sect, drawing on evidence about its faith assumptions, its style, its faith content and its use of religious language, some of it apparently drawn directly from the Christian tradition. This gives way, in Chapter 3, to examination of the historical and other factors that might help to explain the religious nature of management. The question then arises, given that management appears to have significant faith and religious dimensions to it, what can usefully be done with these? The positive suggestion made here is that, rather than denying the reality of the religious nature of management, there is a need for managerial theorists and practitioners to come to terms with this by becoming much more self-consciously 'theologians' of management. The alternative to this is a kind of uncritical fundamentalism that is often to be found within the theory and practice of management.

Subsequent chapters continue to pursue the religio-ethical dimensions of management, but in relation to more specific topics. They can basically be read in any order, and on their own if desired. Chapter 4, 'Words and worlds', examines the words that are used in popular managerial discourse or 'managementspeak' to enquire into their functions. Thereafter, metaphors and specifically religious metaphors that are found within the discourse of management are subjected to critique. Words help to shape the world in which organizations and individuals function and so it is important to be conscious and critical of the way in which they are used if they are to be creative and helpful. Following this, the idealizing, perfectionist tendencies of much contemporary management theory, manifested in techniques such as Total Quality Management, are examined and their implications are assayed in Chapter 5.

Chapter 6 then considers dualistic, exclusivist aspects of management. Management has a tendency to focus very effectively on certain important issues. Unfortunately, its very clarity actually means that certain other important factors are downgraded in importance or ignored altogether. A sense of purpose, optimism and 'organizational goodness' is bought at a considerable price. This kind of perception is developed further in Chapter 7 where the virtues and values that inform managers and the moral community that is the organization are scrutinized. Within this context, systems of individual appraisal can be seen as instruments of social and moral control. A critique of the theory and practice of change management is the focus of Chapter 8. The necessity and virtues of change management are ubiquitous within contemporary managerialism with its very positive orientation to the future. It is, however, not at all clear whether change can in fact be managed, while the cost of change is often borne by those who have least power and influence. Chapter 9, 'Prophets and sages', provides an account and analysis of three contemporary management 'gurus', Tom Peters, Charles Handy and Gerard Egan. These luminaries act as spiritual guides and meaning disseminators within the managerial world so it seems appropriate to look closely at their religious style and characteristics in the interests of evaluating the significance of their work and message. A brief concluding chapter follows this. There is a Coda entitled, 'An essay on management to its religious admirers'. This particularly addresses the issue of how overtly religious groups such as churches might evaluate and respond to the managerial theories and practices that some people are very keen to introduce into the ecclesiastical domain.

1

The nature of management

Although management and managers are now spread throughout society, there is widespread ignorance about what management is and does. It is, therefore, necessary to provide some basic background about the nature and history of management here, before moving towards a more critical stance.

In this chapter, I will first consider the nature of management, then offer a brief history of its practice and evolution. The critique of management in the remainder of this book mainly arises out of, and is exemplified in relation to, the public sector. I shall, therefore, discuss the introduction and evolution of managerialism in that sector and the rise of the so-called New Public Management. The nature and history of management within the public sector has its own distinctive aspects. However, it is relevant to understanding how management has been introduced into other non-business enterprises like voluntary organizations. Analysing the effects of management in the public sector is a good vantage point from which to begin a critique of management generally.

What is management?

Despite the ubiquitous nature of management in most organizations in the modern world, it is very difficult to arrive at a clear, comprehensive, universally applicable understanding of what this activity is and does. Here I shall look briefly at definitions, formal prescriptions, functional descriptions and qualifications for management to try and give a general sense of some of the central elements of this activity. The picture that emerges is far from coherent. At its present stage of development, management is necessarily somewhat elusive and mysterious, even to its theorists and practitioners.

Definitions of management

There are a number of succinct definitions of management. Graeme Salaman, who has tried systematically to categorize the nature and functions of management using empirical research about what managers actually do, suggests that, fundamentally, management is 'getting work done with and through others'.[1] Christopher Pollitt argues that management is 'an activity which is intimately concerned with directing flows of resources so as to achieve defined objectives'.[2] However, these highly generalized definitions are not much help in really understanding what management is all about in practice. For further illumination on this score it is necessary to turn in other directions.

Formal prescriptions for management

One way of finding out what managers do, or should be doing, is to look at a prescriptive pronouncement from a management theorist like Peter Drucker, one of the main inventors and codifiers of the modern management function. Drucker believes that management is a practice aimed at the improvement of organizational performance. It consists of five basic elements or operations.

First, managers *set objectives*, determining what organizational objectives should be, the goals in the area of each objective, and what needs to be done to attain an objective. Objectives are made effective by communicating them to the people who must act to realize them.

Secondly, managers *organize*. They analyse activities, decisions and relations needed and classify the work that needs doing. Then they divide it into manageable activities and jobs which are shaped into an organizational structure.

Thirdly, managers *motivate and communicate*. This is an integrating function by which managers build up teams of people and use decisions on pay, placement and promotion to ensure that those teams work well.

Fourthly, managers *measure*, establishing targets and yardsticks for the organization as a whole, and for the individuals within it, so that performance can be gauged and evaluated.

Finally, managers *develop people*, including themselves.[3]

Drucker acknowledges that these broad formal characteristics could be broken down into sub-categories. Each of the activities listed requires particular skills, qualities and qualifications. He writes:

> Only a manager's experience can bring them to life and make them concrete or meaningful. But because they are formal, they apply to every manager and everything he or she does as a manager. They can therefore be used by all managers to appraise their own skill and

performance and to work systematically on improving themselves and their performance.[4]

Other formal statements about the nature and function of the management role are similar to Drucker's. Fayol, a French pioneer of management theory in the early twentieth century, argued that managers' essential functions were to forecast and plan, to organize, to co-ordinate, to command and to control.[5]

Empirical descriptions of management

To understand what theorists believe the elements of the formal managerial function to be is still to have little idea of what managers actually do. The picture of the apparent reasonableness and coherence of the managerial role as laid out formally in theory can be instructively contrasted with empirical evidence about what managers actually do in practice.

A Canadian management academic, Henry Mintzberg, famously shattered some of the myths that had come to surround the role of senior managers by actually studying their day-to-day behaviour. He found that, far from being calm, reflective systematic planners, managers 'work at an unrelenting pace, . . . their activities are characterized by brevity, variety, and discontinuity, and . . . they are strongly oriented to action and dislike reflective activities'.[6] Instead of using carefully assembled and written aggregated information from formal management information systems, for example, managers favoured oral and 'soft' sources of information such as gossip, hearsay and speculation, often gleaned from numerous telephone calls rather than from paper sources. This led Mintzberg to challenge the idea that management is in any way a kind of science or profession. He concluded that

> the manager's job is enormously complicated and difficult. The
> manager is overburdened with obligations; yet he or she cannot easily
> delegate his or her tasks. As a result, he or she is driven to overwork
> and is forced to do many tasks superficially. Brevity, fragmentation,
> and oral communication characterize the work. Yet these are the very
> characteristics of managerial work that have impeded scientific efforts
> to improve it.[7]

The picture of the over-burdened, over-busy manager who acts as much on hunch and intuition as upon logic and analysis is also found on the other side of the Atlantic. Sociologist Keith Grint's felicitiously characterizes the manager as a 'mimetic pyrophobe'.[8] By this, he means to suggest that most British managers learn, mainly by imitating their peers and superiors, that being busy and active is the most important thing that a manager can do. Fighting fires (i.e. dealing with contingent

emergencies) is a good way of ensuring ongoing busyness. This sub-
verts the need to reflect, to plan, to set objectives and most of the other
constituent parts of the idealized formal managerial role. Actually,

> Fire fighting for managers is probably a misnomer since fire-fighters
> generally have to undertake a lot of physically strenuous activity with
> water and chemicals to douse fires. For managers, the more
> appropriate analogy might be one where fires are suffocated with
> words: linguistic asphyxiation. It does, after all, seem to be the case that
> most management action is involved in the articulation of orders and
> requests to subordinates or peers: management is about talk, if it is
> about anything.[9]

In this vein, Grint makes the radical suggestion that there is nothing
that particularly distinguishes the tasks and roles of managers from
those of many other groups or individuals in society. For example,
parents seem to undertake many of the apparently distinctive functions
of managers when they lead their families, liaise with people about
them, monitor their actions, allocate resources, maintain production,
maintain peace, innovate, plan and control. Grint concludes that

> what managers do does not depend upon the actions they undertake
> but who ascribes to their action the actions of management. In effect, if
> managers are involved in conversation they are managing, they are not
> engaged in idle chatter; but if children are involved in conversation
> they are more likely to be deemed to be engaging in idle chatter than in
> any form of management. Who managers are, in other words, depends
> on who has the power to constitute certain forms of action as the
> actions of managers. [10]

Management, then, is not defined by any particular set of functions but
by some kind of contextual social construction of the designation
'manager'. This leads Grint to argue that the manager's world is at least
as much a world of word and meaning management as one of objective
function or manipulation of reality.

While there may be some general, formal principles of management,
these may be unevenly applied in practice and the actual work of
managers may be rather chaotic and *ad hoc*. Real managers may not do
the things they say managers should do. This contributes to the sense
that management is not the solid, distinctive, professional, expert
activity that it might like to be perceived as from outside. Further
evidence for the elusiveness and vagueness of the management function might be adduced from its frequent inability to measure and give
an account of its own impact. Managers are individuals but much of the
success of their work depends upon the efforts of others and factors that
may be out of their control. It may be very difficult for any particular
manager or group of managers to answer the simple question, 'In what

way does your work enhance the quality of the performance of others
and add value to the enterprise that you are managing?'[11]

Qualifications for management
A sense of the tangibility and clarity of the management functions is not
increased by consideration of the ways in which people become managers. Usually, considering the training, skills and competences
required for a particular role or occupation, such as medicine, gives
some idea of what functions are involved in performing it. There are
moves afoot to clarify the generic, professional nature of the managerial
role across all organizations.[12] Various kinds of educational and training opportunities abound. However, it is still the case that no particular
set of qualifications, skills or competences is required to actually
become a manager.

Gerard Egan notes that most people become managers not because
they are qualified as managers or because they are perceived to have
supervisory or managerial potential, but because they are good at
something else:

> management is the only profession for which no preparation is thought
> necessary. Studies show that few managers, once chosen, receive
> systematic training in effective management. Once 'ordained,' [sic] new
> managers pick up whatever managerial skills they can along the way.[13]

It could be inferred from this observation that having management
skills and aptitudes is innate within people; these are elicited automatically when they are appointed to a managerial role. Another possible
interpretation is that, in reality, people do not really believe that there is
anything important to learn about management. Clearly, however,
there is not a strongly articulated and widely understood core of
essential principles and skills that underlie the practice of management
in such a way that it is believed that these can and should be taught to
all managerial practitioners. Whitley notes that 'managerial skills differ
considerably from other sorts of expertise in their limited standardiza-
tion across industries, their susceptibility to change, their specificity to
situations rather than problems and their diffuse, varied knowledge
base'.[14]

By way of conclusion to this brief survey of some sources of information about the nature and function of management it can be said that
while it is possible to gain some clarity about the formal role, skills and
competences of management, this is a diffuse and confusing field, not
least because it continues to grow and develop. The implication for this
present work is that the managerial enterprise is far less coherent and
far more contradictory and fragile than it might at first appear. Far from

being a solid, clear manipulation of objective skills and realities using universally recognized tools and methods gained from common education and training, management already seems to be de-materializing into the ether and becoming mystical – and I have not yet even begun my critique.

Given the lack of clarity and definiteness about managerial skills and roles exposed above, it is worth pondering the weight of unproven faith and hope that Michael Heseltine placed upon the foundations of management and in the capacities of managers when, as Secretary of State for the Environment in 1980, he averred that: 'Efficient management is the key to the (national) revival . . . . And the management ethos must run right through our national life – private and public companies, civil service, nationalized industries, local government and the National Health Service.'[15]

I shall return to the introduction of management ideas and practices into the British public sector shortly. First, something must be said about the history of management ideas and theories in the present century.

The evolution of management

Management of some kind must virtually always have been part of human social existence. Wherever organization of labour and resources has taken place, a management function must implicitly have been discharged. So, for example, when Stonehenge or the Pyramids were erected, there must have been activities of the kind that now comprise management.

Grint identifies a number of antecedents for modern management. These are human organization in general, the organization of war, Benedictine monastic organization and the organization of trade guilds in medieval society.[16] However, management as we think of it really took off with the advent of industrial society. It found its first theoretical exponents in North America. Most management theories and fashions that have been influential in the UK during this century have continued to originate in North America, and in the private, rather than the non-profit, sector.

There are various ways of analysing and categorizing historical eras, fashions and trends in management. Here I follow Huczynski's typology of historical periods, amplifying it in places from other sources. Huczynski identifies four main historical periods and types of managerial development in the present century: the rational-economic period, the social period, the psychological period and the entrepreneurial period.[17]

The rational-economic period

The rational-economic period started in the 1890s and continued until the 1930s. This was an era of intensive industrialization, the growth of the large corporation, mass production and mass distribution in the USA. A dominant view of human nature was that humans were most interested in maximizing their own self-interest. There was

> an acceptance of the inherited laziness of humans; a perception of labour as bestial or machine-like; the endorsement of the economic nature of the needs and aspirations of working people; and a rejection of unionization and collective bargaining.[18]

This set of circumstances and ideas formed the backdrop for the introduction of systematic or scientific management techniques such as those of Frederick W. Taylor. Taylor believed that all human activities were susceptible to organization along rational lines. Universal, precise, impersonal laws of organization could be discerned, hence the 'scientific' nature of his claims. Taylor, a Quaker engineer whose thinking was perceived as liberal and progressive in his own time, is perhaps best known for his invention of time and motion studies of work. Underlying this technique, which was designed to increase industrial efficiency and to eliminate conflicts between managers and manual workers, lay four principles:

> 1. The development of a science of work to replace the old rule-of-thumb methods by which workmen operated. Fulfilling optimum goals would earn higher wages; failure to do so would result in loss of earnings. 2. Scientific selection and progressive development of the worker . . . . 3. Bringing together the science of work and the scientifically selected and trained workers for best results. 4. Equal division of work and responsibility between workers and management, cooperating together in close interdependence.[19]

Taylor's theories of the scientific analysis and design of activities emphasized controlling the individual worker and determining effort levels. They have subsequently been seen as leading to the devaluing of the worker, who performs monotonous, routine tasks without any sense of autonomy or responsibility, while 'thinking' and planning is left to managers in a division of labour between brain and brawn. Taylorism continues to be an influential way of thinking about management, particularly in relation to designing jobs and organizations to fulfil certain tasks.

The social period

With a changing cultural and economic situation in the USA, management theorists became interested in improving the human relations

within business and industry. The second phase of managerial development can thus be characterized as the social period. This stretched from
the 1920s to the 1950s. It is often associated with theorist Elton Mayo's
emphasis on the informal work group as the centre for managerial
concern and attention.

Social and human relations theories of management highlighted:

- the importance of people rather than mechanics or economics;
- personal existence within the organizational environment;
- the need to motivate people;
- the importance of teamwork which is co-ordinated and requires the
  willing co-operation of the individuals involved;
- the need to meet organizational and personal objectives simultaneously;
- a desire for efficiency that is shared by both individuals and
  organisations.[20]

The social period was more egalitarian and informal than the rational-
economic one. It assumed that being nice to workers and motivating
them more directly was a better way of manipulating them into more
efficient production than using the overt control and measurement
methods of scientific management.

The psychological period

The social period was succeeded by a psychological period which ran
from the 1940s until the 1970s. It included the development of techniques of Organizational Development (OD). Its lasting legacy has
included staff appraisal and counselling, supervisory training and job
design. The theorists associated with this period

1. viewed 'conventional' formal organization as a set of techniques
   embodying specific psychological assumptions
2. asserted that the conventional formal type of organization generated
   individual psychological distress and suggested that managers
   replaced these with more organic structures
3. offered technical organizational prescriptions to improve matters
4. held that managers should trust their subordinates to be more
   responsible for the performance of their jobs
5. suggested that managers should permit their subordinates to
   participate in making up the content of their own jobs.[21]

The entrepreneurial period

The fourth period of managerial development has been characterized
by Huczynski as the entrepreneurial period or the period of guru

management theories. Others designate it as the era of 'new wave' management or of 'culture management'.[22]

At the beginning of the 1980s a new confidence was found in American industry and managerial techniques. This was articulated in well-known works such as Peters and Waterman's *In Search of Excellence*.[23] Heller suggests that 'the central contention of this management idea family is that "the only object of business is to compete with others for the favours of the customer as King" '.[24] It is suggested that five further beliefs are associated with this central contention:

> First, that innovation which leads to improved products and services
> cannot be planned, but is dependent on many 'tries' by many
> employees. Second, that you are more able to 'act your way into
> feeling' than 'feel yourself into action'. Third, that an organization can
> be effectively co-ordinated through its value system and culture, rather
> than through rules and commands. Fourth, that customers are the main
> source of innovation. Fifth, that a strong customer orientation is
> important and has implications for management attitudes and
> behaviour towards staff.[25]

Amongst the features that are highlighted in this approach to management are the importance of organizational culture and the non-rational symbols, beliefs and values associated with it. 'New wave' management also includes a 'rag bag' of prescriptions such as decentralization, small flexible working units, management by contract rather than by hierarchical control, 'doughnut' organizations comprising only a small core of permanent employees who hire independent contractors and consultants as they need to, the importance of innovation and flexibility, the centrality of creative teamwork, empowerment of the individual, employee participation, flattened organizational hierarchies with few layers and the reduction of formal bureaucracy.[26] Within the visionary ethos of the entrepreneurial management theorists, managers are inspirational leaders and manipulators of culture. They try to encourage personal identification with corporate goals and values, high motivation and internalization of constructive attitudes which lead to financial, status and other rewards.[27]

It is interesting to speculate in what directions management thinking might develop in the future. New Age thinking with an overt emphasis upon creativity, holism, intuition and spirituality is one contender for influence in the managerial world. Huczynski quotes one theorist who argues that 'Before long, the spiritual and mystical will penetrate the business world. Business will discover that it's profitable to love your neighbour.'[28] This is, however, to anticipate.

The typology of eras and fashions in management outlined above is a rough and ready abstraction designed to give some idea of how management has developed. The existence of theoretical fashions does not necessarily mean that everyday managerial practice has closely followed theoretical precept. Fashions in theory are not necessarily directly or fully reflected in actual managerial practice, though they may form an important background rhetoric and legitimating discourse.

Furthermore, the eras outlined have overlapped. The theories and practices continue to exist alongside each other. They are not necessarily mutually exclusive and can frequently appear in adapted or synthesized forms. So, for example, the important concept of Management by Objectives (MBO) developed by Peter Drucker in the 1950s is highly compatible with some aspects of scientific management as developed by Taylor in the early part of the century. It continues to be influential in modern organizations that may see themselves as primarily oriented towards 'new wave' management techniques and theories.[29] In the British public sector, management has often shown the characteristics of both a kind of neo-Taylorism and of 'new wave' management.

According to Huczynski, there are very few basic ideas and fashions in management. Those that exist tend to keep on being re-introduced in a slightly different guise. The constancy and basic harmony between what may at first sight appear to be quite different ideas and fashions probably owes much to the fact that the basic needs and functions of business in developed Western capitalist cultures have remained fairly stable over time. The needs to maintain control, to increase productivity and to motivate staff, for example, are enduring.[30]

Management and managerialism in the public sector

Although some management practices and ideas had been present in the British public sector for decades, these became normative and were enhanced in the late 1970s. Before this time, following the pattern of a classic bureaucracy, public services had basically been administered rather than managed. Administered organizations tend to be led by professionals, provide a standard, uniform service, and to act on clear, universalizable rules and procedures.[31] The job of administrators or bureaucrats within such organizations is to ensure that laid down rules and procedures are followed correctly. There is more concern with processes, activities and keeping things going as they are, than with results, outcomes and performance. The latter are qualities more associated with managers and managed organizations. Notoriously, from the point of view of management protagonists, administered public organizations tend to over-supply services and to maximize their budget expenditure rather than identifying priorities and ensuring that performance is maximized and good value for money is assured.[32]

The introduction of management

The Conservative government that took office in 1979 was able to draw upon a wide range of popular perceptions and right-wing ideas to institute more comprehensive management or managerialism within public services.[33] There was dissatisfaction with the inefficiency of bureaucracy, with the arrogance of professionals, with the crudeness and inadequacy of centralized planning to engineer solutions to social problems, and with the lack of responsiveness of public services to their users. Despite cuts during the 1970s, public services were perceived as expensive and inflationary.

> The New Right's perception of the Welfare State was that it was under-
> and poorly-managed, acted as an unaccountable monopoly, was
> professionally dominated, and lacking in client involvement. The
> philosophy of the New Right was that the introduction of markets and
> the process or privatization would bring both the efficient allocation of
> resources and choice to consumers and producers.[34]

Drawing upon this dissatisfaction and ideas drawn from monetarist economists, public-choice theorists and right-wing libertarian philosophers, the government determined to reduce the size of the public sector where possible and to increase the efficiency of what was left. A dose of markets, managerialism and organizational wisdom from the private sector was prescribed to make public services provide better value for money. The pursuit of the virtuous three 'e's' – economy, efficiency and effectiveness – became mandatory. Managers, management techniques and consultants were drawn in from the private sector to shake up the public services in what was essentially a top-down revolution.

It was in these circumstances that Sir Roy Griffiths, the deputy chief executive of the Sainsbury retail chain, was appointed by government to review managerial arrangements in the NHS. He memorably found that, 'If Florence Nightingale were carrying her lamp through the corridors of the NHS today, she would almost certainly be looking for the people in charge', and promptly recommended that generic general management should replace administration in that organization, which it did in 1983.[35] The general management revolution in the NHS was later supplemented with further chastening and invigorating medicine from the private sector. In 1990, new legislation introduced competition and quasi-markets between purchaser authorities and provider trusts. Markets, competition and managers were the means chosen to slim public service down and make it more effective and responsive.

The nature of managerialism

It is hard to distinguish absolutely elements of distinctively manageri-ally derived thought and practice as opposed to, for example, ideas and practices taken from other aspects of business practice or markets in the public sector. There are, however, three main features of the whole 'programme' of management related reform. These are: (a) tighter control of spending; (b) de-centralizing and devolving managerial responsibility to a more local level once financial and other norms and targets have been established at the centre; and (c) the introduction of clear line management. In the pursuit of effectiveness, and especially of economy and efficiency, which have often been given higher priority, there has been enormous emphasis on control of the workforce and budgets, measurement of performance through clear goals and targets, and on saving money through year-on-year 'efficiency savings'.

Key features of the public management project as a whole now include:

- an emphasis on the public as 'customers' and upon user choice (e.g. various kinds of citizen's or user's charters and 'rights' have been introduced);
- the creation of markets or quasi-markets and commitment to com-petition between service-providing agencies so that better value for money is attained (e.g. now hospitals and other providers have to compete against each other for 'business' or funding);
- greater plurality and variety of service providers, using sources both within and outside the public sector (e.g. voluntary and commercial organizations may now be used to provide services previously provided directly within the public sector);
- the separation of the purchasing from the providing role so that public bodies do not themselves organize and provide the services that are to be made available for users (e.g. many local authorities now have to purchase home care and other services from independ-ent commercial enterprises);
- the growth of contractual and semi-contractual relationships in a move away from direct hierarchical or professional control (e.g. now many purchasing groups like councils or health authorities get the services they require by entering into contracts with a particular hospital or care service);
- the clear identification of performance targets and outcomes against which managers and providers can be held accountable (e.g. the waiting lists for certain kinds of clinical conditions now form an imperative for health care providers to work differently or more quickly if they wish to retain particular contracts);

- flexibility of pay and conditions on a local level determined by the local employment situation and the need to provide performance-related pay as a means to workforce motivation (e.g. now individual hospital trusts may pay slightly different rates to employees instead of paying them according to a standard national scale.[36]

Neo-Taylorism and 'new wave' management thinking

Insofar as a real managerial revolution or cultural transformation in public services has been characterized by features such as target setting, measurement against targets, performance indicators, careful activity budgeting, staff appraisal and performance-related pay for those who get 'results', it could be designated neo-Taylorian.[37] However, this approach could be called 'neo-Druckerian'. Many of these features, for example setting targets and measuring performance against them, are to be found in Drucker's work. Indeed, many of Drucker's precepts seem to have been imported directly into public service management, including the need to identify and serve the needs of the customer. This seems a fitting treatment for the mentality of the man who in fact invented the concept of 'privatizing' public services.[38]

The rational, measuring and controlling approach characteristic of both Taylor and Drucker has, however, been leavened with the kind of 'new wave' management thinking that emanated from the 'excellence', 'cultural' or 'entrepreneurial' stream of 1980s management thought. This kind of thinking manifests itself in the language of motivation, flexibility, innovation, development, quality, getting close to the customer and so on which flows around public-service organizations in tandem with concepts like efficiency and economy. The values and practices associated with the Public Service Orientation in management attempt to synthesize traditional public-service values, rational management techniques and ideas and the more imaginative, cultural approach of the 'new wave' management theorists.[39] Critics of neo-Taylorism have also welcomed new emphases upon quality and human resource management as humanizing and liberalizing aspects of public sector managerialism.[40]

The co-existence of two main strands of managment thinking, language and practice – the 'new wave' and the 'neo-Taylorian' – is an important and confusing aspect of life in public-service institutions and other non-profit organizations today.

> The Taylorist or neo-Taylorist approaches deriving from Frederick Taylor's efforts to establish 'scientific management' are primarily focused on the strict control, regulation and supervision of work processes by managers. They rest on an assumption that employees are

fundamentally recalcitrant and productivity improvements can only be achieved by the direct and continuous exercise of management control. 'New wave management' has a more optimistic view of employee motivation and has tended the emphasize the importance of managers 'enabling' or even 'liberating' the creative and productive potential of their workforces, while developing commitment to corporate missions.[41]

Often, it seems that the actual techniques and methods used are those of hard, pragmatic, rationalistic measurement, control, economy, efficiency and effectiveness glossed with a visionary rhetoric of excellence and aspiration.

Blatant contradictions arise in this context. For instance, while much rhetoric dwells upon the importance of users and consumers, those who assess the effect of the introduction of managerialism tend to agree that the position and needs of users have not so far been significantly enhanced.[42] Similarly, it is quite obviously difficult, even impossible, to offer more, better and increasingly flexible services if the real agenda is to save money as a matter of absolute priority. Again, stronger central control conflicts with attempts to make services more locally relevant and accountable. These contradictions in managerial thought, rhetoric and practice form an important basic context for my critique of managerialism.

Whatever the rhetoric of managerialism, be it that of excellence or efficiency, there are substantial shared values in all management systems. Characterizing models of management as permeable ideologies that can carry conflicting, even contradictory messages, Newman and Clarke note that

> conflicts between different models of management are harmonized by their being subject to a higher level of integration. Both models of management fall within the wider ideology of managerialism – the commitment to 'management' as the solution to social and economic problems, particularly those of the public sector; the belief in management as an overarching system of authority; and the view of managment as founded on an inalienable 'right to manage'.[43]

The effects of managerialism in the public sector

Despite the magnitude of change in orientation presented by the introduction of managerialism into the public sector it is difficult to assess its actual effects. Pollitt believes that, minimally, there has been a shift from public- to private-sector provision, there is evidence of increasing cost consciousness, that real savings have been made and, not least, that 'managerialism has made a major impact at the level of rhetoric and vocabulary'![44] More recent, empirically based surveys have been cautious in their findings. Ironically, no baseline measurements or goals were made when management was introduced. Its evolution and effects are iterative and developing. It is, therefore, very difficult to make definitive judgments about what management and managers have accomplished. It is clear, however, that managers themselves feel more influential, while some professionals feel less responsible for their own decisions and destinies.[45] Ferlie *et al.* conclude: 'The overall significance and scale of development of the new public management described in this book are still unclear.'[46] Perhaps this disappointingly cautious conclusion is further evidence for the costly social innovation of management being a mystical phantasm whose effects are more hoped for than actually measurable.

Problematic aspects of public-service management

The problems, as opposed to the concrete achievements of management, have been pointed up very clearly. Managerialism was introduced into the public sector by politicians as ostensibly a set of apolitical techniques, the neutral and acceptable face of New Right thinking, that could effect real changes in power and organization in the public sector:

> By contrast with the professional, the manager is driven by the search
> for efficiency rather than abstract 'professional standards'. Compared
> to the bureaucrat, the manager is flexible and outward-looking. Unlike
> the politician, the manager inhabits the 'real world' of 'good business
> practices', not the realms of doctrinaire ideology. In each of these areas,
> the manager is also more 'customer centred' than concerned with the
> maintenance and development of organizational 'empires'.[47]

Unfortunately, this way of construing management leaves out many aspects that are vital to public service, not least the fact that public service is paid for with taxpayers' money. It is, therefore, necessarily situated within the domain of political decision-making and electoral accountability.

The wholesale, uncritical introduction of management and organizational principles from the private sector which has characterized the introduction of managerialism into public services, has been criticized for over-simplifying and riding roughshod over the nature of the public domain:

> The values of the public domain are, seemingly, not perceived as
> relevant to management theories. Organisational models assume the
> values of the private even when their focus is the public. This has
> meant that many activities of public bodies are implicitly defined as
> outside the concern of management: protest, politics, public
> accountability, citizenship, party conflict, elections, public debate,

inter-authority co-operation, and civil rights. The public domain has been simplified. Such public events and processes are even perceived as interferences . . . .[48]

Other problems with public service management include the relationship between management and professional judgment and knowledge, the locus of decision-making in service provision, the accountability of 'directors' of public bodies, and the effectiveness of markets or quasi-markets (including the loss of trust between 'competitors' and the expense of contracting). These issues must be put alongside the putative successes of managerialism.

Conclusion

This chapter has provided introductory material about the nature and evolution of managerial ideas and practices. In particular, it has given an account of the introduction of management into the British public service sector. The introduction and practice of management in the public sector has been dwelt upon at some length here for two reasons. First, it forms the background to the chapters that follow. Seeing management methods and ideas introduced into the public sector provides a good opportunity to assay the strengths and weaknesses of management as a whole. While there are particular issues that are specific to the public sector, many of the critical themes that emerge could equally be applied directly within the private sector. Secondly, while the introduction of management into the public sector has its own specific history, many other institutions have experienced the same kind of trends and problems, particularly other parts of the non-profit sector where managerialism is now seen as the correct way to run any kind of enterprise.

Both the accounts of management in general and that of the introduction and functioning of management in the public sector have exposed curious anomalies and inconsistencies within the ideology of management. Management is difficult to define, its theory appears in many respects to be incoherent and subject to the whims of fashion, its application is often uneven and its actual results and effects can be very difficult to assess. An activity that looks very solid and coherent at first sight appears to disintegrate under scrutiny. Even a cursory inspection of management theory and practice seems to reveal more that is unknown and assumed than properly accounted for and understood. This preliminary, tentative judgement will be further explored in the chapters of critique that follow. In the first of these, I set out a case for seeing management as, in general terms, a kind of religion.

2

Management as religion

When I gave up being employed as a theologian to take up a post in the NHS, I naively believed myself to be moving from a world of faith, the unseen, the spiritual and the speculative, into a world that would be concrete, realistic, pragmatic and concerned with indisputable verities of expenditure and economics. The metaphysical and the intangible, I thought, would have little to do with the managed world of the NHS. People would have empirical evidence for what they did, and plan their actions rationally on the basis of firm information and well-tried techniques that were scientific and logical. I completely failed to perceive the religious nature of management. Although management is strewn about with tough, practical-sounding talk and scientific-seeming techniques and technologies, it is full of metaphysical beliefs and assumptions. These are often unsupported by any kind of evidence; sometimes they exist in flat contradiction to such evidence as is available.

In this chapter I will begin to outline a case for management being regarded as a kind of religion. It is my contention that management functions in many ways as a religion, incorporating, mostly unwittingly, some aspects of Christianity (though significantly neglecting others). Indeed, management, particularly that which is influenced by 'new wave' thinking, can instructively be construed as having many of the characteristics of fundamentalist sectarianism. To establish this speculative, suggestive hypothesis, I will first look briefly at the nature and meaning of 'religion'. I shall then examine some of the evidence that suggests that management might be characterized as a religious activity. Thereafter, I will point up something of the specific religious content of managerial theory, belief and practice in the interests of discerning more of the precise nature of this religion.

What is 'religion'?

The last chapter showed that management can be difficult to define and identify precisely. Unfortunately, 'religion' is equally difficult to pin down. Looking at world religions, there are so many different ways of believing and behaving that it can be very difficult to identify any elements of commonality between faith communities.[1] Illuminating, comprehensive and meaningful definitions of religion are hard to formulate and apply.[2]

Theorists in disciplines like anthropology, sociology and psychology have their own distinctive ideas about what constitutes religion. They tend to focus on the functions of religion or religions, not upon the content of faith or belief in a particular kind of God. Religion has thus been seen as, amongst other things, a defence against anxiety and chaos (including the fear of death), a series of illusions that allow people to cope with their instincts and desires, a consolation and anaesthetic against the reality of oppression, a way of binding communities together, even, on occasion, as a force for change and liberating the oppressed! The moral philosopher Alasdair MacIntyre argues that religions should mostly be regarded as ways of expressing important feelings and emotions:

> Carnap and Ayer both extended the emotive theory beyond the realm
> of moral judgment [*sic*] and argued that metaphysical assertions more
> generally and religious assertions more particularly, while they purport
> to give information about transcendent reality, actually do no more
> than express the feelings and attitudes of those who utter them. They
> disguise certain psychological realities with religious utterances.[3]

There are many ways of understanding and defining the nature and function of religion and religions, so it is important to adopt a working definition. Here, I take my definition from the cultural anthropologist, Clifford Geertz. He suggests that religion is

> (1) a system of symbols which acts to (2) establish powerful, pervasive,
> and long-lasting moods and motivations in men by (3) formulating
> conceptions of a general order of existence and (4) clothing these
> conceptions with such an aura of factuality that (5) the moods and
> motivations seem uniquely realistic.[4]

Geertz's definition is broad and minimalistic. Clearly, there are many aspects of social life which could be described as religious in these terms. So, for example, the capitalist market economy with its belief in the real value of symbolic pound notes backed up by extensive ideologies formulated by economists would be a religion. Features that are often associated with religion such as faith in that which cannot be rationally established, specific belief, transcendence, worship and ritual

are not mandatory here (though when it comes to analysing management as a religion, most of these elements are actually present, with the
possible exception of worship of some kind of transcendent other). As
to the function of religion, my working assumption is that it acts as 'a
panacea, a blessing, a comfort, a source of all meaning, a path to
identity, morality, wholeness, progress, worth'.[5]

Evidence for management being seen as a religion

A prima facie case for seeing management as a religion, or at least a
substantially religious activity, can be made by considering: (a) the faith
assumptions of management; (b) the religious style and order of management; and (c) the faith content (i.e. the actual beliefs that positively
inform management) and the religious language found in management
theory and practice.

The faith assumptions of management

In the Nicene creed, Christians are invited to affirm their faith in 'God
the Father Almighty, Maker of Heaven and Earth, And of all things
visible and invisible'. The belief in supernatural entities, with the
invisible being regarded as important as the tangible and the visible,
might seem to have everything to do with an ancient, childish world of
religion, but little to do with the practice of modern management.
However, much of modern managerial practice depends upon unproven and unprovable faith assumptions about reality. Here are just a few
examples of activities that are often deemed central to management.
One quickly finds oneself in a world of faith assumptions and rituals
rather than empirically based knowledge and ratio-instrumental action.
I take my examples from the sphere of public service.

The market and the elusive consumer
In the public sector there has been a radical shift away from concentrat-
ing on what producers want to produce (courses in education, different
kinds of treatment in health care, etc.) to looking at what consumers or
users actually want. This is a move from 'product-centredness', concen-
trating on internal processes and what the organization offers its clients
whether they like it or not, to 'market-centredness' in which organizations look outwards and at outcomes in a quest to treat clients like
sovereign consumers. The change is deemed desirable because it makes
organizations more efficient and responsive. It also ensures their long-

term survival. The success of the market-centred organization would seem to be guaranteed so long as adequate market research is carried out on new products to ensure that they meet consumers' needs and wishes.

The irrationalities and limitations inherent in this sensible-sounding market model have been known about for some time.[6]

In the first place, it is difficult to know who the potential consumers of a product are. A recent book reveals that the concept 'consumer' is a diverse and flexible as that of 'community' – it means all things to all people.[7] Even if the appropriate potential users are identified for market research purposes, they may not really know what their present and future needs will be. Furthermore, they may not tell the truth about their needs and opinions. Even if they do, these may have changed by the time a product comes out.

The consequence is that many products that are well market-researched actually do very badly. Others, that may have been developed in 'product-centred' ways, may be enormously successful, perhaps due to the fact that they create a need rather than responding to one. The Open University, for example, was not something that consumers asked for, but that has not stopped it from being very successful.

It seems to be the case that it is very difficult to predict how the market will behave and what people will want. This makes the selection of new things for production a matter of, at best, informed guesswork. In this context, market research activity functions as a kind of ritual to help to cope with the anxiety of uncertainty and the need to commit oneself in a very uncertain environment.[8] The belief that market-orientation and its correlative market research will ensure relevance and success thus turns out to be a matter of myth and debatable dogma rather than indisputable fact. This has not stopped it being treated as one of the underpinning verities of management in general and public-sector management in particular.

Planning

The USSR used to have a series of five-year plans that were supposed to guide the country's economic activity. These were ultimately discarded because actual economic activity (or, rather, the lack of it) bore little relation to what was in the plans. In the UK, similarly, there was at one time much faith invested in central rational planning for social benefit and change. It was this kind of belief that underlay the running of the NHS, for example, for many years.

Central, rational planning was abandoned as inappropriate simultaneously with the managerial and market reforms in the public sector. Localities and autonomous units such as hospital trusts were left to determine their own futures as business entities within a market. One of the first things that many such institutions did was to re-invent the five-year plan, this time dignified with the epithet 'strategic'. Now, many public-service organizations give hundreds of person-hours to formulating strategic plans which include identifying objectives, esti- mating strengths, weaknesses, opportunities and threats (SWOT analysis), analysing critical success factors, eliminating risk and map- ping out the new products that will come on line and those that must be discontinued. In one such institution it is often quipped, 'We take ten months to formulate the plan, then two months to implement it, then we start writing the next plan!'

Quite apart from questions of time-scale and proper use of human resources, it is questionable how useful this kind of planning really is. Organizations must have some sense of where they are going and what they are trying to do. The trouble is that the more specific plans are, the more futile often they prove to be. In organizations and the environ- ments around them, so many crucial factors can change so quickly that plans quickly become irrelevant.

In 1995, for example, many universities made the assumption that they should plan to expand. In the following year, these plans became almost irrelevant as actual templates for action because public funds were dramatically reduced. This is just one graphic illustration of the limits of strategic planning. Only in a totally static environment would it be possible to ensure that a plan was correct and susceptible to full implementation – and in those circumstances one does not need a strategic plan which is designed to cope with change. Cleverly notes the ephemerality and relative uselessness of plans in pointing out that,

> failure to achieve the planned target is very, very rarely punished.
> Making an egregious loss may be punished. Activity that brings the
> company into disrepute may be punished. Actions that offend the
> senior directorate will certainly be. Refusal to take part in the
> formalities of the planning procedure will be. But failures to meet any
> particular target will as often as not go unnoticed, except perhaps by
> the bureaucracy that develops to administer the plan.[9]

Strategic planning may be helpful as a tool of social control or insofar as it helps people to think about what they are doing in the present and to be aware of some of the things that might arise in the future.[10] However, the belief that these plans act as real maps or charts of organizational action is often unfounded, a matter of faith. Like relig- ious faith, much of what strategic planning does is to help people to feel they have some sense of control and direction in the midst of chaotic, unpredictable reality. The planning process allows managers to feel that they are doing something and serves as a ritual activity that brings a sense of efficacy. This is, of course, an important function.

Leadership
Another key factor to enter the public sector with managerial and business methods is the importance of leadership. Rosemary Stewart begins a book on the subject thus:

> *This book has a mission.* This mission is to persuade you, the reader, that the NHS needs leadership and that you should be leading, and preparing yourself to be a better leader. There *are* opportunities for leadership even in junior jobs.[11]

It has become a contemporary orthodoxy that all organizations need good leadership. While administrators carry out policies and are publicly accountable, managers realize the visions of leaders by providing objectives, targets and reviews. Leadership, on the other hand, 'is *discovering the route ahead* and encouraging and – personality permitting – inspiring others to follow. Hence leadership is most needed in changing times, when the way ahead is not clear.'[12] Turning to the battlefield for instruction, Stewart approvingly quotes the soldier-philosopher, Field Marshal Lord Slim:

> there is a difference between leadership and management. Leadership is of the spirit, compounded of personality and vision; its practice is an art. Management is of the mind, a matter of accurate calculation ... its practice is a science. Managers are necessary; leaders are essential.[13]

This view of the leader as inspired, charismatic, heroic philosopher-visionary who can safely navigate the turbulent waters of change is more that of a hoped-for deliverer than an everyday reality within organizations. Although 'approximately every six hours, somewhere, someone publishes a paper on leadership in English',[14] the nature of leadership is not well understood. Some theorists argue for certain innate personal traits as being the essence of good leadership. Others believe that appropriate skills and attitudes can be cultivated. Some locate the essence of leadership within the individual, while others believe that leaders are actually brought into being by particular situations in which they are identified or thrust into the role of leader by others. Individuals are studied; some are found to have none or few of the traits that should characterize effective leadership while they are enormously successful in particular circumstances (e.g. Stalin and Hitler), while individuals who have no apparent skills or charisma are found to be very successful.

The only thing that can be safely concluded here is that effective leadership, like being market-focused and strategic planning, is an elusive, perhaps longed-for chimera, a kind of holy grail for managers. This is not to say that leadership does not exist, nor that it is inessential. It is just to acknowledge that it is difficult to grasp and analyse in any concrete way. Leadership is thus another part of the myth and faith world that surrounds contemporary management.[15]

The 'bottom line'

Many people working in the public sector believe that the driving force behind the changing and shaping of services is the 'bottom line', that is the need to balance the books and not move into deficit. In the private sector, the bottom line is clearly associated with maintaining profitability, not just with avoiding deficits. The bottom line of profit and loss may, therefore, be seen as determinative within management of all kinds. It is one of the few apparently objective measures whereby the success or failure of an organization and its managerial staff might be judged. This is why it has often been used as a clear indicator of competence or incompetence when government tries to evaluate public services.

However, rather than being an absolute clear line of demarcation that reveals the objective truth, it appears that the bottom line is a construct. Accountants cannot categorically judge financial figures as being correct or in balance. All that an accountant does is to certify that in his or her opinion the accounts are correct and that they give a fair and true view of the affairs of the organization being audited, including any profit accrued by that organization. There is much scope here for figures to be construed in different ways, to be categorized differently, and for 'creative accounting' that puts the best gloss on what is actually going on. This is not because accountants are lazy or dishonest. It is just that it is almost impossible at any particular moment to have any kind of 'objectively true' picture of an organization's financial performance, especially if it is a large, complex organization. As in religion, interpretation of the 'facts' presented is all. There is room for diversity of opinion as to the meaning and significance of sets of figures.[16] It was presumably this kind of subjectivism and relativism that allowed one set of accountants to say that a particular District Health Authority was working with a substantial surplus whilst another set of accountants later found that that Authority was running a £16 million deficit!

Here again, then, what seems on first sight to be the solid, defining basis for evaluating organizational and managerial effectiveness turns out to be in large measure a matter of point of view and faith – what individuals and groups take to be significant, unquestionable and factual. The concept of the bottom line serves as an unquestionable guiding symbol or myth. As in religious faith, a fundamental belief in the veracity of certain assumptions and methods is then allowed to structure and shape reality and activity in very important ways.

Performance-related pay

A significant innovation that came with general management into the public sector was the possiblity of performance-related pay for those individuals who perform in excess of their agreed annual performance targets. Building on the Taylorist idea that human nature is corrupt and essentially venal, performance-related pay is supposed to enhance individual and organizational performance by giving individual workers an incentive to work harder. Unfortunately, there is little evidence to substantiate this claim. It has long been known that individuals do not work for money alone, so extra pay represents a crude and partial incentive.[17] Moreover, reflective management theorists like Drucker recognize that incentive payments soon become regarded as rights, that they quickly lose whatever power they have to exact better performance, and that they introduce envy, resentment and dissent into work teams that have to co-operate on doing jobs together by individualizing performance.[18] None of this has prevented the British government continuously and vigorously defending performance-related pay, even in the face of studies from the Institute of Personnel Management which show that it has no beneficial effect in the public sector.

Here, again, we are in a world of faith, irrationality and ideology. This is a world in which beliefs and hopes are more important than facts or empirical realities. It is a place where the paradoxes and inconsistencies often associated with religion are commonplace.

General credulity

Management theorists and practitioners, like other members of society, are vulnerable to adopting unprovable but undergirding myths about the fundamental nature of existence:

> the dogmas of religion and superstition have been widely challenged and debunked as capitalism and science have delivered unparalleled improvements in material standards of living. But ancient dogmas have been intertwined with and/or superceded by modern, secular myths – such as the understanding that science guarantees progress, that markets ensure freedom and efficiency, that affluent consumption is the route to happiness, and that experts know best.[19]

Occasionally, there are overt and extreme lapses into credulousness. In autumn 1996, senior fund managers in London banks have asked for astrological predictions about the future of the markets to be brought to them as part of their work of scanning the horizons of the future. My own institution, dedicated to reason and the pursuit of truth, and firmly secular in most respects, recently published an institutional horoscope in the staff newsletter – this at a time of funding crisis and great uncertainty about the future. The bank managers might argue that consulting astrologers allows them to think about possibilities that would not otherwise occur to them, while the editors of the Open University newspaper would probably say that publishing the horoscope was 'just a bit of fun' and that 'nobody really believes in that kind of thing'. Maybe so, but actions can speak louder than words and somebody thought the chart had some value.

Faith in even the most tawdry aspects of the intangible seems inevitable even in the most rational of managed organizations. All of which would seem to provide evidence for Alasdair MacIntyre's assertion about management technique and effectiveness that,

> all too often, when imputed organisational skill and power are
> deployed and the desired effect follows, all that we have witnessed is
> the same kind of sequence as that to be observed when a clergyman is
> fortunate enough to pray for rain just before the unpredicted end of a
> drought; that the levers of power ... produce effects unsystematically
> and too often only coincidentally related to effects of which their users
> boast.[20]

Or, as one of my colleagues puts it: 'We know that managerial interventions can and do have enormous effects, but the trouble is that we don't know which interventions will have particular effects in specific situations.'

The process of showing that key aspects of management rest upon myth, symbol, ritual, faith and unprovable assumption could be extended indefinitely. The point, however, is not to give an encyclopaedic account of the faith assumptions behind basic managerial practices but to show that these kinds of assumptions are to be found. Furthermore, they are not just on the margins of managerial theory and practice, but in central aspects of management such as leadership, the orientation to markets and accounting.

It is the existence of a large measure of basically uncritical faith that structures a practical orientation to reality that leads to the notion that perhaps management might usefully be seen as a religion. This impression is amplified and clarified when one goes on to look at the religious style and order of management, some of its more explicit faith content, and the religious language in which it is often expressed. Once again, I shall illustrate my argument from the context of public-sector management.

The religious style and order of management

The case for seeing management as a kind of religious activity is strengthened by an analysis of the introduction of management into the National Health Service. This brings to the fore some of the major and overt religious features of at least some kinds of management, especially those that are based on 'new wave' principles referred to in the last chapter.

It was the research of two ethnographers, Philip Strong and Jane Robinson, that first alerted me to the possibility that there might be a large religious component in the kind of management first introduced into the NHS in 1984. They write of that introduction:

> Chairmen of health authorities, directors of finance and personnel, community physicians, nurse managers, general managers and aspirants to management would sit, several hundred strong, and listen to the *prophets* of the *new order* .... In the heady atmosphere that a day off work can induce, a *dream* was outlined; a *vision* that was both organisational and *moral* ... but this was not just another way of restructuring the health service, it was also a *crusade*. ... Down the tatty corridors of the NHS, new and dedicated heroes would stride – the general managers. Inspired by their leadership a new sort of staff would arise.[21]

Strong and Robinson go on to describe general management as 'a *doctrine*, not just of firm leadership and corporate structure, but of cost and quality too'.[22]

> General management is both a theory and a practical discipline. As a theory, it is not something that has been conclusively and scientifically demonstrated to be superior; nor, perhaps, could it ever be for it operates in that most complex of worlds, the social arena, the home of the soft, not the hard sciences. Thus the only way practical managers can proceed is by using a subtle brew of hard evidence and gut feeling, of official statistics and qualitative data, of both careful analysis and the charismatic enthusiasm of management gurus, variously stirred. *General management, in short, is a philosophy, a paradigm, a doctrine.*[23]

Strong and Robinson approach general management in the NHS as dispassionate ethnographic researchers. The fact that they use language with religious overtones to describe some facets of the management revolution prompted me to explore this phenomenon further in religious and theological terms rather than just accepting it at face value.

In fact, the kind of general management that was introduced into the NHS in 1984 has many the features of charismatic, fundamentalist, aggressive, conversionist, evangelical North American sectarianism.[24] I have drawn on a number of personal impressions and different sources, literary and other, to create this broad caricature or ideal type of religious management style. Here are some of its main characteristics:

- *commitment* is required from all members of the organization, however lowly or badly paid they are;
- the *past is discarded* and disavowed as a time of darkness which has no value except as a foil for the virtues of the new, different ways of doing things within the community of the converted;
- a strong sense of *corporate identity* is required – members of the organization must stick together and adhere to a set of common values against the world (the customers?) outside;
- the *individual* is important to the organization – he or she must believe in what he or she is doing and be *converted* to the aims of the organization. Thus she will find a sense of purpose, community and belonging;
- *perfection* (quality assurance, excellence) is to be sought by all members of the organization;
- *leadership* is directive, and comes from above (compare the place of God in Christianity);
- there is no long or elaborate *hierarchy* of leadership but the short hierarchy is very clear and definite;
- leadership is based on *charismatic authority*, not on professional training or knowledge. Anyone, from any part of society, can be a manager so long as they are qualified by personal gifts and competences;
- no-one can say what the essential features required for management and leadership are with any certainty. Instead, *the managers, like the true prophets, are known by their fruits*, or meeting individual performance targets;[25]
- managers, especially senior managers, are required to exercise extreme *inner asceticism and self-control*. They must be devoted to the organization and give unlimited time to their jobs as a sign of the seriousness with which they accept their vocation. Only thus will they receive the manna of performance-related pay and experience the fruits of organizational salvation;
- before the judgment seat of individual performance review the manager is *personally and uniquely responsible* for the success or failure of their organizational stewardship. Sin and salvation are ultimately personal;
- *evangelizing* the organization and clientele is important – hence the emphasis on what are enigmatically called communication skills and organs such as corporate newspapers and leaflets;

- *theories and statements* about the organization must be clear, simple and indisputable. They should be accepted and retailed by all organizational members;
- because of their charismatic authority managers are in a unique position to *identify the vision* towards which the organization should be working and to empower their followers to bring this vision to reality;
- to reinforce their own authority and confirm their own *identity, vision and inspiration*, managers may from time to time go to a rally at which they will be inspired by a wandering charismatic leader who will give them a simple, practical and uplifting session on the need for excellence or time management. This will be easily assimilable within six to eight hours and will not require further elaboration. The wandering charismatic will have his own vocation confirmed by the size of the cash collection from participants. (Convention centres are preferred to tents for these occasions, but the media and messages used will be similar to those of Christian evangelists);
- *pour encourager les autres*, from time to time successful charismatics or gurus like Tom Peters and John Harvey-Jones will write easy-to-understand popular tracts explaining in narrative form, with concrete personal examples and testimonies, how they have succeeded and how others can appropriate the grace of success and become heroes of faith if only they can become like the author.[26]

The style traits that I have outlined and characterized as religious have come into British public-sector general management from the American private sector. In due course, I will try to show that American private-sector management ideas and practices are inextricably bound up with, and directly and heavily influenced by, certain kinds of Christianity. In the meanwhile, it is worth noting that the introduction of distinctly religious-seeming features into public life was probably more than a coincidence or a gimmick under the 1979 Conservative government.

One of the features of recent Conservatism has been a turn to the overtly religious, publicly signalled by Prime Minister Thatcher by her use of a prayer of Saint Francis upon her assuming office in 1979, and by her later 'Sermon on the Mound' to the Church of Scotland General Assembly in Edinburgh. Mrs Thatcher certainly had a place for a kind of individualistic, meritocratic, simplistic Christian belief in her own philosophy. Her coming to power began a moral and value revolution as much as social and political one. The basic worldviews and doctrines of Christian-influenced Conservativism and Christian-influenced managerialism converged with the introduction of the latter as an engine for change into the management of the public sector. The religious nature and style of management was consonant with the political and spiritual order of the day.

The faith content and use of religious language in management theory and practice

The religious traits identified above were accompanied by certain important faith assumptions and by quite a lot of overt religious language.

The faith content of management

The faith content of management generally, and 'new wave' management in particular, is characterized principally by forward-looking optimism. The forces of humanity and nature can, given the right motivation, reasonable resources and clarity of purpose, be harnessed towards a desired future. Combining elements of ratio-technological instrumentality, such as breaking down problems into soluble goals and targets which can then be dealt with by individuals or groups, the management revolution is also suspicious of reason and rational planning. Too often in the past, it is believed, rationality has led to paralysis by analysis, abstraction and heartlessness, negativity, an unwillingness to take risks and a denigration of the role of values.[27]

The rediscovery of values, often inseparable from creating a religious vision of the world, lies near the heart of the management revolution. Peters and Waterman, whose work was very influential in public-sector management, wax lyrical as they claim that 'so much excellence in performance has to do with people's being motivated by compelling, simple – even beautiful – values'.[28] They suggest that 'good managers make meanings for people, as well as money' and they argue that 'Instead of brain games in the sterile ivory tower, it's shaping values (manangement's job becomes more fun) through coaching and evangelism in the field – with the worker and in support of the cherished product.'[29] The company or organization should become a community of the faithful finding meaning and productivity together as they colonize an ever-expanding future and wrest from it blessing for themselves and their customers. Having developed their key values the point is then to act, for actions speak louder than words and, of course, they reinforce faith.[30] The faith of the managers can be summarized as 'I believe, therefore I can do.'

It seems clear from this that managers, like many other groups in society, for example counsellors, priests, politicians, accountants and businessmen, are involved to a considerable extent in the metaphysical realm of deep hopes, values and assumptions. Even as they talk of elements of 'realism', practicality and pragmatism; and scan spread-sheets and accounts, the managers are acting on a faith in the intangible world of values, hopes and assumptions. Part of what managers manage, perhaps ultimately the most important part, is a reality-shaping transcendent dimension through which they and their subordinates perceive needs, tasks, their own place in the world and the nature of their organization. This could be designated the spiritual aspect of management if 'spiritual' is understood to mean something like,

> the way in which a person [or organization] understands and lives within his or her historical context that aspect of his or her religion, philosophy or ethics which is viewed as the loftiest, the noblest, the most calculated to lead to the fulness of the ideal or perfection being sought.[31]

Religious language in management

The overtly religious nature of management reaches its apotheosis in some of the language that is used. Here evangelical revivalism appears to have unbridled sway. The process of determining organizational direction and structure is governed by visions (what people most want to bring into being), mission statements (very short statements of what the organization believes itself to be trying to do) and doom scenarios (what will happen if desired action to achieve objectives is not taken). It is possible that the vivid apocalyptic language of early Christianity has its greatest contemporary currency within British public and voluntary organizations, leaving churches and overtly evangelical groups in the shade! It will be important to give more critical attention to the vivid revivalist language and shining metaphors that characterize much of the language of management later.[32]

Conclusion

In this chapter I have tried to establish the case that management is a substantially, if mostly implicitly, religious activity. By exposing the fact that many key management activities are based upon faith assumptions and myths, that they have ritual aspects and that they exist alongside paradoxes, irrationalities and contradictions, I suggested that management should be seen as having a substantial element of faith within it. Management is, amongst other things,

(1) a system of symbols which acts to (2) establish powerful, pervasive, and long-lasting moods and motivations in men by (3) formulating conceptions of a general order of existence and (4) clothing these conceptions with such an aura of factuality that (5) the moods and motivations seem uniquely realistic.[33]

As a system of symbols, beliefs and practices it acts in many ways as 'a panacea, a blessing, a comfort, a source of all meaning, a path to identity, morality, wholeness, progress, worth'.[34]

Going on from this, I showed that the type of 'new wave' management that was influential in the the public-management revolution in the 1980s seemed to have many overtly religious elements within it, some of them drawn more or less directly from the Christian tradition. The task immediately ahead now is to try and account for this religious nature of management. It must then be asked how such religious faith should be dealt with or treated, given that faith is not brought into being or dispelled by argument or reason.

3

Understanding management as religion

Management appears to have substantial faith and overtly religious components. Some of these seem to be directly derived from the Christian tradition. In this chapter, I shall attempt to account for the religious elements and content of management in general terms. I will then consider how religious faith and practice might be critically dealt with in the context of management.

In the first part of the chapter I shall suggest, speculatively, that the religious nature of management emerges partly from present human needs and partly from preceding historical factors. The religious and faith elements of management are not accidental, coincidental or, in fact, avoidable. Insofar as they continue to meet human needs they cannot be dispensed with at will, though they may be ignored. The point, therefore, is not to deny or denigrate the non-rational, religious and faith aspects of management but to become conscious of them, to be critical of them and to ensure that they play a positive role in personal and organizational life. In the second part of the chapter, therefore, I argue that there is a need for an insider, critical 'theological' stance towards management which goes beyond naive, uncritical belief to consciously acknowledge and work with faith and religious elements.

Accounting for religion and faith in management theory and practice

To over-simplify grossly, two main groups of factors may help to account for the faith and religious elements within contemporary management. One set of factors concerns the present situation and needs of managers. Here, I suggest, faith and religious elements are probably mainly a response to the anxieties, uncertainties and need for control inherent in the managerial condition in contemporary society. The second set of factors cluster around the historical influence of overt religion upon the evolution of management theories and practices.

Some kinds of North American Protestant Christianity may have been
particularly influential here.

The need for faith and religion in contemporary managerial practice

Faith and religious beliefs and practices do not exist in a vacuum. While
some believers would maintain that a religious faith is a direct response
to some kind of divine reality or revelation, social scientists, as we saw
in the last chapter, tend to see religions as a system called into being and
shaped by human needs, both personal and social. Religion has been a
response to many kinds of situation. It may act as a defence against
anxiety, chaos and even death. It can be a way of allowing people to
deal safely with their instincts and desires. It may provide comfort and
consolation in situations of oppression where nothing can be changed
for the better. Often, religion has served as a kind of social cement,
welding communities together under a common system of meanings,
symbols, rituals and institutions. (The Latin root that lies behind the
word religion means 'to bind together'.) Sometimes it has acted as a
force and point of unity for change and liberation.

Religion performs many functions in different times and places and
has a variety of uses that are not necessarily mutually exclusive. It
makes sense, therefore, to characterize the functions of religion as being
polyvalent and multi-variant. If, however, it is accepted that it acts as 'a
panacea, a blessing, a comfort, a source of all meaning, a path to
identity, morality, wholeness, progress, worth', then it is possible,
bearing in mind and not excluding the other functions of religion
mentioned, to begin to speculate upon why managers might need
something like a religious faith and belief.

The contemporary social context

Managers are not the only group in contemporary society who adopt
broadly religious beliefs and practices. Late twentieth-century society is
often characterized as a secular one in which the practice and influence
of formal organized religion is declining. However, it can be argued
that the nature of religious belief and practice is simply changing. Many
people claim to have religious beliefs and New Age religious and
therapeutic movements of all kinds appear to flourish. Some com-
mentators argue that it is not that people do not believe, but that they
are prepared to believe fairly indiscriminately in almost anything. One
of the main differences between the present and previous generations
is, however, that modern 'believers' tend to select their beliefs and
practices *à la carte*, from all manner of sources and traditions, to meet

their own individually perceived needs or preferences. In a sense, moderns have become 'consumers' of belief, as they have of other commodities.[1]

One of the reasons for a strong, continuing interest in religion and belief in the population generally is probably a sense of anxiety and insecurity in a rapidly changing, unpredictable world.[2] Anthony Giddens notes that the modern world is a 'runaway world: not only is the *pace* of social change much faster than in any prior system, so also is its *scope*, and the *profoundness* with which it affects pre-existing social practices and modes of behaviour'.[3] He goes on to argue that it is when things are changing fast that people most need the traditional comforts of faith and religion to support them and give them a sense of belonging and orientation in the world. Ironically, the social conditions for stable faith and religious structures are necessarily lacking. This in itself provokes considerable anxiety. Perhaps this sense of general social anxiety is further fuelled by the advent of the millennium which seems to be producing a sense of 'pre-millennial tension' in many parts of society. One does not have to look far to see many groups and individuals looking for beliefs and structures that will sustain them personally in this period.[4] Millennial Christian sects in particular seem to flourish in this kind of environment. Perhaps it is within the context of the rise of these kinds of sects and New Age beliefs that the concurrent rise of 'new wave' management with its gurus, religious language, and spiritual ideas and practices should be situated.

The managerial task
Managers share the anxieties of their contemporaries, but they may often find themselves experiencing them more acutely. For managers are often the very people who are called upon directly to initiate, channel and control the bewildering changes confronting societies and organizations. This was the case when general management was introduced into the British National Health Service. A relatively small group of people were appointed to change the ethos and *modus operandi* of a very large, staid, professionally led organization. It is not surprising in circumstances like these if managers feel the need quickly to find strong, motivating symbols, words and practices that will help them to cope with personal and organizational anxieties. This may help to explain the strong attraction of the quasi-religious 'new wave' management teachings that were so influential in public-service management in the 1980s. It cannot be expected that anxious people with an enormous, confusing task to perform in an unstable environment can survive without some kind of faith. Nor will this faith and commitment to belief systems be ironic and critical in the first instance. The task is too

big and too urgent for people to question the faith assumptions upon
which their continued survival may depend.

The managerial situation

The key to the need for elements of basically non-rational faith and
religion in the theory and practice of management probably lies in the
actual situation of managers. This is a somewhat insecure, unsure and
precarious one.[5] Managers usually do not have the security of owning
the enterprises that they manage. Often they are employed on short-
term contracts. People tend to become managers having done
something else in which they may have been able to use particular skills
and knowledge to execute specific functions. By contrast, the managerial function is often rather vaguely defined. It consists of large amounts
of responsibility over a wide variety of tasks which may, therefore, be
difficult to define and execute. Managers' efforts are mostly dependent
for success on the work and efforts of others. This can make it difficult
to evaluate what difference their contribution actually makes. At the
same time, employers and peers have high expectations of the management function. The success of any enterprise is deemed to depend to a
large extent on managerial effectiveness.

There are further huge and unpredictable uncertainties associated
with the managerial role. It is difficult to exert total control, or to
guarantee particular outcomes, in an organization that is heavily
dependent upon human beings. Managers have to be responsive and
responsible to several different audiences or 'stakeholders' in their
enterprises, such as owners, the workforce, consumers, and indeed
themselves and their own interests. The main resource of managers, the
workforce, is unlikely to behave always in rational and predictable
ways. Customers may be even less co-operative.

In such a complex, confusing situation which amplifies other sources
of anxiety, it is to be expected that managers will need the security of
some kind faith or religion, albeit this is often not couched in the terms
and assumptions familiar in formal, theistic religion.

The tools of management

The main and perhaps the only real tool that managers possess to carry
out their considerable responsibilities is that of language. What managers do is 'primarily achieved through language'.[6] Reviewing the
limits of rationality and effectiveness in management, Grint writes: 'the
world of management is one of infinite constructions, where what
managers do is to construct their worlds through language . . . .'[7]

In this context, managers seek to find a measure of security and
certainty with a mixture of faith, ideology, over-busyness and

concentration on technique and statistics. The alternative might be despair, loss of self-confidence and abandonment of the managerial role.

Apparently rational systems and ideologies such as Total Quality Management, Human Resource Management or Management by Objectives provide legitimation, solidity, technique and rationale that give a sense of security and purpose in what might otherwise appear to be a shapeless world. They provide the words, symbols and practices that might help to keep chaos at bay. Given the precious security of some kind of working faith that allows organization and individual to continue to exist, if not to flourish, it is of considerably lesser importance whether a set of ideas or practices have an empirical basis. The continuing existence of many unproven or even disproven theories of management bears eloquent if disregarded witness to this. The currency and value of theories and practices depends not upon their objective correspondence with truth but upon their ongoing utility to particular groups of humanity.

Motivating words that appear to grasp reality at its roots and to give a sense of purpose and direction are common in religious faith systems. They become particularly important at times of increased insecurity, risk and change. It is no accident that management uncritically ingests more overt faith elements at times of radical social transition. In circumstances of uncertainty and threat people find firm, even overt faith symbols and rituals such as those provided by the 'new wave' management theorists enormously attractive and important.[8] These aficionados of culture, belief and ritual offer a way of coping with uncertainty that legitimizes a sense of confusion and unmanageability within organizations while providing a sense of control and motivating symbols that could help to structure the chaos. I will be discussing these theories and their influence later in the book. It should not be forgotten at this point, however, that it is not just in situations of radical change or cultural theories of managment that elements of faith are to be found. Fundamental, mainstream aspects of management like leadership, effectiveness, accounting and marketing, as we have seen, are not necessarily free of non-rationality, paradox and unprovable assumption.[9]

The historical influence of religion upon managerial theory and practice

In the beginning God created the heavens and the earth. The earth was without form and void and darkness was upon the face of the deep; and the Spirit of God was moving over the face of the waters. And God said, 'Let there be light'; and there was light. And God saw that the light was good .... (Genesis 1.1–4a, RSV)

The contemporary anxieties and insecurities of managers may partly account for the need for, and prevalence of, faith and religious elements in contemporary management. However, it does not really do much to account for the specifically Christian beliefs, language and assumptions that seem to have some prominence here. To understand this Christian influence, it is necessary to look briefly and speculatively at historical sources and interactions between formal, organized religious traditions and management.[10]

The general influence of the Judaeo-Christian tradition
As the quotation at the head of this section suggests, since its inception the Judaeo-Christian tradition has had an intense interest in subduing the forces of chaos and providing structures of meaning, authority and control. The myth of creation, where God wrests order and substance out of chaos and formlessness, stands at the head of a tradition which tries to create undergirding myths and meanings whereby social life and organization can proceed in a satisfactory manner. Alongside occasional eruptions of charismatic leadership and radical change emanating from the prophetic tradition, an emphasis on social order, correct procedures, control, obedience and authority persists through-out both parts of the Bible. God acts as the apex and guarantor of the whole process.

The Judaeo-Christian tradition has been so pervasive in Western society that it would be suprising if any major activity was unaffected by its words, ideas and practices. There is strong general affinity between the concerns for hierarchical order and control within the religious tradition and the needs of modern organizations. It might even be speculated that ideas like the basic recalcitrance of workers prevalent in Taylorist views of managment owe something to religious concepts of the fallenness and waywardness of humanity. Perhaps the ecclesiastical practice of discipline by private disclosure of sins in confession may have influenced the modern system of individual appraisal. Whatever the possible specifics, the broad cultural influence of the Judaeo-Christian tradition upon all aspects of Western society must be remembered when attempting to assess the prevalence of religious and faith elements within management.

The influence of the Church
For centuries the Christian Church was really the only multi-national 'managed' organization in the world with defined roles and structures culminating in obedience to the Pope. Ritual obeisance is always made to its general primacy as a place where management in some form was practised in histories of management. Grint, for example, sees

Benedictine monasteries as one of the original places where complex organization and timekeeping structured corporate life. He, therefore, sees religion as one possible fount of modern management ideas and structures.[11] Unfortunately, a full account of the influence of Catholic ecclesiastical managerial structures and beliefs upon contemporary managerial practice is not available. Arguably, it might reveal little anyway, for it seems reasonably clear that the main point of intersection between religious ideas and practices and those of modern management has been predominantly in Protestant North America.

The influence of the reciprocal relationships between business and religion in the USA

The modern disciplines of management emerged in North America. Most new ideas and theories that ultimately become influential in the UK are imported from that continent. So, for example, much of the 'new wave' management theory is American in origin. Henry Mintzberg asserts that America has had a 'love affair' with managers and the management process.[12] America also continues to have a love affair with religion:

> The American character derives from two fundamental themes. One is the essential religiosity in the American consciousness; the other is the abiding belief in the power of human effort to bend the world to human purpose. Americans order their place in the world around the idea that their natures have been forged out of experiences which give them a special capacity to absorb adversity and to mold out of it a transcendent good fortune.[13]

Americans have a much higher rate of active participation in organized religion than those in most other developed Western countries. It makes sense, therefore, to try and locate the prevalence of ideas and practices in management that have overt religious and faith resonances within the historical relationship between business and religion in North America.

I have been unable to locate a direct account of the historical interaction between religion and actual managerial practices. However, this can be approached somewhat obliquely through Laurence Moore's history of the relationship between US religion and business, *Selling God*.[14] Moore's book is a delight to read. Its insights, if tangential, are so suggestive for understanding some features of modern management that it is worth giving some account of it here.

Selling God argues that business and religion, particularly Protestant religion were inextricably intertwined in nineteeth-century America. There was no established religion or denomination that had an official relationship with the state. This meant that different religious groups had to compete with each other to attract adherents. They also had to compete with other aspects of culture, for example the theatre and reading. Thus Protestant religious groups directly entered the market-place for faith.

Moore argues that the shape of religion was deeply affected by adopting the market mentality, meaning

> the imperative to expand, the association of growth with innovation, the reliance upon aggressive publicity, the assumed importance of building networks that linked the local to the national, the habit of thinking in tangible exchange terms that allowed a quick calculation of returns (converted souls or its measurable equivalent, moral behaviour) . . . .[15]

Religion had to commodify and sell itself to perpetuate its own influence. Religious groups entered into popular entertainment activities such as the mass publishing of novels (religious groups pioneered mass communication and big business in this way), or laying on public lectures.

Business and political life were reciprocally influenced and shaped by Protestant religious values and ideals. Businessmen saw religion as a good preparation for commerce. They supported religious preachers who would preach a gospel of cleanliness and godliness compatible with capitalist expansion to their workers. Such was the influence of religion that some 15,000 business conventions in the USA in the 1920s held sessions devoted to religious inspiration in business.

The Social Gospel movement, which flourished amongst liberal Protestants at around the turn of the century, baptized business. It saw consumerism as the way to social and moral reform which would help to realize the Kingdom of Heaven on earth. Protestant churches were keen to import Taylor's principles of scientific managment. Journals focused on managing religious organizations were founded. In a book entitled, *The Man Nobody Knows*, published in 1925, Bruce Barton characterized Jesus as a salesman/businessman, canonizing the businessman as the religious hero of the times (an example later followed by Norman Vincent Peale).[16] Over a period of more than a century 'Commercial culture in America developed new forms of "worldliness". At the same time, it developed new ways to be "religious".'[17]

It is in the powerful synergy and cross-fertilization between business and Protestant religion in nineteenth- and early twentieth-century America that one is perhaps most likely to find the most powerful and direct religious influences on modern management. *Selling God* begins to locate some traits and practices that are evident in management today.

It is in the Social Gospel movement, perhaps, that the origins of a sense of business being an almost holy, vocational enterprise that can do no harm and contributes only positively to society lies. Here, too, possibly, are the roots of managerial optimism and the sense of the market as the place of almost divinely sanctioned opportunity for all. The moral nature and tone of managerial theorizing may derive something from the religiously attributed importance of using business and the market as a place of social and moral improvement. Again, the santification of consumption and consumerism as a way of actively improving and morally reforming society may have its origins here. The virtues of self-control and conformity that illuminate the work of contemporary management writers like Peter Drucker were important aspects of American Protestantism in the last century. It is tempting to see the creation by American religious entrepreneurs of camps for recreation and instruction as forerunners of the modern management retreat.

Above all, it is within the Protestant attempts to successfully sell God that the origins of the ideal type of the modern management guru might be located. Moore outlines the widespread importance of theatrical religious lectures and revival meetings where people paid to go and be entertained and morally elevated by speakers.[18] Oral communication was linked to fun and entertainment rather than to work. The evangelists who spoke carefully groomed themselves as actors who could speak, very sincerely and in an arresting way, without notes, holding the attention of mainly one-off audiences for long periods of time. The mood of such meetings would be carefully engineered to provide emotional excitement and uplift, but also, paradoxically, to ensure social control and discipline. The meetings entertained and transformed people by taking them out of their normal settings. They also moved individuals towards individual responsibility and moral behaviour. The 'audience' paid to hear morality preached as a kind of entertainment or commodity.

All this may sound improbable until one considers the style and habits of US management gurus like Tom Peters who charge people high fees to attend 'revival' meetings at which, according to Huczynski, they basically tell people what they already know, but in a theatrical, involving and gripping way.[19] The modern management guru seems to imitate his nineteenth century forebears in almost every detail – even down to providing the souvenirs and follow up materials that Moody and Sankey sold to their enthusiastic audiences. Perhaps there is more than a passing resemblance between the style and content of modern televangelists' religious revivalism and the style and content of the new wave management theorists.

Following sociologist Thorstein Veblen, Moore suggests that religious leaders 'blazed the trail in bringing the world to modern sales techniques'. Beside Christian propagandists, business salesmen were useless:

> When the latter peddled their 'soap powders, yeast-cakes, lip-sticks, rubber tires, chewing-gum and restoratives of lost manhood,' they appealed to 'the same ubiquitously human ground of unreasoning fear, aspiration and credulity' as salesmen of the 'sacred verities.' What they had not quite mastered was the final untroubled skill with which religious merchants promised much and delivered nothing. Secular advertisers handicapped themselves by feeling it necessary to pass a visible product over the counter.[20]

This review of Moore's work has not accounted in any direct or detailed way for the influence of certain Christian ideas and practices upon management specifically. However, it may have provided some general indication of where some of the most overtly religious aspects of management may have come from. It seems more than likely that Christianity, or at least a certain kind of Christianity, has had a direct and continuing influence upon management. Given the continuing American love affair with both management and religion, it would be very unwise to conclude that contemporary management does not continue to be significantly influenced in shape and content by religiously based practices, assumptions and beliefs, even if their religious origins are not readily apparent.

Having now established the existence and importance of religious, faith and non-rational elements within management, my next task is to ask how these might be dealt with in a positive, useful manner.

On having a critical faith

Recently some management theorists have become interested in the cultural, informal side of management. They have begun to explore the realms of the non-rational, the symbolic, the ritual and the mythical, recognizing that organizations have a complex, shadow side to them which is not easy to control with ostensibly rational techniques.[21] Many of the so-called 'new wave' management theorists and 'gurus' have fallen on these cultural and anthropological approaches with enthusiasm. They probably hope that by understanding the non-rational and the 'unmanageable' aspects of organization, managers will actually be better able to understand, manipulate and control them![22] No theorist, as far as I know, has gone so far as to suggest that at least some of these aspects of organizational life and behaviour might be appropriately designated as religious, though clearly they are often to be found in religions.

That management is, to some considerable extent, a religious activity and that is laden with faith assumptions, myths, metaphors and symbols may not be congenial to managerial theorists and practitioners. Since the Enlightenment, faith of any kind has been viewed with suspicion. The high ground of knowledge and practice has been occupied by an assertion of the supremacy of reason and of empirical evidence. Western society presents itself as a rational-instrumental culture that prizes facts over beliefs. Faith is thought to be the same thing as fiction or delusion.

In these circumstances, it is understandable that while management may admit to some non-rational aspects that have to do with the murky world of organizational culture, it basically wants to believe itself to be a politically neutral, rational, empirically based activity which provides proven, non-value laden techniques that accomplish useful organizational ends. In this lies management's claim to social and professional respectability.[23] Most managers, even if they were to acknowledge that there are non-rational, symbolic and cultural aspects in management would resist identifying their activity as in any direct sense religious. Religion, they might suppose, belongs to their own childhoods and to the childhood of humanity.

In relation to acknowledging management as a substantially religious activity which often rests upon faith elements, a number of responses are possible. It could be completely denied that management has any religious elements. Alternatively, it might be accepted that management does have a few 'religious-seeming' elements and assumptions, but that these are coincidental or unimportant. Again, it would be possible to acknowledge that management does indeed include these elements, but that they need to be eliminated because they impede management's becoming the rational, scientific discipline that it should aspire to be. On the other hand, it could be recognized that religious practices and assumptions are often integral to managerial theory and practice. Indeed, they may be in some ways necessary and functional. If this is so, it is important to learn to identify, criticize and befriend these. Faith systems are inevitable and, where they have a living existence, people have a real need of them. The point, therefore, is not to abandon faith, but to understand it. And it is at this point that theological methods and insights might be of some help:

> The language of faith is irreducibly symbolic, imaginative,
> metaphorical, embedded in texts, stories, traditions; yet it is always
> pressing towards thoughts, concepts, doctrines. The metaphorical and
> symbolic character of language is not something to be avoided .... Yet

theology cannot simply remain within the symbolic mode; it must
attempt to saturate the symbols of faith with intelligibility. The symbols
themselves seek intelligibility: Symbols give rise to thought (Ricoeur).
the heart has its reasons (Pascal). Faith seeks understanding (Anselm).[24]

The role of theology

Within the overtly religious sphere of churches and religious groups,
the role of articulating, assessing and evaluating inhabited religious
belief without necessarily seeking to destroy it and in such a way that it
actually supports humane practice is undertaken by the discipline of
theology. Since the Enlightenment, theology has subjected religious
beliefs and practices to rational scrutiny. This has permitted the critical
assessment of the strengths and weaknesses of faith and has helped to
get religion into proportion without destroying it. Instead of supporting an unquestioning total worldview with a terrifying God at its
centre, theology has helped to place religion in the service of humanity,
questioning its excesses and empowering human beings to have a
critical faith. Becoming critical of faith, while not abandoning it, is
emancipatory, empowering work. It might do much to answer the
critiques of management that emphasize its narrow, manipulative,
conformist, stratified functionalist view of itself and the world in which
it is situated. It could widen the horizons of management just as much
as taking on critiques from other kinds of human practice and discourse.

Some possible benefits and advantages of a theological approach

Here are some of the possible benefits and advantages that might
accrue to management theory and practice, were it to adopt a critical
theological stance in terms of methods and insights in relation to its
working faith.

Critical awareness of the use of language, metaphors and myths

Religious and theological language used by theologians has been
refined over many centuries. The subject-matter of theology, God, is
certainly not available for direct objective scrutiny. This means that
theological language perceives itself to be distanced from the reality
about which it tries to speak. Metaphors and myths in theological
discourse are intensively scrutinized, refined, and compared with
others.[25] They are not uncritically accepted or employed in an
undisciplined way (except by fundamentalists or poor theologians).
There is a recognition that metaphors, myths and models carry with

them unintended and possibly harmful or distorting secondary meanings.

Myths and metaphors can, if unexamined and uncriticized, act ideologically to impede reflection and inhibit emancipation and fundamental change. Pondy notes that myths and metaphors often function to 'place explanation beyond doubt and argumentation'.[26]

> He also argues that 'in myth the ordinary rules of logic are suspended, anomaly and contradiction can be resolved within the mythical explanation' ... and that they can therefore fulfil important managerial functions. ... closure is understood to be achieved through the use of metaphors and myths – devices that effectively exclude alternative and potentially disruptive representations of organizational reality.[27]

As a critical discipline, theology can render the service of helping management theorists and practitioners to become aware of, and evaluate more carefully, the myths and metaphors by which they live.

Self-awareness and sensitivity about language, metaphors and myths is not often to be found in management where people use words like 'mission', 'vision' and 'crusade' without seeming to have much sense of secondary and possibly unintended meanings inhering in them.[28] Language and the way it is used is important. It shapes the fundamental way in which people perceive their worlds and the organizations in which they work, forming their reality. It is desirable, therefore, that managers and their critics should become much more conscious of the ways in which it is used in the fundamentally religious work of shaping worldviews, values and assumptions.[29]

The creative nature of faith

There is some debate about whether management is a science, a practice or an art. Perhaps it has features of all these activities in it. To recognize the faith and metaphor constructing aspects of management is consciously to emphasize the artistic, creative dimensions of management. Once it is accepted that, as in theology, words, images, stories and metaphors can legitimately and usefully be minted to create truthful new understandings and directions, then management can be more overtly acknowledged as a real artistic activity. Theologians aim to be critical as well as constructive in using the words and images that comprise the language of faith. However, it is important that criticism does not extinguish the kind of creativity that gives faith new insight and purpose. The art of telling truthful stories rather than, say, 'lying with statistics', is one that could usefully transform understandings of management.[30]

Truthfulness and self-awareness

Religions have often been used ideologically to deceive self and others, particularly in the interests of the socially powerful who wish to control the world. They present themselves as a seamless robe of meaning which is internally consistent and which cannot be challenged. Such religions can be narrow and oppressive. They over-simplify the nature of reality and easily become morally vicious.

One of the tasks of theological thinking at its best is to ensure that religious schemes and stories are true and correspond to reality rather than to the interests of particular powerful groups. By critically examining the content of belief, theological methods may help prevent belief from falling into self- and other-deceptive fundamentalism. The capacity to criticize and be honest about the limits of faith is a virtue that management could usefully acquire, rather than simply requiring unthinking acceptance of 'official' reality as determined from above. This would empower and legitimate critics and individuals. It would also allow management to be a broader activity that takes more factors into account in understanding and trying to operate within reality.

A broad horizon for self-criticism

Part of the essence of theological thinking is the need for criticism of self and others. Readers will be aware of the extensive debates over heresy within the Christian tradition. In retrospect, these often appear distasteful or futile. However, they do bear witness to the fact that it really is worth thinking out what is the case and what is correct and incorrect. One of the advantages of working with the theological tradition is that it provides a matrix of critical, sometimes contradictory, questions that prevent people from just emphasizing one truth or insight to the exclusion of others. So, for example, those who insist that human beings have an important part to play in creating things are also invited to reflect upon the fact that often they fail or get it wrong.

Management theories, by contrast, often present themselves as homogenous and incontrovertibly true, a kind of universal panacea. It would be extremely useful if such faith systems were to be subject to serious criticism from the inside as to their limitations, self-delusions and partial distortions. This would help managerial theorists and practitioners to get themselves into proportion. As I suggested earlier, and will develop later, I think it is possible to argue that in some ways management is a kind of Christian heresy insofar as it takes the future-oriented, hopeful aspects of Christianity but ignores concepts of flaw and harmful effects that are inherent in that religion. It is this kind of bias that needs to be interrogated and redressed by a quasi-theological perspective within the faith of the managers.

Critical understanding of transformational knowledge
Transformational knowledge is 'soft knowledge':

> [It] involves intuition, wisdom and mystery in contrast to technical
> control . . . . Transformational knowledge is 'a peculiar amalgam,
> different from the methodological knowledge sought by the humanities
> in their academic and scholarly pursuits. Members of the
> transformational disciplines are always faced with the 'messy' aspects
> of human life.[31]

Transformational knowledge could be called practical wisdom. It arises from people's experience of living and their dialogue with this experience. It is both knowledge in action and knowledge as action. It operates in the transitional realm of fundamental emotions, fears, hopes and understandings that are not necessarily easy to express verbally, but which are fundamental to human existence. This kind of knowledge is very difficult to measure or assess. However, it has an enormous effect on people's capacity to judge and act.

Theology takes such action-guiding, but intangible, knowledge and understanding very seriously, seeing it as the way faith can actually work itself out in practice. Clearly, managers do have and act upon knowledge like this. It is possible that they undervalue its importance and significance because it is not 'scientific'. Understanding and valuing transformational knowledge and the way it expresses itself in action, symbol, story and ritual from the inside might enrich the managerial task and help managers to be wiser, not just more efficient. It widens the horizons of what kind of knowledge is useful in managing organizations away from the simply rational and positivist paradigms that express themselves in facts and figures. This then provides a richer and more complex epistemology for managerial theory and practice.

Learning from other religious traditions
Much articulated wisdom and understanding of what it is to be human and to live and work together with other human beings is to be found in the world's religious traditions. Once management is seen as a faith system with its own implicit beliefs and 'theologies' it is possible to begin to think of conducting 'inter-faith dialogue' with other religious traditions and learning from them. Again, this can widen the critical horizons within which management operates. For example, the Christian tradition offers two thousand years' worth of thought and dispute on what it is to be human and how people should relate to each other in communities. Whether or not one accepts the faith claims of that religion, it is possible to gain from it important and fundamental critical questions such as:

- what sort of world do we believe that we are in?
- what are the beliefs and objects that we serve; are these worthy of service, or are we engaged in a kind of idolatry?
- where do we believe life is leading?
- what should be done to make human life worth living?
- what responsibilities do we have towards insiders and outsiders to our community/organization?
- how do we evaluate and deal with questions of good and evil?

Or again, it could be useful to think more directly about the 'spirituality' of an organization, thus embracing its material and immaterial, its internal and external reality, rather than hiding behind more partial and vaguely militaristic terms such as staff morale.[32] Management has often been arraigned for being insufficiently aware of its context and intentions. Perhaps questions and insights derived from religious traditions might serve to enrich its capacity to be self-critical and humane, even if it might be mainly a question of learning from other religions what they have done wrong!

The features I have outlined are described as theological because they come from my own understanding of the theological tradition and how it can usefully exercise a critical function. However, I would suggest that they should commend themselves to many people as sensible, humane points for constructing an insider critique of an important activity. While I am drawing on the method and theory of theological endeavour here, I am not suggesting that people who wish to adopt this kind of critical stance need to develop a faith in any particular kind of metaphysic or God.

Conclusion

If management is, at least in part, a religious activity containing the myths, metaphors, narratives, rituals and symbols that are normally associated with religion and faith systems it is better to be conscious of this fact and work with it rather than to deny or ignore it. By developing a self-consciously critical 'theological' perspective, it is possible to become more aware of the deep values, myths, metaphors, hopes and assumptions that form an important part of managerial activity.[33] This might or might not contribute to organizations and managers becoming 'better' (though the adjective 'better' begs the question in this context). However, it will increase the potential for examining the values and choices and perspectives that form the essential prerequisites for effective judgment and responsible action.

As self-conscious 'theologians', managerial theorists and practitioners could open themselves up more directly to external scrutiny and internal debate about their faith systems. There could be much more direct dialogue about their attitudes, hopes and assumptions. They might also be better able to recognize the essentially artistic and creative aspects of mangerial work. Managerial authority might then become more the authority of the artist who creates through imaginative performance in human relationship rather than that of the commander who coerces.[34]

If managers fail to recognize the religious nature of their activity and to work self-consciously with it, they might be in danger of being unrealistic and other-worldly. One of the most criticized aspects of evangelical Christianity is that it cuts people off from the world and fixes their lives within a sectarian community where all attention is fixed on the world to come, not the world as it is with its present needs. The mystical manager who is unselfconsciously absorbed in shaping the vision of his or her sectarian organization according to the tenets of the latest wandering charismatic pamphleteer runs the risk of failing to see some of the real needs of organizations, and the world outside. To ignore important dimensions of faith and belief where they are present is to be unrealistic and 'theological' in the ideological sense of that term.

Quite enough has now been said to establish the case for management being seen as having a substantial religious content and for the theoretical value of having some kind of self-conscious theological analysis of this. The value of any analytic perspective lies in its power to be illuminative in practice. It is high time to see what this kind of analytic perspective reveals.

From this point onwards, I will focus upon particular themes and issues arising in management, especially management in the non-profit sector. As I indicated in the Introduction to this book, I do not intend to pursue the religious, ethical and worm's eye perspectives slavishly in creating a critique of management. I am, however, keen to give priority to these perspectives or concerns when this seems relevant. One way of keeping the religious dimension and critique of management firmly in view is to continue to point up the elements of fundamentalist sectarian thinking and practice that arise particularly in management that has been influenced by 'new wave' thinking. I try to do this in two main ways. First, the chapter titles have been chosen to pick up on religio-ethical themes that arise in the analysis of contemporary Christian sectarianism. Secondly, each chapter begins with quotations from two sources, the Bible and a book entitled *Words, Wonders and Power* by Martyn Percy.[35] The latter is a study of contemporary Christian fundamentalism and revivalism that focuses particularly upon the charismatic sect that centres upon John Wimber in the United States. I hope that framing each chapter in this way will help readers to make direct and indirect analytic connections between overt Christian sectarianism and the kind of religion that management can be in some circumstances.

4

Words and worlds

The Word was in the beginning, and the Word was with God and the word was God. . . . All things came into being through this Word and apart from it not one thing came into being.

(John 1.1–3.)

[I]n Wimber's churches 'words of knowledge', reputedly supernatural in origin, are used to persuade, convict and transform individuals in order that they might respond to God. Although there is some biblical precedent for such approaches . . . the problem with Wimber and his followers' *use* of words of knowledge is that they frequently do not permit a free response or constitute an invitation. They can be tools for persuasion, alteration and coercion . . . .[1]

If you believe the evangelist John, it all started with words. God pronounces, speaks a word, and creation comes into being. Speech and act are one and the same. Maybe words are a good place to start thinking 'theologically' about management. Managers make words, make worlds. They create and perpetuate verbal symbols, myths and narratives that locate and give meaning to their own work and that of others in their organizations. That is why communcation skills are so highly prized in almost all management job descriptions. That is perhaps why managers spend most of their time in oral communication with others.[2] Words create, maintain and renew the organizational world, like blood flowing through the human body.[3] To enter a managed organization is to enter a world of distinctive words. The managerial 'revolution' in the public and voluntary sectors has been as much a rhetorical event as anything else. It is worth thinking critically about some of the words and concepts that form this lifeblood in the body managerial. If words are important, then it is important to attend to what kinds of words are used and to some of their functions and effects.

In this chapter, first, I shall examine some of the words that enter the managerial world and muse upon their function and rapid turnover – there is no one eternal word in management these days. Secondly, I

59

shall consider the use and possible misuse of metaphors in managerial language. I will pay particular attention to some of the specifically religious words and metaphors that have crept into managerial usage, asking what their function is and what effects, intended and unintended, that they might produce. I shall conclude with some reflections upon the need for creative, truthful words and narratives within organizations.

The changing world of managerial language

The language used in management theory and practice changes rapidly. A while ago, I went on holiday for a week. When I came back and picked up the main weekly journal for health service managers, I found that a whole new range of words and concepts had come over the horizon in health service management. On this occasion, they were to do with 're-engineering' the organization and 're-thinking the business of health'. It was this experience that led me to think about the speed of evolution and revolution in the language of management in the public sector. What does it portend that the discourse changes so fast? What is going on?

One easy answer to the latter question might be: 'Not a lot.' The tasks and daily lives of managers continue as usual. The new words simply exist as a kind of background hum emanating from the management schools and consultants. Their job is, after all, to make noise and sell words. In this context, words are like any other product with their own life and decreasing saleability. Management consultants and theorists have to keep on coining words and concepts if they are to have anything apparently 'new' to offer in a rapidly changing environment where there is a high premium upon novel ideas and solutions.

But this hardly seems an adequate answer. Words cost money and becoming a competent user of new jargon requires effort. Change is often painful. Continuity in language is a key component of stable identity and clear communication. Why, then, do over-burdened managers plunge so readily into the chilly torrents of new discourses springing forth ever-new from the gurus' pens? And what is the nature of the language that successfully appeals to them?

Selling words: the successful product

There are some very tight, accurate, meaningful and precise languages flowing around organizations. In the public sector, these are the languages of professionals and technicians such as doctors, architects, civil engineers and physiotherapists. They have a high degree of definition and refer directly to procedures and phenomena that seem to have an objective existence in the world. The words in these technical discourses are different from the popular management words and concepts which are eclectically adopted with alacrity by persons from all professions and none. The managerial lingua franca I have in mind here includes words like 'quality', 'total quality management', 'human resource management', 'downsizing', 'right-sizing', 'strategy', 'doughnut organization' – the list could be indefinitely prolonged.

Characteristically and ideally, words and concepts that become successful within the ambit of management appear to be:

* low in definition and direct reference;
* vague and mysterious in terms of precise content;
* easy to say;
* vivid and radical sounding in metaphorical and imagistic terms;
* radically action-oriented ('doing words');
* polysyllabic, so they sound complicated, technical and difficult to understand.

A word or concept that succeeds in being taken up in popular parlance amongst managers can be drawn from any almost any domain of theoretical or practical endeavour. Systems theory, economics, production engineering, military science, even 1960s anarchism, whence concepts like Tom Peters's 'liberation management' seem to have emanated, have all contributed to the language.[4]

It is an advantage if a word or concept sounds somewhat technical and scientific, giving the impression that complex knowledge or expertise is being communicated.[5] At the same time, the concept or word must be capable of being used and understood completely outside its discourse or situation of origin. It must be easy to understand and say, and it must sound as if it helps to get a grip on the hard realities of, for example, staffing, finance or planning. While it must sound as if it is highly practical and functional, it does not necessarily need to demonstrate its empirical basis or track record in practice. Thus, the language of goal-setting and objectives, for example, can be freely used by managerial practitioners, whether or not this is actually well-based in the area of theory and practice in which it was developed.

It is helpful if concepts become detached from their origins. This helps to prevent critical questions about their validity and veracity being asked. So, for example, it sounds like a useful idea to treat everyone in an organization as a 'customer', as the proponents of Total Quality Management (TQM) suggest. This is an easily understood idea which relates to common human experience in day-to-day market relations.[6] However, a moment's critical reflection will reveal that (a) the sum total of desirable human relationships is not contained in the contractor–customer paradigm; and (b) the concept that everyone can be a satisfied customer is profoundly counterfactual. In life in general, and particularly in the contemporary British public sector, not everyone can have what they want and be entirely satisfied.[7]

A few years ago Neil Postman, in his book, *Amusing Ourselves to Death*, criticized the claim that television was educational. TV is always first and foremost entertainment, he argued. One of the signs he adduced for its basic triviality was that it was undemanding and did not require viewers to learn any skills to participate in watching it.[8] Watching TV does not require the acquisition of skills such as those required of those who want to read, for example, James Joyce's *Ulysses*. A similar comparison can be made between learning foreign languages and acquiring the argot of popular managerial language. The former require considerable time and effort because there is much to be assimilated and fundamental changes have to be made in one's neural pathways. The latter can be acquired and skilfully performed after a brief exposure to a few popular paperbacks, day seminars or board meetings. The implication of this is that popular managerial language is essentially trivial. It lacks the significant content or conceptual richness which would require aspirants to linguistic performance to make considerable efforts to master it. It can be counterfactual, lacking in empirical basis and even downright misleading. At its best, it may conceal hidden shallows. So what function does this dubious 'managementspeak' play in managers' lives?

The uses of 'managementspeak'

Most managers are not wilfully cynical, dim-witted, or self-deceived, yet they often use dubious language and concepts of the kind described above in a most undiscriminating way. Why should this be so? Why do managers need 'managementspeak'? Here are some speculative rationales.

Identity

People who define themselves mainly as managers neither own a business nor do they actually produce a product. Their job is in the realm of oversight; it is necessarily rather intangible. If public-service professionals become managers, they are encouraged to abandon the exclusive, technical language that they have used so far and to adopt a managerial perspective. Conversion to managerialism is signalled by the adoption of 'managementspeak'. Everyone can speak it after a week or two. It helps to form identity and solidarity, as every new convert to a religious cult knows. Like clergy, managers have to convince themselves and others that they are doing something worthwhile, this without the benefit of a divine vocation, antique rituals or special clothes. It is not surprising that language carries a heavy burden here. Once one becomes a competent performer within the discourse of management, it is very good for creating and confusing a group of outsiders who become the 'laity' in this context. When we prepare courses at the Open University, we have to write a glossary of terms for students every time we allow a public service manager to speak on a programme, and I have yet to meet an ordinary member of the public who really understands such basic concepts as 'citizen', 'market', 'purchaser-provider' and 'care manager'.

Theory as therapy

If a language is used when it is not closely related to reality and has little empirical grounding, it may be suspected that, like psychoanalytic language, it is being used therapeutically, to help managers feel better about themselves.[9] Psychoanalytic language has often been arraigned for being non-empirical, non-verifiable, subjective, vague, non-specific, explaining everything and nothing.[10] This does not stop many people from paying good money to use the services of analysts and therapists. What they get from their encounters is a sense of care, belonging, understanding and purpose. These are very important and valuable things; one can fully understand hard-pressed managers wanting them too. The question is, are there other ways or languages for making managers' lives more worthwhile and meaningful than the adoption of 'managementspeak'?

Playing with reality

Play is a very important part of human life. It allows people to integrate themselves and their worlds, to use their imagination, to formulate plans and possibilities, and to develop useful skills. Perhaps play is one of the functions of popular 'managementspeak'. While children fantasize using wooden building blocks to build and imagine houses and cities, managers and other adults play with words and concepts that allow them to see new futures and possibilities. However, if managers need to play, simulate and imagine, like the rest of the human race, it is arguable that this needs to be more directly addressed for what it is. It may need to be more directly facilitated, perhaps with the provision of better quality building blocks. A plunge into the stream of managerial language may be recreational and refreshing. The trouble is that the experience may be visceral and have no long-term effects. Possibly that is why the half-life of many managerial concepts is so short.

The search for meaning, motivation and orientation
One of the distinguishing features of human beings appears to be our
capacity and need for language to construct our world, find our place in
it and create a worthwhile future for ourselves. In a situation of
plurality, change and uncertainty such as society and public services
have experienced over the last decade, many old languages, for example the languages of professionalism and the public service ethic, have
faded or died. We await the arrival of new ones. In the meanwhile,
managers need to get a grasp of complex, confusing realities, to understand, to explain, to predict, to plan and to inspire. In this situation, they
reach out for the latest concepts and ideas, hoping that these will bear
the weight of hope and aspiration. Sadly, they often do not, being of
inferior quality and little substance. However, this in no way negates
the quest for meaningful language. It simply suggests that managers
and management theorists need to try harder to find language that will
have better grip and power.

Simple understandings of complex reality
The reality with which many managers have to work is impossibly
complex and difficult to control and manipulate effectively. The value
of a good concept is that it can radically simplify reality and the tasks
that need to be undertaken to influence it. Particular concepts render
some features of reality visible while making others invisible. So, for
example, if one takes the familiar concept of the market as a kind of
linguistic prism for viewing the whole of reality, then people can be
seen as customers rather than friends (a perception that comes from
private life) or clients (a perception arising from traditional professional
relationships). Or take the concept, Human Resource Management
(HRM). HRM commodifies and aggregates the workforce into one
controllable input into production. This removes from sight the real,
troublesome, unpredictable individual human beings who actually
make up the workforce and who may have to suffer the real personal
anguish of unemployment when businesses are, for example, 'down-
sized'.[11] Simplifying reality conceptually and linguistically makes it
much easier to control and deal with, psychologically if in no other way.
It is a way of revealing and seeing very clearly, as well as of hiding
unwanted factors and becoming selectively blind. In both ways, it helps
busy managers to create a finite, manageable personal and organizational world.

There are some serious implications to all this wordplay. The brief
lifespan of fashionable, designer 'managementspeak' suggests that it
has little staying power. Its capacity to disclose, to inspire, to comfort, to
control and to grip reality is often illusory and limited. It is easy to

throw away and its desultory and passing nature is unnoticed and unmourned as new linguistic weeds are pulled from the dressing-up trunk. Paradoxically, however, language is important. People cannot live without it. They crave and require concepts that will make sense, that will create new possibilities, that will give a feeling of solid meaning and direction in a turbulent, ever-changing world.

The quest for meaning and direction often leads to the adoption of powerful, motivating metaphors. These are the object of examination in the next part of this chapter.

Metaphors and management

Most people think they can get along perfectly well without metaphor. We have found, on the contrary, that metaphor is pervasive in everyday life, not just in language but in thought and action. Our ordinary conceptual system, in terms of which we both think and act, is fundamentally metaphorical in nature.[12]

Put at its simplest, 'the essence of metaphor is understanding one kind of thing in terms of another'.[13] Seeing argument in terms of war is a good example of metaphor in action.

Managerial language is full of metaphorical language and concepts. Managers often seem cheerfully undisciplined and unaware of the language they use to describe what they are doing. Metaphors streak across conference tables and boardrooms like bright comets, making points vividly and excitingly. Unfortunately, like their physical counterparts, these comets have tails of slush and mud in that they have important secondary and perhaps unintended meanings and values that they bring with them from their original contexts. In this part of the chapter, I want to comment on the use of metaphor in managerial discourse. First I shall consider the limits and misuse of metaphorical understandings generally. Then I shall look at the use of religiously associated metaphorical understandings in particular.

Misleading metaphors

In his important study of ethics and business, *Ethics and Excellence*, Robert Solomon 'declares war' on the use of myths and metaphors that distort the nature of reality.[14] Solomon argues that certain dominant metaphorical and mythical understandings lead people to radically misunderstand the true nature of business, to the detriment of all involved. They do this by slipping in value-laden concepts and assumptions that acquire a kind of unchallengeable facticity. This prevents wider thought or exploration of the true nature of business activity in its social context. He writes:

> This book ... is a battle in the war against those myths and metaphors and other forms of conceptual isolationism that lead us to think about business as a game – or worse, as a jungle or a war for survival – and neglect or abandon those virtues and that sense of shared community without which business would not be possible.[15]

Solomon's main point is that many of the metaphors used in business conspire to construe it as a 'ruthlessly selfish and greedy enterprise', rather than as 'a healthy aspect of a prosperous community'.[16] He comments: 'one would almost surmise that the competition for the best business metaphors is akin to a barroom contest to find the least flattering, most offensive, and unethical image for business life and the business world'.[17]

Solomon wonders at the kind of language that is habitually used in business:

> I have often marvelled at the abyss I observe in so much of the corporate world, between the polite, friendly faces and proud, cooperative conversations that I see and hear whenever I enter the offices of a successful corporation and the truly frightening images that get thrown around once the conversation gets more free-floating and abstract. 'It's a jungle out there', I hear all the time, and 'It's kill or be killed.'[18]

In response to this kind of rhetoric, Solomon points out that 'bankruptcy today is rarely fatal, and however horrible six months unemployment may be it hardly compares with the war victim or refugee images invoked on its behalf'.[19]

Many of the metaphors and myths to which Solomon objects have become implicitly accepted in management practices of all kinds and in all sectors of society.

Solomon first arraigns 'macho' myths and metaphors. These include: the Darwinian concept of the survival of the fittest; the military concepts of enmity and battles; the concept of organizations being like machines; and the concept of business as a game which is fun and which has winners and losers. Disputing the adequacy of these metaphors, Solomon points out that: survival actually depends largely upon co-operation; the point of business competition is to produce products and services, not to wipe out some putative 'opposition'; organizations are full of people, not moving parts; most people see their involvement in business as a way of earning a living rather than playing some kind of game.

The next myth to be challenged is that of 'abstract greed' which holds that greed without specific desire should be the motor for business. This, he points out, has nothing to do with real wants, needs or expectations. In fact, it

> militates against them, making the workplace not a joint venture
> defined at its best by the gamelike virtues of good sportsmanship, team
> spirit, and mutual fun but, at its worst, a cut-throat competitive
> nightmare. It is a set of myths that allows and encourages the vices to
> parade as virtues, selfishness to overwhelm mutual goals and fellow
> feeling, mutual destructive competition to win out over cooperation
> and real efficiency.[20]

Solomon questions the validity of the myth of the 'profit motive' in the same way. He argues that 'to single out profits rather than productivity or public service as the central aim of business activity is a falsification of most people's motives, and just asking for trouble as well'.[21] He comments:

> The most dangerous metaphors are those that present themselves not
> as metaphors but as straight matter-of-fact description about the ways
> of the world. ... It is the narrow-minded language of the profit motive
> that gives rise to public suspicion and many of the dubious practices
> that are the object of that suspicion.[22]

Turning next to the application of game theory to business, Solomon welcomes some aspects of this model, for example, ideas of rules, exchange and even fun. However, he finds the inevitable aggression, competition and self-interest associated with the need for there to be winners and losers to be unhelpful. Business is a set of human relations, not just the application of abstract quasi-mathematical rules that game theory pushes it to be.[23]

Finally, Solomon questions the 'self-gratifying image of the lone Wild West champion taking on all comers and "proving" himself against every challenger'.[24] This is designated the metaphor of 'cowboy capitalism'. It is condemned, because it over-emphasizes competition of all kinds for its own sake while minimizing the equally important needs for creativity and cooperation. Against all these myths and metaphors, Solomon proposes the need for a sense of corporate belonging and working together within a social context if business is actually to perform its role of providing appropriate products and services.

Solomon's work is extremely illuminating on the subject of the limits of myths and metaphors. Metaphors that are uncriticized or that are not situated within an ecology of counter-balancing metaphors can easily distort the nature of reality, or at least the nature of a reality that is worth aspiring towards. People easily become fascinated by one-sided,

powerful images. They can forget that adopting them may have unintended side-effects that may be harmful. Unfortunately, much of the
unthinkingly aggressive, competitive and individualistic language that
surrounds business has crept into all corners of managerial life. It can
cast a considerable shadow over the lives of individuals and organizations.

In the British public sector, for example, the language of competition
and 'business' has destroyed alliances and co-operation between individuals and institutions. They may now see each other as enemies
competing for domination over territory and budgets rather than as
collaborators seeking the common public good. Thus, people working
in educational institutions may seek to withold ideas and educational
technology from one another. Those working in the NHS may be
desperate to take business from other providers of services because,
'It's a jungle out there, and if you don't win you lose.' Hospital trusts
within the NHS are battling for their own survival. This is a laudable
objective for competitive, independent organizations. However, pursuing it may do little to ensure that public money is best used in the
interests of maximizing health care for the population. Competition
may inadvertently become a way of eliminating or curtailing services
that people need, rather than making them more effective or
economical. In some circumstances, particular metaphors may almost
literally be something to kill for or to die by, rather than being something to live by.

It is within this general context of proper anxiety about the kinds and
uses of metaphors and myths in management that it becomes appropriate to look at some of the uses and implications of metaphors in
managerial parlance that appear to emerge from religious language and
experience.

Mystical metaphors

One of the remarkable features of some kinds of managerial theory and
practice is the prevalence of language and metaphors drawn from
religion, particularly apocalyptic, millennarian Christianity. Not since
the earliest days of the Christian Church, if then, has the language of
visions, missions, doom scenarios and the like had such widespread
currency. It is pertinent, therefore, to look more closely at these concepts and their origins to discern what some of their unintended
implications and side-effects might be. What do they render visible and
invisible in organizational life?

The particular words that I have selected for consideration, vision
and mission, are good places to see that (a) metaphors are often

polyvalent (that is to say they have many different meanings, primary and secondary, some of which may be overtly emphasized to the exclusion of others); and (b) metaphors have histories that may add to and affect their meanings.

Vision

Visions are what managers as strategic leaders are supposed to construct for their organizations. They provide a clear sense of where the organization is trying to go and what it is trying to do. However, vision is a polyvalent concept with a variety of meanings and backgrounds. Not all of these are likely to be prominent in the minds of managers when they use this term.

In the first instance, vision may be understood as a human sense. Arguably, vision is the most powerful of all the senses. The person who can see has immense power which is lost to the person who is blind. Information that can be presented visually is usually much more quickly and fully assimilable than information presented in other ways – consider how quick it is to scan a page instead of having to listen to a tape to get the same amount of information.

It is possible that this latent sense of vision as powerful, top-down looking is present in managerial uses of vision. It certainly underlies the use of the idea of vision within religion. In the Judaeo-Christian tradition, visions come from the creator, God. They are given to specially chosen charismatic figures like prophets who then have the power and authority to demand that people change their ways. Visions are used to challenge habits and traditional ways of doing things for the better. Those who 'see' them may be regarded as having power from 'above'.

Often, biblical visions and visionaries were subversive of the status quo and critical of the powerful. However, there was a real problem with visions. It was sometimes difficult to tell whether they were from God or from some other source. There were false prophets who claimed to have had visions, but their visions were false and misleading. This sometimes only became apparent when the false prophet's vision was followed and disaster ensued. Since biblical times visions have perhaps been a bit less common in orthodox religion. They tend to be the province of groups revolting against oppression of some kind and wanting to assert their own authority on the basis of a divine mandate to true discernment of reality. They are often perceived to be suspect by established members of society who do well out of things as they are.

This little background sketch hopefully usefully complicates and enriches the use of the metaphor of vision in managerial parlance. It makes clear both the physical and religious origins of the term. In turning up possible secondary meanings, it should allow a more adequate evaluation of the strengths, weaknesses and uses of the metaphor.

On the one hand, talking of organizational vision might be seen as beneficial. It has connotations of changing things for the better, not accepting an unsatisfactory present, thinking imaginatively about the future, and subverting the powers and arrangements that presently exist. As such, the concept of vision is alluring and motivating.

However, emphasizing these features of vision may conceal other important and not so positive implicit meanings. These might include a sense of arbitrariness (God does not consult people about the content of visions), top-down planning, the need for unquestioning obedience in the face of self-authenticating revelation (as non-rational revealed and imaginative things, visions cannot easily be rationally challenged), and a sense of required compliance and passivity as mere mortals have to execute radical change in order to fit in with a divinely ordained new order.

By being future-oriented, visions may devalue good aspects of the present that need to be preserved. Furthermore, there is no guarantee that any vision is authentic and worthwhile just because it is described as a vision. Visions may motivate and guide, but they may also be used manipulatively to subordinate human wishes and strivings to the will of another which is disguised in visionary form. No-one can really see into the future. Just because something is called a vision does not mean that it is automatically good, true, unchallengeable, right and useful for the organization.

Mission

In managerial activity, mission is the way that vision becomes a clear statement about where an organization is going and what it conceives its main purpose and aims to be. Often the mission of an organization is incarnated in a short mission statement that tries to set out as clearly as possible what the organization aims to do and become.[25]

Like vision, the metaphor of mission carries the connotations and meanings of a very mixed past. The word 'mission' does not actually appear in the Bible. However, the activity of the early Church, carrying the gospel of Christ to all corners of the earth and endeavouring to obtain converts to Christianity, has come to be understood as one of the primary meanings of mission. The concept of mission often carries the connotations of being commissioned by a higher authority, God, to undertake a particular task, such as making all people believers, and then single-mindedly pursuing this, against all odds, until it is complete. This kind of understanding presumably underlies the military use of the term where mission is used to describe the purposeful exploits of combatants as they undertake their duties in the service of their commanders. In both the religious and the military contexts, there are connotations of obeying orders, having a clear and 'higher' important purpose, being obedient to a superior power or powers, doing what has to be done at almost any cost to realize the task that one has undertaken and outreach beyond one's immediate confines to fundamentally change people and the world.

While contemporary theologians have now developed more complex, critical and less aggressive views of mission and missionary activity, it is difficult to shake off the associations outlined above. Within the managerial world the concept seems to connote clarity of purpose, obedience to higher authority, urgency, outwardly directed activity and the need to do everything necessary to change the situation as required.

There are negative implications to using the concept of mission uncritically. These flow from the secondary meanings that may be implicit in it. Mission may appear to justify narrowness, imperialism, conquest, and changing others and the world rather than living alongside them. The implicit radical, militant, invasive, sectarian, dualistic overtones of this concept may energize outreach at the expense of seeing people outside the organization as 'objects' to be saved. Christian mission has involved the deaths of thousands of the heathen, as well as the exploitation through colonialism of millions more down the centuries. Mission seems to imply a dualistic world view in which one group of people feel empowered to achieve their own aims at almost any cost to others outside their own particular tribe or group. It is thus unfortunately consonant with many of the other metaphors that inform management and, indeed, the Christian tradition of war against evil. These often tend to be aggressive, red-blooded and thrusting.

By way of concluding and summarizing these critical observations on the metaphors of 'vision' and 'mission' it may be pertinent to recall the fictional example of Mrs Jellyby in *Bleak House* by Charles Dickens. Mrs Jellyby is a lady with a large number of children and a downtrodden, taciturn husband. She is a woman driven by a single overwhelming vision, that of doing good to and converting the Borrioboola-Gha in Africa. To this vision she devotes all her energies, resources and time, neglecting her family's present needs and interests and depriving them of care and nurture in the interests of the glorious things to be achieved in far-away places. On the wedding day of their eldest daughter, Caddy, Mr Jellyby, a man who spends much of his time leaning his head against a wall in apparently dejected silence having been worn down by years of visionary zeal becomes uncharacteristically voluble and offers his daughter the following advice: 'Never have a mission, my dear child.'[26] Living with visions and missions can be a tiring business. At the end of the day, they may be worthless, or at any rate not worth the cost which they exact from other people.

Despite living in a secular society, religiously derived metaphors continue to be powerful. This is not surprising, because a main purpose of religious language is to be transformative and motivating.[27] It is very difficult to think of a metaphorical way of talking of future hopes and plans that would have anything like the clarity, accessibility, comprehensibility and galvanizing power in shorthand terms that 'vision' has. Other, more appropriate, metaphors might be available, but they may be difficult to identify and deploy in the managerial world as it is. Metaphors like mission and vision may have unintended meanings and side-effects that come into play when they are used. It is worth thinking critically about all the meanings that might inhere in managerial metaphors to ensure that they do not contain unhelpful ambivalences – and perhaps to discover whether there are additional helpful meanings that might be amplified and brought to the fore.

Considering the nature and meanings of mission and vision makes clear the fact that while metaphors may reveal some aspects of reality very clearly, they may hide other, equally important aspects. This may be to the detriment of some of the issues and people involved. If managers are to engage in shaping fundamental worldviews, values and assumptions using powerful, motivating, mythical and metaphorical understandings, they would do well to consider and discipline their metaphors. Their secondary meanings may inadvertently shape a reality which is contrary to their primary intentions.[28] They should also consider whether the dominant metaphors in their discourse should be counter-balanced with others that might reveal equally significant but different aspects of existence. There is scope here for managerial artistic creativity in minting more adequate, truthful, comprehensive, action-guiding metaphors.

Conclusion

According to some sociologists, in postmodern societies like ours, grand narratives and common languages within which everyone can situate and understand their lives, such as Christianity or Enlightenment rationality, are now dead.[29] So, for example, the consensual myth that sustained the British Welfare State for perhaps 40 years is now disintegrating. Where there are few signposts and certainties, there is a drive to re-mythologization and a quest to find new words and narratives that will make sense of individual and organizational existence. Within managerial discourse, there is a contest between languages and metaphors drawn from many quarters (economics, sociology, manufacturing, engineering, systems analysis) to find some kind of linguistic security or dominance.

The contested, fragmented, incoherent, desultory nature of discourse within management theory and practice is destined to continue for the foreseeable future. This is not entirely to be regretted. There are many story-tellers and linguistic performers, some of them very inventive and creative, on the scene.[30] This allows a kind of democracy and pluralism which was not possible while the old monolithic myths and narratives prevailed. The casualty here may be creative, accurate, comprehensive metaphors and myths. A good myth or series of metaphors can be worth many thousands of pseudo-scientific concepts. Consider the lasting value and influence of children's fairy stories or stories from the Bible like the parable of the Good Samaritan. Management can be an art as well as a science. In the end, good art may be worth more than bad science. Fairy stories, if they are really illuminative, might actually be more revealing than thousands of computer printouts or organizational audits: 'To survive, you must tell stories.'[31] The challenge to managers here is more openly and courageously to become authors of their own organizational myths and guiding metaphors, instead of hiding behind the half-baked, truncated, dislocated and distorting metaphors of 'managementspeak'; to become creators of truthful fiction which everyone can understand and enjoy, rather than purveyors of tepid pseudo-scientific jargon.

If discourse and words are vital and inevitable, it is important to pursue vigorously the most illuminative language, myths and narratives within which to situate the practice of management. In the film *Educating Rita*, there is a moment when Rita's mother weeps during a pub sing-song with the family. When her daughter asks her what is wrong she says that she is upset because she does not think much of the songs she knows: 'There must be better songs to sing,' she says. Maybe it is the same with management. Perhaps there are better words to use, more adequate myths, metaphors and stories within which to situate managerial activity than those that come from war, mass production or religious fanaticism.

5

Ideal and reality

Be perfect therefore, as your father in heaven is perfect.

(Matthew 5.48)

Fundamentalists are generally committed perfectionists, and part of the reason for the proliferation and diversity of fundamentalist churches lies in that relentless drive towards doctrinal and spiritual purity that in the end divides rather than unites.[1]

One of the ways in which much contemporary management theory and practice strongly resembles fundamentalist sectarianism is in its idealism and perfectionism. Perfectionism and idealism have been part of Christianity since its earliest beginnings in the ministry of Jesus. They have sometimes elicited remarkable lives, like that of Saint Francis of Assisi. On the other hand, the call to perfection and an ideal kind of life has often led to despair and the abandonment of any kind of aspiration to virtue at all. This because it seems too difficult and unattainable, even with the assistance of divine grace and forgiveness administered through the Church.[2]

A kind of perfectionism and a search for ideal standards is most evident in the managerial world in movements like Total Quality Management and the 'search for excellence'. In this chapter I shall briefly examine some of the idealizing and perfectionist trends in recent management theory and practice. Some of the possible and actual effects that managerial perfectionism might have in reality upon organizations and individuals, particularly in the public sector will then be considered. It will be seen that, as in Christianity, perfectionism has very ambivalent effects that may not be entirely to the benefit of the consumer who is ostensibly their object and rationale. Idealized standards can induce destruction and despair as well as improved performance into public service. The ideal may be the enemy of the good. There is, therefore, a need to make standards more realistic and humane.

The language of perfection

The language of ever-elusive, unattainable ideals fixed far in front of current performance has been an integral part of the 'new wave' management theories that have been so influential in the public sector over the last 15 years. Driven by the idealized vision of the wholly satisfied 'customer as king', a whole stream of ideas and practices that aim at radically improved organizational perfomance have been formulated. These have begun to flow round all parts of the British public sector.

Perhaps the greatest exponent and advocate of customer-focused perfectionism and idealism is Tom Peters. In a series of influential managerial paperbacks, Peters has consistently argued that to be successful organizations must stay close to their customers and ensure that they meet their needs. Indeed, they must be obssessed with the service and quality that customers require.[3] In his latest book, Peters advocates a new ideal – the pursuit of WOW. WOW is 'stepping out (individuals at all levels in a firm and independent contractors) and standing out (corporations and other organizations) from the growing crowd of lookalikes'.[4]

Always strong on the rhetoric of ideals and striving, Peters's essentially moral vision of the successful organization challenges any sense of complacency or contentment with what already exists. Here, however, I will look at a slightly more systematized and less extreme version of managerial perfectionism, Total Quality Management (TQM).

Over the past few years, there has been increasing interest in finding standards and mechanisms that will guarantee and improve performance in all parts of the public sector. Some organizations have chosen to introduce conformity to a British Standard, others have adopted the workforce improvement method of Investors in People. The principles and systems of TQM have appealed to many. Like most other management philosophies, TQM originates in US manufacturing industry, though it was mainly developed in Japanese industry. Morgan and Murgatroyd, who have attempted to introduce TQM into the public sector, argue that it is 'a general philosophy and set of ideas which has paradigm wholeness – an entity of related concepts, beliefs and working practices that have come together from different authors and cultural directions over a period of some thirty-five years'.[5]

While there is a good deal of variation in the exact application of TQM there are some common denominators:

> TQM is total in the sense that it must involve everyone in the
> organization, and that this total management approach is about both

systems and a culture that impinges on all the internal detail of working in the organization .... There is also the important assumption that decision-making in respect of all the detail should be based on data.[6]

Key features of TQM systems include building quality into every aspect of the process of production, ensuring that all members of the organization feel responsible for quality, and the use of teams to improve quality. Couched in the language of corporate endeavour, mutual responsibility and democratic empowerment of all members of the organization,

Total Quality Management assumes that quality is the outcome of *all* activities that take place within an organization; that all functions and *all* employees have to participate in the improvement process; that organizations need both quality systems and a quality culture and that these are the responsibility of management.[7]

Although developed in private-sector industry, Morgan and Murgatroyd believe that TQM can be applied to the public and non-profit sectors. Here processes could be enhanced in the production and delivery of services so that 'waste is eliminated, measured efficiency is enhanced and costs are reduced'.[8]

There are, Morgan and Murgatroyd admit, critical issues about using TQM in the public sector. It may be difficult to define and measure quality and to identify the nature of the 'customer' who needs to be satisfied in a situation where services are intangible rather than objects and clients do not necessarily pay directly for what they get.[9] Professionals may feel displaced by having to subordinate their expertise in teamwork. Employees generally may be disillusioned if they do not get paid by results, or if the money saved by quality improvements is then cut from services rather than being re-invested. Morgan and Murgatroyd believe, however, that these problems can be overcome.

It is not necessary to have a detailed knowledge of the techniques and methods of TQM (quality circles, data collection, etc.) to get a feel of its idealizing, visionary mood. This becomes explicit at some points. For example, it is suggested that for TQM to work, senior managers must be 'obsessed' with quality: 'It is the single-minded obsession of the chief executive and other senior managers with issues of quality which must bring about total organizational change.'[10]

Morgan and Murgatroyd commend the practice of setting 'outrageous improvement goals' as well as being committed to small improvements in quality.[11] Benchmarking, or measuring one's performance against the best performers in the field and then trying to match it, is applauded.[12] At the heart of TQM lies the ideology that each is the customer of the other, whether inside or outside the organization, and that customers' needs are sacrosanct.[13] Thus, every person within a quality chain in an organization is bidden to examine themselves in relation to the following:

- Who are my internal customers?
- What are their *true* requirements?
- How do I find out what those requirements are?
- Do I have the necessary capability to meet those requirements? If not, what must I do about it?
- Do I continually meet the requirements? If not, what are the reasons?
- How do I monitor changes in requirements?[14]

The whole of this process is, predictably, driven by a corporate, values-based vision that is linked to the needs of customers. The endpoint is a kind of consumer utopia: 'A philosophy and culture of never ending improvement, TQM leads first to customer satisfaction then to customer delight.'[15]

It is clearly legitimate for an organization to try and improve performance, to save money, or to provide a valued service that customers or users actually want. My concern about TQM is that, like many other product and service improvement devices, it aims to do this in large part by appealing to ideals and perfection.[16]

There may be nothing wrong with ideals and the quest for perfection, 'getting it right and getting it right first time', in some circumstances. If, for example, a workforce is well-paid, securely employed and properly consulted about a realistic organizational vision then it may be very useful to have idealized standards to pursue. However, if the quest for idealized quality, for example, is pursued at the expense of actual quantity or simply to save money, the gap that can open up between ideal and reality can be very unhelpful. Thus, for example, customers seeking services from the NHS might feel rather disillusioned and cynical if they are assured that the quality of services is getting better when their real and immediate needs are ignored. While in some circumstances the gap between ideal and reality may be a spur to greater efforts and tangible improvement, there are situations in which it can result in very negative consequences. It is this gap that I will now explore in relation to the creation of idealized standards of service and care within the public sector.

The consequences of perfectionism

Perfectionism and idealization do not necessarily make the world a better place. They can have curious and unintended consequences. This can be clearly seen in developments that have taken place in the British public sector over the last few years.

Anyone who uses public services will probably be aware that almost all public organizations, from universities to social service departments, are now besieged by dissatisfaction, complaints and even litigation from discontented 'users'. It was not ever thus. Members of the public used to accept many things, for example waiting for ages in hospital outpatient clinics or for repairs on council houses, more or less as a matter of course. The wait was expected, if tedious, and the job would get done in the end – no use moaning. There was broad if grudging acceptance that things were just like that. There was considerable congruence between people's relatively low expectations and what they actually received, and so a measure of acceptance of services as they were.

While apparently uncritical acceptance and low expectations may in themselves be problematic, they are as nothing compared to the real and sometimes irrational fury and discontent which consumers now display. People act as if they are deeply hurt and disillusioned by public services at the same time as those services claim to be more user-centred, empowering, responsive, sensitive, individualized and so on. Something appears to have gone profoundly wrong here.

The roots of idealization

The roots of the problem may lie in a rather unhelpful kind of idealization. This idealization has, in many ways, been deliberately fostered by politicians and managers.

In the first place, idealization has been created by politicians. Keen to commend new ideas, policies and institutional reforms, politicians appeal to people's infantile wants and fantasies to get them to assent to fundamental changes. 'If you vote for us, then all your problems will be solved and you will get more of what you want' is the key message here. To get people to accept fundamental change, it is necessary to present them with a positive alternative. The vision of better, more responsive public services that give users more of what they want is a seductive one for the average citizen, especially when it relates to such fundamental areas of life as health, shelter and support for everyday living. It is this kind of vision that informed the promulgation of various kinds of 'citizen's charters' for public services. In 1991, the government's 'Citizen's Charter' on health stated:

The Government is committed to:
- improving the Quality of NHS provision at all levels;
- increasing the Choice available to everyone within the NHS;
- raising the Standards within the NHS, describing clearly what those standards are and what can be done if they are not achieved;
- ensuring as taxpayers we receive the best possible Value For Money.[17]

Raising the expectations of the population is an important part of engineering fundamental change in social institutions. However, if reality turns out to be very different from the ideal vision, people may not forget that they were promised something more and something better. Their idealization remains intact and, crucially, unrealized.

Within the context of a highly politicized environment where government has consciously sought to raise the expectations of the public, a second main strand of idealization has been the introduction of commercial management ideas and methods into what is now seen as a market-place of services and care. Here again, much of the language of management has involved extensive use of the rhetoric of ideals.[18] Sober, even boring, British institutions like universities and hospitals now claim to pursue excellence and promise TQM that delivers to the customer exactly what he or she needs. This seductive vision has been vigorously sold to members of the public. Naturally, they hope for something better than they had before.

That a certain amount of 'hype' and rhetoric may be necessary to get anything really to change, to motivate and to inspire, is not in dispute. The British public-service sector still contains many idealists who are inspired by powerful ideologies such as those upon which the Welfare State was founded. They were very willing to adopt and promulgate the new language of consumer care in the market-place. After all, who would want to argue that customers should not be served, or that quality should be anything less than good? And there would, perhaps, be few problems with these ideals, but for the fact that, on the whole, few of them have been realizable. The politicians and service managers appear to have made fulsome promises, appealing to the fantasies of users and workers alike, that they are simply unable to keep, largely because of lack of resources.

Political and managerial idealizing aspiration made a promise that the budget and reality cannot keep. Thus, for example, far from finding that new community care arrangements deliver more to so-called customers, many users find that they have less than they did before and that it is more difficult to get even what they do receive with the paraphernalia of means-tested services and benefits. A cocktail of raised ideals and expectations mixed with diminished resources and fewer services is an explosive one. The stage is set for a bruising confrontation that is likely to hurt users and service providers alike as the rather barren nature of reality seeps into consciousness.

It is worth noting, by way of contrast, that there is nothing like the degree of consumer disillusionment with traditional private business and industry that there is with British public service. This cannot be because the market gives people what they want when they want it – try buying a single screw or a book that has gone out of print: 'Sorry, there's no call for it these days.'[19] People seem willing to accept not getting what they want in the real market place with its unresponsiveness and inflexibility. It is public services that they have idealized and with which they are chronically disappointed. This provides evidence, perhaps, that public services often appeal to basic infantile needs and fantasies of nurture and care (food, clothing, housing) so that any kind of deprivation is felt as fundamental, unwarranted injury to the person.

The pernicious effects of idealization

Even in a pragmatic country like Britain, it is often thought to be a good thing to have ideals towards which one can aspire. It is important, however, to realize that ideals are not necessarily good in themselves. Some kinds of idealization and perfectionism can be extremely unhelpful and oppressive, creating false, unrealizable hopes for users and service providers alike.

Effects upon service users

Over the last few years, users of public services have been encouraged to see themselves as important, significant customers who have the same kinds of rights and choices as purchasers in a supermarket. The rhetoric runs that if people want or need a service to which they are entitled and it is not delivered, or it is not delivered in the way the user desires, then there is something wrong. Nothing should be too good for the sovereign consumer.

Unfortunately, the reality is rather different from this. Beneath the veneer of charters, 'rights', customer-focused language, individual attention and personalized service are public services that simply cannot deliver even basic goods to many users. Perhaps it is significant that complaints departments often seem to be the most responsive parts of public organizations. While they may be able to say 'sorry' nicely and very sincerely, they are not necessarily in a position to change anything, or to ensure that anything is done differently in the future.

In a situation where rhetoric and reality are often almost entirely divorced, users, with their raised but unrealistic expectations, feel disappointed, manipulated, used, traduced, deprived, cynical and very angry. Having been promised the earth, they are left with a handful of dust. The greater the expectation that has been built up, the deeper the disillusionment that comes when expectations are not met. This painful disillusionment alienates users from public services which then lose their basic support and confidence. The long-term consequences of this could be tragic if it contributes to the demise of public services. It will be particularly unfortunate for those who most need public services, namely those whose needs will not be met from any other source.

Effects upon service providers

Idealization can also have a corrosive effect on service providers, particularly those who directly encounter the public. If users have been encouraged to indulge their fantasies of omnipotence and insatiability, providers have been set up as omniprovident parental figures who must provide everything that is asked for, more or less on instant demand.

Faced with increased, not to say impossible, expectations and standards emanating from managers and politicians above and from users below, and without adequate resources to meet these, providers have only a limited number of options. They can admit to failure and inadequacy; this may lead to a sense of pervasive shame, and the paralysis and immobility of demoralization that accompanies it. Or, they can deny their imperfections and inadequacies, in which case a sense of continuing goodness and effectuality is preserved at the expense of self-deception. In the case of face-to-face providers, individuals may attempt to live up to the ideals of service that have been thrust upon them, in which case they may risk burn-out. They can ignore or deny the ideal, in which case they provoke the wrath of users and managers alike. Or they can distance themselves from expectations, standards and ideals, in which case they risk falling into a kind of objective cynicism which is not good for them or those with whom they have to do. If all these stratagems fail, they can split the world in two and blame the users who are the source and rationale for the idealized standards in the first place. They can vent their rage and frustration upon members of the general public who are apparently the cause of such anxiety and frustration.[20] In the last resort, providers can actually abandon the pursuit of ideals and perfection altogether by leaving the organization voluntarily – or by being sacked. None of these options are healthy or attractive from anybody's point of view. They are unlikely to improve individual or corporate health.

It is particularly unfair and unfortunate that much of the dissatisfaction that disillusioned service users feel is likely to fall upon the heads of employees at the bottom of the organizational hierarchy. These are the very people who have least power to make fundamental alterations in budgets, standards and practices. They are unlikely to be consulted about the nature and goals of the service that they have to deliver and will often be on low wages and perhaps temporary contracts. It is people like this, for example care assistants and home care workers, who have to take the full brunt of public anger in response to disappointment.

The outcome of idealization of public services in the present socio-economic climate appears to be basically negative for both users and providers. It can be expressed as MADD – Mutually Assured Denigration and Disillusionment. MADD is bad for users and providers, individually and corporately. It can only blight the existence and functioning of much-needed public services.

On abandoning perfection and ideals

As I said earlier in this chapter, the pursuit of ideals and perfection may be legitimate and feasible in some contexts. Within the well-funded, private companies described by theorists like Peters and others where workers really feel responsible for organizational visions and policies and are properly rewarded for their efforts and forgiven for their (inevitable) mistakes, the challenge to strive for the heights seems an appropriate one. Even in other, less ideal contexts like British public service, it certainly does not seem adequate to always accept things just as they are without seeking to reorient and improve them. However, as the case of introducing idealized standards into public service illustrates, the quest for the perfect or the ideal can actually be counter-productive and even destructive.

Overtly religious organizations often espouse ideals which may be perceived to be hypocritical, unrealistic, destructive or ridiculous. Often such groups have to abandon them, modify them or find mechanisms whereby adherents who cannot live up to them can receive forgiveness or encouragement. This experience leads me to suggest that in management, as in religion, there may often be a case for striving for and accepting the 'good enough' and the imperfect, rather than holding out for the ideal. Religious thinkers and philosophers have recognized for centuries that the search for the ideal can blind people to the value of the good. Certainly in the public sector where users are also co-producers of services, there is much to be said for an alternative to the relentless pursuit of the ideal. I will conclude this chapter by considering the pursuit of the 'good enough' in public services in a little more detail.

The concept of 'good enough' is borrowed from the domain of psychoanalysis.[21] Recognizing that reality is hard and imperfect, and that children cannot get everything they want exactly when they want it from their parents, child psychiatrist Donald Winnicott coined the term 'good enough' parenting. He argued that satisfactory parenting is not a matter of perfection or living up to an ideal, but of giving children a secure and beneficent environment which is adequate to allow them to grow up to maturity. Ideals, he recognized, were unrealistic and de-skilling. Indeed, they could be positively harmful.

The point, then, is to accept that that which is less than ideal may be usable and acceptable. Psychotherapists like Winnicott recognize that, generally speaking, it is more healthy not to have a huge gap between ideal and reality. It is certainly less painful and destructive.[22] Narrowing the gap between ideal and reality in therapy is not a recipe for stasis or accepting everything as it is. Rather, it provides a firm basis for identifying what is really wanted, what is truly desired and what is realistically worth striving for individually and together with others.

Presently, users and service providers are caught up in colluding to idealize public services. Encouraged by managerial and political rhetoric, users feel that the services are a kind of omniproviding parent that should respond immediately to their every need, however unreasonable. Providers aspire to unbounded parental providence, feeling unable to be honest and say openly that some services cannot be provided, or not in the way or to the extent that users might like. Both users and providers need to change, to pull in their projections, and to work together towards a different kind of mutual responsibility that is oriented towards the production and consumption of services that are adequate, or 'good enough'. Legitimate, reasonable and feasible expectations that are shared need to replace destructively unrealistic ideals.

The pursuit of 'WOW' must be replaced by a more sober and realistic quest for 'good enough' management, particularly in public services. This aim will probably not thrill the heart, nor does it make much of a dynamizing mission statement. However, it may be a good way for both users and providers to begin to engage in taking renewed mutual responsibility. This is serious, adult work of citizens and workers alike and it sounds dull, like many other aspects of adult life. But until providers cease aspiring to be Santa Claus, treating users as children who need to be protected from the awful truths of reality, while users act like adolescents who accept no responsibility for anything, MADD seems destined to stay.

Attaining 'good enough' means that ways must be found to enable real user and citizen participation in decision-making and policy processes. There must be a rebirth of mutual accountability and involvement of a more direct kind than is presently apparent.[23] Life without idealizing fantasies is likely to be tough. However, there are very few people who can actually afford to live in cloud-cuckoo-land while much-needed public services, and those who deliver them, crumble under the weight of unrealizable, idealized expectations.

6

Dualism and demons

They are of the world, therefore what they say is of the world and the world listens to them. We are of God.

(1 John 4.5-6a, RSV)

Be sober, be watchful. Your adversary the devil prowls around like a devouring lion seeking someone to devour.

(1 Peter 5.8, RSV)

In a sense, some form of dualism is inevitable for most fundamentalists. The vigorous modernism and pluralism of contemporary society require a response from a community whose power ideology is under threat, and that response is nearly always divisive.[1]

One of the main characteristics of Christian religious sects is their dualistic attitude to 'the world'. (Dualism here is used loosely to denote making a division between good and evil, between inside and outside.) This is related to traditions going right back to the life and work of Jesus that the world is an unsafe place, in the thrall of evil, which must be escaped from, or overcome, by those who want to be saved. Very quickly in the history of Christianity, members of the church came to think of themselves as belonging to an exclusive, elect community that was inspired by and close to God – a separate realm of salvation – while the rest of the universe was godless.[2]

The self-identification of some Christians with God and goodness meant that they could easily find it difficult to conceive of themselves as capable of harm and wrongdoing. Whatever the Church did was good and right, because it was inspired by, and followed the will of, God. Ironically, an inability to see any negative or shadow side to the life and actions of the church and a determination to do good by their own lights led to much actual evil being perpetrated by Christians down the centuries. The crusades are a graphic example of Christians being absolutely convinced of their own righteousness and of the folly and evil of the benighted 'heathen'. This justified the coercion and destruction of the latter.

Over-identification with God or the good, and an inability to acknowledge negative or harmful aspects of one's own community's position and actions, seems bound to have baleful effects. Historically, Christian communities have often maintained a strong sense of their own goodness at the expense of demonizing and destroying outsiders. They have denied or externalized the shadow side of their own existence, fighting it outside rather than acknowledging it within. When this has happened, Christianity has itself, paradoxically, become devilish.[3]

Churches and Christian groups do not have a monopoly on the denial of their own potential for evil and harm. Many modern managed organizations appear to fall into similar kinds of denials and exclusions, often with comparable negative effects. In this chapter, I want to look at some of the dualisms and exclusions to which managerialism is prone and to examine some of their implications. My basic thesis is that when reality is over-simplified, or important aspects of it are downgraded, excluded, denied or ignored, then there is every prospect that harmful effects will ensue. The single-minded, clear adoption and pursuit of one kind of 'good' or truth to the exclusion of other goods and truths is likely to give rise to at least some serious negative outcomes. Indeed, there is no more sure way of corrupting or tainting good than by pursuing it too narrowly and too vigorously. Mary Midgeley, a moral philosopher not a theologian, argues that wickedness is often the result of the myopic pursuit of a single aim or goal that is in itself worthwhile to the exclusion of others that are also important.[4]

This exploration of the denied, negative side of managed organizations is not a figment of the theological imagination. I discovered the concept of the darker or shadow side of organizations in a critique written by two management theorists who write: 'Rarely is the darker side of management theory and practice acknowledged or considered, and then most often it is presented as an aberrant and avoidable deviation from the normal state of affairs.'[5] All I will attempt to do here is to develop this kind of critique with a little occasional help from the Christian theological tradition.

Folklore, rather than theology, offers the following two myths about the devil. The first is that the devil travels in straight lines.[6] The second idea is the well-known myth that the devil has no shadow and no reflection. Contained in these myths are two important insights into the nature of harm and destruction. The myth that the devil travels in straight lines seems compatible with Midgeley's thesis that ruthlessly following any line of action to the exclusion of all else is likely to have evil effects. The notion that the devil has no reflection or shadow might be taken to suggest that people or organizations who cannot see or reflect upon themselves but simply exist without any critical awareness of themselves or their actions are likely often to do harm. It may be useful to bear these two images of the nature of evil and harm in mind as the exclusions and negativities that may often shadow modern managed organizations are considered.

I propose to start my examination of this topic by constructing an ideal type or caricature of the modern managed organization. This emerges from my own 'worm's eye' experience. It should make it easier to see what is excluded and denied, and why this might be so. I will then go on to examine a number of crucial exclusions that are often made and the implications of these. These include failure, social and political context, truth and criticism, and the past. All these exclusions occur because management practitioners and theorists tend to conceive of management too narrowly and uncritically. They have too clear and too coherent a vision. The cost paid for this clarity is that managed organizations may be less socially and humanly beneficial than they could be. The solution, as many non-theological critics would also agree, is that management must become a more self-critical, widely based activity that embraces more of its surrounding context and reality. Driving in a race with the mythical devil on the coachman's seat may be exhilarating and profitable in the short-term. In the long run, however, it is likely to end in chaos, destruction and tears. Owning the shadow side of management is going to become increasingly important if that activity is to make a more positive contribution to society and the future of humanity.

Understanding the ideal type of the modern organization

People suffering from cancers are sometimes asked to draw a picture of their diseases on a piece of paper. The visual images that emerge seldom look like illustrations in medical textbooks. However, they can be useful in assisting the individual and those who want to help her to understand what the significance of the disease is for them personally. Adopting the 'worm's eye' perspective that I outlined in the introduction to this book, I now propose to outline a sketch, caricature or 'ideal type' of the modern managed organization as it appears to me from my experience and reading. It is not any particular organization that is described here, but rather an abstracted representation of how many managed organizations seem to arrange themselves, whatever their specific context and rhetoric, particularly within the contemporary British public sector. I suspect it can be found in the churches, charities and the private sector as well as in the public sector.

The modern managed organization can be characterized thus:

- The purpose of the organization is sprung from a *vision* of what the organization is there to do – in a changing world, this is a vision of where the organization is aiming to go, not a statement of where it is, or what it likes doing best.
- The organization's vision is inscribed in its *mission statement* or general statement of purpose – ideally a single sentence encapsulating the organization's philosophy and direction.
- This statement is explicated and concretized through a number of constitutive *aims*.
- These aims are broken down into *objectives*.
- People working in this kind of managed organization have some aspect of the organization's aims and objectives to address. Occupational *roles* and *job descriptions*, together with the skills and competencies needed, are, or should be, directly related to tasks sprung from organizational aims and goals.
- To perform the tasks necessary to achieve objectives, organization members need job-related training (not education) to acquire observable and demonstrable *skills* and *competencies* which fit them exactly for their organizational role.
- To ensure that organizational and individual efforts are progressing towards the realization of the vision, *measurable targets and performance targets* must be identified and implemented.

A few features of this symmetrical, well-ordered arrangement may be noted. First, in principle, everybody in the organization should be trying to achieve the same aim and moving in the same direction, thus eliminating friction and waste. Secondly, the organization functions as a hierarchical pyramid with vision at its apex. Thirdly, as one moves from the top to the bottom of the organizational pyramid, the vision/mission becomes incarnated in ever-more specific and concrete tasks and skills.

Some important organizational exclusions

The simplicity and clarity of this vision-driven, mission-led organization described above is both its strength and its weakness. Management theorists like Peter Drucker have provided powerful apologias for this kind of arrangement.[7] In this context, I want to point up its weaknesses, and particularly the ways in which important issues and aspects are excluded from organizations that basically construct themselves around this kind of model.

Vision and the exclusion of the past

The modern, managed organization is forward-looking, trying to shape its own future in desired ways, often via an official plan for change. There is nothing wrong with this in itself – clearly, organizations cannot spend all their time dwelling on the present or the past. However, far from dwelling on past or present, these aspects of existence are almost completely ignored. Sometimes it seems as if the only thing that matters is the colonization of the future.

There are several potentially negative aspects to the exclusion of past and present in managerial thinking. First, to collude with an entirely future orientation is to deal in a realm of speculation and unreality which is essentially unknown and unmanageable. The capitalist economic order in general often trades on non-specific hopes of better things to come on the morrow; deferred desires and needs will in due course be plentifully gratified. However, nobody actually knows what tomorrow will bring (for example, a stock exchange crash or a cut in government grant). To place all hope upon colonizing the unknown is a dangerous, risky enterprise. This is particularly so if the shadow cast by a future orientation has negative effects on the present, as is often the case in organizations. The anouncement of strategic plans and visions can make individuals and groups feel displaced or insecure, thus reducing the capacity of an organization like a hospital to actually deliver good services today.

If the present and the good things (as well as the negative things) it contains are often devalued in managerial thinking, the past is almost a dirty word. Like converts to sectarian Christianity, many managers seem to regard the past as having value only insofar as it provides a negative contrast with the present and the future. It is a thing to be discarded and repented of. Drucker sees one of the most important jobs of managers as working out which 'old' practices and products should be jettisoned.[8] Handy and other theorists turn their attention constantly towards the beckoning, benevolent future, bidding managers to recognize the second curve of the 'S' that means that they need to get on with changing the ways of the past before they are overtaken by obsolescence.[9]

The denial and abnegation of the past is a troubling phenomenon. For most individuals and groups, much of their self-identity actually resides in their sense of the past and the events and stories that emerge from it. Often, people derive real strength and courage to face the troubles of the present and the anxieties posed by the future by resorting to some sort of version of a great tradition that gives a sense of place and purpose. Organizations, too, are products of their past in many ways. It seems sensible in this context to remember the psychoanalytic dictum that those who do not remember are forced to re-experience what is repressed.[10]

In the NHS, an organization with a history if ever there was one, there appears at the moment to be a mixture of amnesia and denial about the past. Managers talk about the NHS before the 1990 reforms as a kind of pre-managerial, pre-market forces dark age. It is presented as full of bad practices and poor performances with nothing to offer the present or the future except quaint, nostalgic myths and a few dusty core values.[11]

The exclusion or denial of an organizational past that is fostered by some contemporary ideologies of management requires further investigation than can be offered here. However, some of its problematic and possibly harmful effects can be pointed out. First, denying the past and failing to understand former successes and failures means that nothing useful can be appropriated from it. This may help to ensure that past mistakes are destined to be repeated while any wisdom and learning that might have been gained is lost. Secondly, past performance is often a source of considerable pride and esteem. To fail to recognize this may be to demoralize and denigrate individuals whose own pasts are tied up with the organization.[12] Finally, in some cases, too determined a denial of the past may lead to individuals and groups leaving the organization or withdrawing their goodwill and effort from it. Valuable expertise and skill that may be needed again in a truly uncertain future may be lost – this could be very expensive to replace.

Pursuing a future-oriented vision seems to require making the present uncomfortable and problematic while denying, repenting of or demonizing the past. This kind of exclusive thinking is not unproblematic. It may be humanly, organizationally and even ecologically harmful and destructive. A place needs to be found for understanding and living happily with past and present in any management theory which is humanly sensitive and ecologically sympathetic.

Optimism and the exclusion of limitation and failure

Managed organizations have an official ideology of confidence and optimism that they can attain their objectives and ensure their own survival. Stewart, for example, points out that NHS managers have to inspire confidence in others. They must, therefore, appear more confident than they feel and keep their negative feelings and attitudes to themselves.[13] This is probably desirable in many ways. Organizations that perceived themselves to be ineffectual and futile would be in a poor position to do anything, rather as individuals suffering from depression may find themselves disabled from effective action.

The problem with having too great a sense of optimism is that doubts, limitations and failures in organizational performance may be ignored or denied. One of my Business School colleagues asserts that organizations persistently under-report management experiments and initiatives that do not deliver the results that they are expected to. Many of the more visionary management texts talk about the need to make mistakes and to learn from failures. However, my own experience is that people very seldom want to recount their experience of failure and the lessons they have learned from this. In practice, failure is frequently either ignored or punished; it is seldom welcomed as a real learning opportunity. The texts written by successful business people and management gurus almost never give detailed accounts of specific failures and the valuable lessons that have emerged from these.[14]

The prevailing ideology of the 'gospel of success' precludes a proper understanding of the limits and harmful effects of individual and organizational activity. Unnuanced optimism and denial of problems and doubt is oppressive and unrealistic. This might be thought a particularly relevant factor in the non-profit sector where limited resources often prevent the ideal from being realized. Incapacity to acknowledge and understand limitation and failure distorts reality, making it one-sided. It may prevent employees and managers being honest about their own limitations and failures so that important and potentially damaging mistakes are 'covered up'. This cannot be helpful to employees, to managers, or to the society in which organizations exist. Sometimes there are very good reasons for managers and organizations to feel pessimistic, for example when they contemplate the baleful effects of some of their activity upon the public or upon the environment. Balanced realism is important if they are to play a responsible and responsive role in society.

Clarity and the exclusion of diversity
The point about formulating a vision and a clear mission statement that is then turned into action through the identification of aims, objectives and tasks is that this gives a very clear direction and purpose to an organization.

For some organizations, it may be entirely appropriate to have a very clear and narrow purpose. However, gaining total clarity is likely to exclude activities and purposes (and ultimately people) that might themselves be desirable and important. For example, it could be argued that churches and other kinds of voluntary organizations might exist for a large number of purposes that may be to some extent conflicting or incompatible, such as providing friendship for the members and providing a high standard professional service to the community.[15] Similarly, members of the public may legitimately expect to get a number of different things from public services. This being the case, it is reasonable that there should be ongoing and unresolved debate upon what such services should provide. That is the nature of politics in a society where groups have different interests and needs and public services are situated within the political domain.[16]

Lack of clarity and purpose may be very unhelpful and wasteful. However, excluding diversity of opinion and vision can itself be problematic. Exclusion of purposes and persons can be pernicious. It may create feelings of rejection and anger that can backfire on an organization. For example, if a public-service organization decides that it is not interested in providing services for a particular group of users it may find them uninterested in supporting the continuing existence of the organization in the future. Similarly, if an organization gets rid of particular categories of staff because they are not necessary to the realization of its well-defined purpose, it may find that it does not have the diversity of skills it needs at a later point to tackle new eventualities. At one level, the identification and pursuit of very clear, measurable goals and aims may simply mean the arbitrary neglect of sensible, laterally relevant activities that may be in the long-term interests of an organization.

Autonomy and the exclusion of effective accountability
A key feature of the modern managed organization, such as the hospital trust or the school that has opted out of local education authority control, is its autonomy and its capacity to determine its own vision and future plans. This is an advantage if it allows those who manage organizations to have a real sense of responsibility for their corporate destiny, or if it enables the organization to become more flexible and locally responsive. The danger with this kind of independence, which mirrors the autonomy that private-sector organizations enjoy, is that it may be unclear to whom the organization is accountable and whose interests should be served.

It has been a long-standing criticism of private-sector institutions that, despite the rhetoric of becoming ethical and serving wider communities locally and beyond, they adopt objectives and purposes that may not be in the interests of the wider public.[17] Such organizations are often accused of failing to take account of the social and political context within which their activity is situated and of being ultimately self-serving. This is a serious matter for private business which is often inadequately addressed.[18] It is of even more fundamental importance when it comes to non-profit and public organizations where accountability to the wider community is crucial.

There is increasing anxiety about the 'democratic deficit' in public services run by boards of directors or governors that are not directly elected or appointed by the local community. It is often unclear how citizens can be effectively involved with shaping the goals and types of services that should be available, and how the managers of such services might be held publicly accountable for their actions. If this problem is not addressed, there is every possibility that appropriate, acceptable services may not be delivered. Similarly, those who work in these organizations may feel that they do not have much public man-date and support for what they are doing. The exclusion of effective accountability is, therefore, potentially a harmful effect of a managerial ideology that prizes 'managers right to manage' in autonomous organ-izations that have little direct responsibility to the community and to society in general.

Competence and the exclusion of the human and unpredictable
The vision and purpose to the managed organization is broken down into aims and objectives which eventually become the basis for the job descriptions of individuals. Within contemporary understandings of Human Resource Management, individual role occupants are then required to have the specified, observable, measurable skills and com-petences needed to perform their allotted tasks. Of course, it seems very sensible for individuals to know what they should be doing and to have the wherewithal to do it – nobody would want to have a job for which they felt entirely unequipped. However, there are problems inherent in the specification of very particular observable competencies and skills that can form the basis for, for example, National Vocational Qualifica-tions (NVQs).

The main objection to an emphasis on observable skills and com-petences is that types of skill and knowledge that are not easy to specify may be neglected or downgraded. For example, the kind of under-standing and wisdom that comes from life and which may be very valuable in, say, caring relationships may be disregarded. Similarly, the tendency to break jobs and occupations down into analysable units may in fact distort the holistic nature of a job. Nurses, for example, protest that the performance of their job is more than applying atomized skills.[19] Much that is of value to the actual performance of a job may not be recognized in the competence-based organization. This may down-grade individuals' sense of their own worth and job satisfaction.

The idea of skills and competences existing almost independently of understanding is narrow and suspect, presenting a view of the person as only valuable as a performer. I can be seen to perform, therefore I am of (economic) value – what I think or feel is irrelevant. Alvesson and Willmot note that, 'the concept of "competence" is crucial in presenting people as manageable commodities rather than unpredictable and self-willed agents'.[20] The dominance of a skills and competences orientation may therefore have dangerously narrowing and dehumanizing tendencies in organizations that are necessarily comprised of human beings and which need to serve human purposes. They may be seen as part of a managerial temptation to denigrate the essential humanity of organizations:

> Managers may try to make employees, suppliers or customers act
> predictably, like well-oiled machines. But people are wilful. Indeed, the
> orgins of the term 'management' can be traced to the Italian word
> *maneggiare*, which means 'to handle a horse'.[21]

The identification of relevant and demonstrable standards of skills and competence is clearly value-laden and ideological. It requires some individuals to conform to the implicit values of a hierarchically constituted standards authority. This moulds them according to its own immediately perceived needs and values. Ironically, NVQs and other competence standards which are couched within the rhetoric of preparing people for the future and for change are likely to be highly conservative. This is because they are based on the experiences, interests and views of those who are at the top of organizations. They may, in fact, discourage just that kind of imagination and flexibility that will be needed to respond effectively to an uncertain future. Conformity to well-defined and established standards is of infinite value to an organization, but only if nothing is going to change radically. From the point of view of higher education, Barnett writes:

> Profound societal, international and ecological change ... denies
> validity to the notion of competence if by that term is taken to be any
> set of behaviours, activities or responses that will tomorrow carry the
> value that they have today.[22]

Measurement and the exclusion of the intangible

The specification of standards and outcome measures in organizations ensures that individually and corporately things continue to move forward towards the organization's ultimate purpose. They provide benchmarks against which performance and progress can be measured, giving something specific towards which the organization can aspire and allowing a sense of achievement when they are attained.

To be useful, outcomes must be specific, observable and measurable. The problem here is that there is a tendency to concentrate on things which are easy to measure and quantify, particularly, of course, on financial measures which are very clear and well-developed by accountants. It is easier to measure the number of days a patient stays in hospital, for example, than to evaluate the nature of the experience that he or she may have had in the hospital. There is an inexorable pull, therefore, towards focusing upon things that are seen rather than unseen. A target or outcome that is clearly specified may be pursued vigorously and at the cost of pursuing less well-specified but equally important ends.[23]

Equally, there is a pull towards valuing outcomes and end products rather than processes, and quantity rather than quality. Measuring quantity, indeed, can become a surrogate for measuring quality and intangibles. Thus, managerial attention can quickly become concentrated on meeting measurable goals and targets, and especially on the financial 'bottom line'. This may displace thinking about wider factors that might be highly pertinent, particularly in organizations that deliver services to other human beings which of their very nature must have elements of process, subjectivity, unpredictability and intangibility.

Many of the things that are most valued in life and human service provision are not easily susceptible to measurement or accurate prediction. The experienced process of eating a gourmet meal on a French hillside is qualitatively different from eating a sandwich in the works canteen, but the measurable outcome is the same – one takes on enough calories to be able to continue living. Furthermore, people do not always know what they will find valuable in advance of receiving it. A common experience amongst students, for example, is that subjects that they did not think they would get much out of yield surprising rewards and benefits that could not have been predicted.

An individual's inner experience of events and people may be more significant than their external, measurable outcomes. So, for example, a chance word from a lecturer or carer may be more useful than the course as a whole or the treatment the carer came to deliver. Furthermore, the process of receiving a service or partaking in it may be at least as important as the outcome. Understanding, wisdom of body or mind and experience may be intangible and unmeasurable, but they have considerable, if elusive, value. A certain openness to the depth and breadth of life may in itself be valuable:

> As with competences, outcomes represent a form of closure. They
> predetermine the required characteristics students should end up with.
> Both terms are part of a language of prejudging, imposition and
> inevitable narrowness. They spring from a particular form of reason –
> instrumental reason – and seem to broaden its domination in the wider
> society . . . so further marginalizing other forms of action and reason.[24]

The management theorists who argue strongly that, with enough thought, most, if not all, worthwhile, desired human experiences can be measured against sensitively constructed standards may be right in this bold assertion. However, in many organizations an emphasis on measurement constrains the scope of organizational attention in such a way that much of human value and significance is excluded.

The actual process of measurement may in itself be invasive and costly (consider the cost in terms of effort, time and personal stress that has gone into various assessment exercises in schools and universities). There is a danger that in trying to measure everything and know everything that is going on, important aspects of reality are actually hidden.[25]

Finally, the specification of standards and targets may actually encourage some organizational members to strive for less rather than more. It is possible to work down rather than up to a target for some people. All these factors may help to make an obsession with measures and outcomes actively diminishing for managers, staff and organizational clients alike, especially in human services.

Organizational goodness and the exclusion of evil

The modern, managed organization is led by a value-driven vision. It believes its activity to be of great worth. Organizational literature proclaims the value of the organization's aims (e.g. many universities say they are 'seeking excellence in teaching and research') and also the high quality of its performance. Of course, it is good if organizations believe both in the value of their work and superiority of their products. This may help to provide a sense of high morale and justifiable pride amongst employees. However, no organization is free of faults and weaknesses (often known all too well by their employees) and no activity is free of negative or harmful effects. It is important, therefore, to consider the effects that overt denial of any kind of evil may have in and for organizations.

One exclusion that often occurs here is that no-one overtly and fundamentally questions the aims, ends and methods of the organization. So, for example, it seems to be forbidden to question whether the production of armaments or junk food is a worthy end of human endeavour. Whatever the organization does is deemed to be essentially good because the organization does it. If this end is questioned, then the critics are often encouraged to change their point of view or perhaps to leave the organization. This situation has occurred often in the NHS where critics of the aims and methods of the new organizational rulers have often found themselves rather quickly dismissed.[26]

If organizations cannot admit to an evil or dark side within themselves then a good place to locate it is outside. Here the language of warfare and cut-throat competition is used to create enemies ('competitors') whose products can be criticized and derided and who can be seen as dispensable. Such discourse, which is pervasive in many modern organizations, accompanies the creation of a sense of permanent threat from outside. This helps to get organizational members to pull together for their common good. The problem is that it may create unhelpful and unnecessary enmity and suspicion between organizations which may not ultimately be helpful. For example, if universities see themselves as being involved in a price war against each other to attract students, then costs may indeed fall for students, but so might the standards of the courses which the universities concerned offer. The losers will ultimately be the students. Demonization of outsiders corrodes co-operation and trust. This may be very harmful in public and non-profit organizations where these elements may be very important for the long-term public good.

The secretiveness and paranoia that have sprung up in the name of competition between organizations and colleagues who used to work together seem in many ways antipathetic to the needs of users of all kinds, as does the costly charging and billing process that goes along with quasi-commercial contract relationships. Similarly, it may encourage a combative or conflictive attitude on the part of service users and consumers who begin to think of public organizations and services as adversaries to be sued. It will be a long time before many organizations have the maturity to be able to adopt a stance which does not involve implicitly demonizing opponents, competitors and even 'customers' while failing to acknowledge the harmful effects of their own practices and activities.

It would be possible to go on to document further examples of important exclusions from the modern managed organization. For example, although the rhetoric of participation and corporate 'ownership' of organizational purpose abounds, the views of people at the 'bottom' are seldom really attended to. This is symbolized by the fact that most organs of communication, for example organizational newsletters, are basically controlled by senior management and are mainly used to disseminate information from the top rather than to collect it from below. As we will see in the next chapter, there is often a strong ethos of compliance and obedience in modern organizations, despite their lip-service to creativity and empowerment of organizational members.

Another exclusion may be that of having truly worthwhile social purposes. The desire to be successful and to survive as an organization can actually blind managers to issues of long-term value and purpose. Alvesson and Willmott give a cautionary account of the US Pepsi Corporation and its chief executive, John Sculley. This can serve as a salutary warning even to those who do not work in the private sector. Discussing Sculley's single-minded obsession with beating the Coca-Cola Corporation, they write:

> Sculley and his colleages appear to have behaved like the members of a religious cult whose prospects of salvation were measured in the sales of sweetened water. In this context, it became unreasonable to ask: What is the purpose of the Pepsi Corporation? Does it accomplish anything socially valuable? Work was self-evidently purposeful so long as more sweetneed water was sold, and the ultimate prize was to outsell Coca-Cola. A person working for the Red Cross, saving people from starving to death ... could not not have been more committed than Sculley was to increasing Pepsi's sales. Through rigid codes (e.g. dressing), and through carefully orchestrated rituals ('public hangings' for poor performance), discipline and conformity at Pepsi were tightly maintained. ... [E]xecutives willingly subordinated their working lives to a strict logic of winning market share. Friendship, family and other interests were pushed to the margins. This corporate hegemony was so strong that no sign of complaints, doubts or questioning was tolerated. When working for Pepsi, the purpose was self-evident and unquestioned .... To doubt, or to become deflected from this purpose was *heresy*.[27]

Conclusion

Precisely because of the clarity of its profile and purpose, the modern, managed vision-driven organization can cast a very clear, dark shadow. It can easily be, or become, myopic, hierarchical, centralized, unegalitarian, self-centred and self-determined, aggressive, competitive, suspicious, dualistic, conformist, slightly paranoid and, surprisingly, conservative. Its narrow, instrumental view of people and of reality precludes much that is of value in human experience and it is wildly over-optimistic in its view of controlling the future.

Even in the public and voluntary sectors, managed organizations may be in danger of creating important exclusions and dualisms that may be harmful, both to individuals inside and outside the organization, and to wider society. While I may have overdrawn the negative aspects of modern organizations, their narrowing and diminishing effects on human possibility are real. Their potential for exclusion and harm is often ignored for reasons of survival and trying to preserve a sense of organizational goodness. However, it is the very fact that it is ignored that makes it most pernicious and dangerous. The only way to come to terms with exclusions is for them to be recognized, owned and re-integrated by organizations. Managers and others need to recognize and critically understand the shadow cast by their organizations and their activities. Seeking to travel in straight lines towards a single vision that is defined from the top may bring harm and unintended ill-effects in its wake. All of which is to recognize that the power to be creative and be effective is not inevitably to do good.

In trying to point up some of the demonizing and dualistic tendencies in modern managed organizations it is very important not to demonize them. Any kind of organization or human activity of significance, whether managerial or other, has the potential for benefit and harm. Administered organizations, insofar as they exclude innovation, choice and flexibility might be just as vulnerable to critique on the grounds of important exclusions as their newer, managed counterparts. There is no ideal kind of organization which does no harm and includes everything that is worth including. However, managed organizations, particularly in the non-profit sector, need to become aware of factors that are excluded and the implications of this so that they can assess whether particular exclusions are helpful or not. Managers acting and thinking on their own within organizations are not necessarily in the best position to judge this. They need the input of outsiders, customers and citizens if they are to live up to their potential for human benefit and social usefulness.

7

Virtues and values

Be sure of this, that no immoral or impure man, or one who is covetous (that is, an idolater) has any inheritance in the kingdom of Christ and of God. Let no one deceive you with empty words, for it is because of these things that the wrath of God comes upon the sons of disobedience.

(Ephesians 5.5–7 RSV (adapted))

If fear of the world forms part of the basis for ecclesial identity, an equally strong ingredient is that of obedience .... Fear and obedience – either of God or those agents who represent him – often leads to an emphasis on holiness.[1]

An important part of membership of a fundamentalist religious sect is rigorous adherence to that sect's moral code and ethos. One of the things that distinguishes those who are saved from those who are damned is their distinctive, strict morality. This is born out of loyalty to the sect and its leaders, as well, perhaps, as from fear of exclusion and exposure to the wicked ways of the world. Sect members are required to live in a moral enclave. They strive to make their lives conform to the norms and mores of the group. If they respond positively to the carrots and sticks of sectarian discipline, they may hope to inherit the earth. If they fail to do this, they may find themselves consigned to outer darkness, to the place of wailing and gnashing of teeth.

In this chapter, I want to explore some aspects of the morality of managers, particularly in the public sector. First, I will look at attempts to think about ethics in public-service management. The attempt to think consciously and officially about ethics in management generally is welcome. Nonetheless, the problems raised in trying to do this in the public sector are considerable and solutions so far adopted are at best partial.

Managed organizations do not lack values, norms and approved behaviours, many of which are implicit, to which organizational members are required to conform. Corporate ethos pervades all aspects of an

100

organization's life, work and culture. One of the points where it is ensured that this ethos is adopted and adhered to by individuals is within the context of Individual Performance Review (IPR), or appraisal. The second part of this chapter is, then, a critical examination of the appraisal process as a tool of 'virtue formation' or social control. I will argue that appraisal is such a complex and problematic activity that its persistence as a key tool of management is mainly due to its symbolic importance in affirming hierarchies of power and 'managing the individual heart'.

The third part of the chapter provides cautionary material about the virtues of loyalty and obedience within the context of managerial control. In it, I shall look at the way in which the desire to ensure obedience and loyalty can lead to the suppression of truth and dissent. Notwithstanding the rhetoric of empowerment and participation, many public-sector workers now find themselves in a position where they feel that they cannot speak out about issues that concern them. The plight of the 'whistleblower' who tells the truth outside the organization for the sake of the public good is becoming increasingly prominent as employers in the public sector equate loyalty with blind obedience and uncritical silence.

Ethics and values in management

Ethics in management theory

Ethics and values are of fundamental importance in much of the management theory that emerges from the private sector. Peter Drucker, for example, takes an impressively high moral view of both the ends and means used in business: 'To Drucker, the business organization, as any organization, is "a human, a social, indeed a moral phenomenon".'[2] For Drucker, 'The business enterprise produces neither things nor ideas but humanly determined values.'[3] Businesses do not exist for the sake of survival or profit. These are but means to the higher ends of innovation and marketing: 'The purpose of business is not to make a profit. Profit is a necessity and a social responsibility.'[4] Drucker is acutely conscious of the context and responsibility of business, seeing it as necessary for the production and maintenance of social and human goods. He describes the ethical responsibilities of management, allotting to it the task of becoming 'the keeper of society's conscience and the solver of society's problems'.[5] Drucker sees this approach as a philosophy of management based upon objectives and self-control.[6]

Recognizing the value-laden aspect of every aspect of management, including various kinds of measurement and control, Drucker demands high individual and corporate ethical standards of managers. They must respect the individuals with whom they work and manifest fundamental qualities of integrity and character:

> if [the manager] lacks in character and integrity – no matter how knowledgeable, how brilliant, how successful – he destroys. He destroys people, the most valuable resource of the enterprise. He destroys spirit. And he destroys performance.[7]

For Drucker,

> Nothing better prepares the ground for ... leadership than a spirit of management that confirms in the day-today practices of the organization strict principles of conduct and responsibility, high standards of performance, and respect for individuals and their work.[8]

Drucker sums up his vision of ethical managers in socially and morally responsible, value-creating businesses thus:

> together the managers of our institutions – business, universities, schools, hospitals and government agencies – are the leadership groups in the modern society of organizations. As such they need an ethics [sic], a commitment and a code. The right one is the code developed more than two thousand years ago for the first professional leadership group, the physician: 'Above all not knowingly to do harm.'[9]

The rhetoric of ethics and values, expressed in the high tones of moral vision, runs deep in some parts of management theory.[10] It is difficult, however, to evaluate how far moral vision affects practice. Within the British public sector, finding ways of articulating and interpreting ethical and value issues for managers and groups has been problematic. The importance of recognizing and dealing with these issues in management has been equalled by a corresponding ignorance of how to do it.

I now propose to look at concern for ethics and values within public service management as a way of highlighting some of the problems that arise when organizations and their managers aspire to be ethical and moral.

Explicit concern about ethics in the public sector
Explicit concern about ethics and values has only recently become an important feature of organizational management in the public sector. A number of factors have contributed to this change.

First, the whole management function has become more important and significant. It has been revised and upgraded to become more 'professional'. There are now, for example, attempts to specify common standards and skills for managers. It is usual for professions to have a code of ethics to which members are required to adhere. This helps regulate standards, as well as enhancing clear professional identity.

At a more practical level, significant decision-making and responsibility have been devolved downwards to smaller independent purchaser and provider units. In the absence of precise central guidance, many managers perceive a fairly urgent need for greater guidance and for more skills of value judgement, for example in trying to determine how resources should be deployed on behalf of a local community. In the past, it was mostly professionals who were perceived as needing to make overtly ethical decisions; now this responsibility is shared by managers.

Ethical and value issues become both more apparent and more contested when radical change takes place. Custom, tradition and 'common sense' can no longer serve as a complete guide to behaviour. Public service organizations have undoubtedly experienced radical change over the last few years. Many of the changes which have taken place have been driven by a powerful moral vision of free-market values. This has served to make ethical concerns more visible.

There is now an ethical and value 'market-place', as much as in any other kind of market-place, in the public sector. Lack of specific guidelines coupled with organizational change and fragmentation in public services controlled by local contract rather than direct central management means that the details of responsibility and judgment are not filled out. Individual managers at the local level therefore have a clear responsibility to formulate and choose their own values and ways of realizing them.

Public bodies have become much more politicized and overtly value driven. Politics, however, which from Plato onwards has been the art of debating social values and determining the public good, has been edged out of the public domain with the exclusion of elected, representative politicians from responsible bodies. This has left an ethical vacuum which contributes to the present need to develop managerial ethical codes, competence and awareness as a partial substitute. As in the world of business, from which managerialism has taken much, the place of politics is taken by ethics. At the same time, the consensus on the Welfare State and the meaning of the public-service ethic has disappeared.[11] We are in a period of exploration and change.

Ethical issues and dilemmas
That managers in the public sector face important ethical issues and dilemmas is not in doubt. Here is a list of issues that might face any manager in health care:

- How are the competing interests of the individual patients and patients as a group to be reconciled?
- How are competing principles of individuality, privacy, preservation from harm, informed consent and professionalism to be harmonized?
- How should scarce resources be allocated between different needy and deserving groups?
- What weight is to be given to patients' preferences/beliefs?
- Does respect for the autonomy of individual patients override the health of the nation, for example in immunization and screening campaigns?
- Which professionals should have the dominant voice in making decisions about individual patients or indeed about the allocation of resources?
- What is the role of managers in inter-professional disputes?
- To what extent should managers act as champions of those like elderly and mentally ill people whose rights may be threatened?
- When is it right to intervene in someone's life for their own benefit but against their will?
- What significance and resources should be given to health promotion and illness prevention for the sake of generations yet to come when present needs of sick people are still unmet?
- What responsibility does the manager have to the general public as opposed to the health care services?
- How much should a manager tell members of the public about health service plans – what obligation does she have to inform and consult with the public about proposals which may affect their future?
- What personal ethical and religious beliefs and practices should be tolerated and encouraged by the manager within her organization?
- How should a manager behave ethically towards her employers and her employees?
- How should ethics impinge upon contracting with its competitive and therefore secretive implications?
- What is the relationship between the law and ethical principles, for example that of confidentiality?[12]

These issues have been supplemented and sharpened by various difficulties and problems that have arisen recently. For example, there are concerns about probity in corporate governance, corruption and failure of judgment in public bodies, and the increasing need to make conscious, controversial decisions about the use of ever-scarcer resources. In these circumstances, it is not surprising if public-service managers feel a bit at sea, rather confused and isolated, terribly responsible for many things at different levels and needing to get it right first time, without really knowing what 'right' means any more.

Strategies for filling the ethical vacuum

In the absence of any clear, easily accessible guidance from ethical tradition and of authoritative consensus on methods to be used or values to be adopted, various strategies have been employed to fill the ethical vacuum between legal requirements and individual conscience in public-service management. Central government has tried to provide guidelines for corporate governance to enhance its reliability and credibility.[13] Professional bodies like the Institute of Health Services Management have issued statements of values which provide some guidance for managers, but only at a high level of generality.[14] There is some impetus towards providing detailed codes of practice for managers that are modelled on the professional codes of, for example, doctors or nurses. Here there is the danger either of vagueness or over-specificity for managers who may have to deal with very different issues in different contexts in different ways. To help overcome these problems, some people suggest that the main thing is for organizations at a local level to develop their own philosophies and codes, formulated as a kind of ethical 'Ten Commandments' which can be hung upon the wall of every office and against which behaviour may be measured.

Some managers repose much of their hope for responsible, ethical decision-making and behaviour in consulting with the public by various means, for example using referenda or reference panels on priorities and resources. The idea is that if the public decides then the decision must be right. This is, however, to miss the obvious point that the majority may not be right. In practice, such populist methods often yield results that would be professionally unacceptable, giving, for example, low priority to mental health needs or the needs of the elderly. Another method that may be used to supplement management decision-making is the employment of utilitarian techniques like 'QALYs' (Quality Adjusted Life Years). Here the benefits in terms of treatment versus likely improvement in quality of life over a period of time can be weighed in the balance and so resources can, in theory, be distributed to those who will most benefit from them.[15] This has some affinities with ideas such as Evidence-Based Medicine which allots treatments only on the basis of their tested success rather than on the basis of arbitrary professional judgement.

All the above techniques and intitiatives contain elements of arbitrariness and subjectivity. At best, codes, QALYs and the rest are simply guides and aids to judgment. They cannot remove the responsibility for judgment, decision and action from individuals and groups of human beings. Managers play a crucial role in ensuring that appropriate decisions are made in ethical ways. To do this they need the confidence and skills of appropriate ethical judgment and discernment. If these skills and this confidence are not easily to be found (and presently they are not) a real vacuum of moral responsibility can emerge.

In such a vacuum, essentially moral issues and decisions may be cast into financial terms. Some managers may feel tempted to let the rights and wrongs of policies and decisions rest upon 'market forces'. The process of contracting for services will then sort out what is going to happen. For others, the necessity to exercise ethical judgment and to take moral responsibility may be abrogated to uncritical obedience and loyalty to some kind of higher authority. When obedience and loyalty become the total method and content of managerial ethics, there may be untoward consequences. A culture of intimidation and conformity may emerge. The cost of not becoming competent in the area of ethics and values is, therefore, very high.

The inevitability of values and ethics

While attempts to help managers manage more ethically in both private and non-profit organizations are still in their infancy, this does not mean that organizations lack ethos, norms and practices, some of which are explicit, others implicit and unacknowledged. Organizational members 'swim' in a sea of values, adding their our own value preferences together with the ethical decisions and performances to this sea. It is not a matter of choosing whether or not to have ethics and values in management. Rather, it is a question of which values should be selected and affirmed and whether to be unconscious and uncritical or conscious and critical of them.

In the next part of the chapter, I examine one of the ways in which ethos and values are inculcated in the individual by the process of Individual Performance Review (IPR). I will argue that, whatever its putative advantages and benefits, one of the main functions that IPR performs is that of confession in medieval Catholicism. It is a means of engendering conformity and control in the individual. This judgment is based on looking at some of the criticism of IPR that shows that many of its practices, assumptions and outcomes are so problematic that it cannot be demonstrated that IPR is actually useful within many organizations. When problematic practices continue to be pursued, one must look behind their obvious uses and the rationales that are advanced for them to ask whether they serve a different purpose from that which is overt.

Governing the soul: appraisal and Individual Performance Review

Appraisal, or IPR, is, in some ways, the most personally immediate sign and sacrament of the modern managed organization. In most organizations, some kind of appraisal or performance review is now mandatory for employees. It has been one of the elements of private-sector management practice that the British government has been most keen to promote right across the public sector. Many charities and non-profit organizations have also introduced it voluntarily in the name of good management practice.

The nature of appraisal
Systems of appraisal, and the uses to which it is put, vary between and even within organizations. Three elements are typical of all appraisal schemes. First, it is usually individual performance that is the subject of appraisal; individuals are usually appraised by a single other individual who often has direct managerial oversight of their work. Secondly, appraisal requires assessment of past performance against previously agreed goals or targets. Thirdly, goals and targets are set for future performance.

Appraisals may take place annually, or more or less often. Appraisal can be is linked to the judgment of whether an individual should receive additional reward (e.g. Performance Related Pay) or to the planning of career development and discerning training needs. Some appraisal systems use a standard form or format for all employees of a particular kind. Others work with a 'blank sheet' upon which the appraisee assesses him or herself and writes his/her own long- and short-term objectives and how they will be attained within a particular time period. Like many types of management technology, appraisal is usually aimed at ensuring that employees understand and assimilate the objectives and goals of the organization and their function within it so that they can bend their efforts to the corporate purpose. Being linked to the overall future-oriented vision, aims and objectives of the organization, the setting of performance goals and targets inevitably contains an imperative to personal change. Although some goals and targets will be about maintenance, that is carrying on doing what needs to be done, the implicit thrust of much appraisal is towards change and development.

The advantages of appraisal
In a history spanning more than 40 years, appraisal has become steadily more universal throughout organizations and a staple element of personnel management. It has many enthusiasts and defenders. It has been

characterized as 'a key management system by which the effectiveness of individual managers is assessed and developed'.[16] Its advocates argue that it has many benefits. It gives managers a chance to assess the human resources at their disposal and objectively to review the work and skills of their subordinates so that they fit in with overall organizational needs and objectives. It permits a systematic and objective view of an individual's total performance. Career counselling and career development can be planned using appraisal. It can also be used for planning succession to different posts, assessing suitability for promotion, for identifying problems and poor performance, and for improving performance.[17] It is a 'tool for increasing managerial effectiveness through managerial learning and developing the capacity to learn how to learn, at both an individual and a corporate level'.[18]

From the appraisee's perspective, appraisal may allow for the recognition of past achievement, a sense of being supported, open communication with superiors, and knowledge of how their role and efforts contribute to the overall organizational task. Regular appraisal permits weaknesses and training needs to be identified and remedied, as well as giving a sense of progress and movement within an occupational role. Flanagan asserts that, 'At its best, IPR stimulates, provides clarity of purpose, increases effectiveness and reinforces personal development.'[19]

Problems with appraisal
From this kind of description, it might be concluded that appraisal is a kind of universal panacea for the management of people, the holy grail of personnel work. However, even protagonists of appraisal point out some important limitations of this activity.

For appraisal to be effective, a large number of conditions must be met. The objectives of any appraisal scheme must be very clear. If too many objectives have to be met, for example reviewing past performance, deciding on performance-related pay, identifying development needs and opportunities, then a scheme may well fail to meet them. Similarly, some purposes and objectives may conflict; for example, it is unlikely that someone is going to be honest about their failures and performance defects if the appraisal is to be used to determine pay or promotion prospects. Organizational objectives and definitions of effectiveness must be clear if appraisal is to be used to set individual targets. If appraisal is to work well, it should be introduced with the active consent of the workforce. Furthermore, it must be an integrated part of a whole philosophy and style of management, not an afterthought, or a 'bolt-on'. This is particularly important if the needs and opportunities identified in appraisal are to be followed through. If there is no action as a result of appraisal, for example if time and money for training are not forthcoming, then people may become cynical and detached about it. Successful appraisal schemes should be flexible and develop over time with the changing needs of the organization. The people who act as appraisers have to be skilled. They and their appraisees will require time to prepare for appraisal. It needs to be understood that honesty in appraisal sessions will not be punished and a non-judgmental attitude needs to be cultivated.

Beyond these ideal conditions, which are often not met in appraisal, there are a number of specific criticisms that protagonists make of appraisal systems. Some kinds of appraisal tend to focus on the traits and personality of the individual being appraised rather than upon actual behaviour and observable performance. The creation of goals and targets that extend only, say, over a twelve-month period can create a short-term view of the individual's role and function. Frequently, appraisal does not acknowledge or deal effectively with the fact that individual performance is often dependent upon, and embedded within, group activity. Then again, appraisal can be too static and infrequent; objectives may be set but not revised over time as situations change, leading to the 'OOOPs' phenomenon – 'objectives ousted by other priorities'.[20]

Appraisal easily becomes an end in itself, detached from other aspects of organizational life such as planning, pay and training. This makes it essentially a time-consuming irrelevance. It can also become too complex and too general, failing to provide swift, accurate and specific feedback to appraisees. If insufficient time is given to the development and implementation of appraisal schemes they often fail. If they are too rigorous and judgmental, appraisees may not be honest. They may then try to select low and loose aims and targets that they can easily fulfil. This can actually lead to diminished rather than improved performance.[21] Flanagan acknowledges that, 'At its worst, [IPR] ruins careers, causes personal resentment and anger, and creates disharmony and consequent inefficiency and ineffectiveness.'[22]

This kind of criticism and confusion around appraisal coming from its enthusiastic protagonists is deepened when the critics of appraisal are consulted. Sociologist Keith Grint, for example, highlights the fact that one of the basic assumptions of appraisal may be very problematic: 'Built into the appraisal system, of course, is an assumption that performance will improve with appraisals or that performance will decrease without appraisal.'[23]

Often, managers fail to enquire into the actual efficacy of their appraisal schemes once they are established. Grint points out that very few appraisal schemes avoid distortion to produce an objective measurement against some kind of measurable standard. They are distorted by the 'Halo Effect' (whereby assessment based on one specific criterion distorts assessment of other criteria), the 'Crony Effect' (where assessment is distorted by the personal relationship between appraiser and appraisee), the 'Doppelganger Effect' (where the rating reflects the similarity of character or behaviour between assessor and assessed), and the 'Veblen Effect' (whereby all those appraised end up with moderate scores). Furthermore, most appraisers do not like to give very negative assessments of others.[24] Grint cites research that shows that less than 20 per cent of appraisals are undertaken effectively in the USA; the more senior managers are, and so the more important their individual performance is, the less likely they are to be effectively appraised.

Grint concludes that appraisals do not in fact reflect or measure against reality. They actually construct reality, the performer and the performance:

> In effect the appraisal constructs rather than reflects the appraised and this should be borne in mind when any appraisal system is adopted and deployed. *Caveat emptor* should perhaps be required as a government health warning on the front of all appraisal schemes.[25]

Not surprisingly, he claims,

> there seems to be considerable though not universal dislike of and dissatisfaction with all performance appraisal systems to some degree; though some are clearly more popular than others, and the level of popularity seems to vary with position and result.[26]

If appraisal is actually such a useful and effective part of organizational management, giving feedback on performance and oiling organizational wheels, Grint argues, one might well expect senior managers to welcome appraisal from their subordinates. In fact, appraisal is almost invariably top-down. This leads to the suspicion that appraisal is not just to do with maximizing performance:

> If, as the CEO [Chief Executive Officer] may imply, the medicine is entirely safe and positively health-enhancing, then let us see the CEO directly involved too. On the other hand, if upward appraisals are not involved in any change towards a more participative style then subordinates might be justified in questioning the intentions of the superordinates: are they concerned with empowering subordinates or just exploiting them in more subtle ways?[27]

Grint concludes that, 'Rarely in the history of business can such a system have promised so much and delivered so little.'[28]

The critique of appraisal outlined above has been mostly constructed from sources that enthusiastically commend this activity as a key management tool. It shows that there are so many imponderables and things that can go wrong with appraisal, both in theory and practice, that it must be seen as a highly problematic activity. Most people working in managed organizations will recognize the difficulties and practical problems that arise in its implementation (hasty implementation, lack of employee participation and consent, failure to be non-judgmental and to follow through on needs identified etc.). Nothwithstanding the fact that some people actually value appraisal and may feel that they get a great deal from it, the ubiquity and popularity of appraisal schemes which are time- and money-consuming would seem to require an explanation that goes beyond vigorous assertion of their self-evident value.

Appraisal as a mechanism of social control

At least one important, if often implicit, function of appraisal is to contribute to organizational discipline and social control of the individual employee. The modern managed organization is panoptic.[29] There is a drive to know, understand and control everything that goes on inside it. Over the course of the present century, a major area of endeavour, particularly in psychology, has been to comprehend and control not just the bodies and behaviours of employees, but their minds and emotions as well.[30] The aim is to ensure that all organizational members have internalized the norms of the organization and behave accordingly. This desire finds expression in Drucker's aspiration that managers should be self-controlled from within rather than simply conforming to external norms:

> Management by objectives and self-control makes the interest of the enterprise the aim of every manager. It substitutes for control from outside the *stricter, more exacting and more effective control from inside*. It motivates managers to action not because somebody tells them to do something or talks them into doing it, but because the objective task demands it. They act not because somebody wants them to but because they themselves decide that they have to – *they act, in other words, as free men and women*.[31]

This aspiration is consonant with a less enthusiastic observation about social control in organizations from P. D. Anthony:

> The end result is to be able to propose to the worker that the social system is his in that it, like his work, has been constructed in order to take account of his wishes and his needs so that its objectives become his own. The end result is achieved when the application of authority

and power is no longer necessary to assist in the achievement of the organization's goals because the goals have been internalized by those who are to pursue them.[32]

The aspiration to control people from within, or rather to have them control themselves, is part of a turn to the individual self as the place where social control is mediated.[33]

To produce employees who have internalized organizational norms and values, even to the level of conforming their emotional responses to that which is organizationally acceptable, requires concerted effort and considerable technology. The one-to-one, confessional aspect of appraisal is one important way in which people learn to internalize, or at least be constantly aware of, the fact that their performance and behaviour is constantly being monitored. Performance and values may not be much altered by appraisal in concrete terms. However, the very process of having to account for one's work and activity reinforces the important value that individuals are personally responsible and must account to those who are 'above' them.

This is paralleled in the practice of sacramental confession within the Catholic Church. Again, this may or may not have helped people to live more virtuous, saintly lives. One thing it certainly did was to embody the idea that ordinary church members were under surveillance, if not by God directly then by his earthly representatives. The power of the Church to insist that people went to confession reinforced and made real the right of the Church to survey and control people's lives and souls. Writing of the twin rituals of excommunication from the Church and confession to obtain rehabilitation, Hepworth and Turner note: 'The presence of these complementary rituals provide, at least in principle, the possibility of a double confirmation of the authority of those in power and the validity of their moral universe.'[34]

This helped to create an ethic of obedience and respect for authority based on anxiety about sin and wrongdoing underwritten by a discourse of reward and punishment after death. The power of inescapable surveillance from above to discomfort and bring about conformity should not be underestimated now, any more than it was by religious authorities in the past:

> One of the major elements of the belief systems of the ancients is the perception that all human beings are totally exposed both in thought and action to their gods. This has the principal effect of inspiring mortals with a sense of guilt, well aware that in everyday life they constantly behave and think in contravention of the rules laid down by their gods, provoked in such behaviour and such thoughts by personality factors and their responses to situations.[35]

If appraisal systems are organizational 'cultural artefacts' that send out 'clear cultural messages', at least one important cultural message that most appraisal schemes send out is that people's lives and behaviours are constantly subjected to critical gaze from above.[36] Even if individuals find ways and means to hide or partially hide from the all-seeing, appraising eye (which they do), the right to appraise undergirds the right to manage.[37] It is an outward, powerful and visible manifestation of the ethos of top-down control that has enormous potential to produce guilt and shame in organizational members. This occurs almost independently of any particular values and behaviours that might be commended in any specific organizational appraisal process. As such, it can be a powerful symbol or sacrament of the absolute need for employee loyalty and obedience.

Paradoxically, the existence of highly visible external methods of surveillance like appraisal testifies to the continuing recalcitrance and ungovernable aspects of the humans who comprise the workforce, just as the existence of the confessional witnesses to the ineradicability of sin. Equally, as we have seen, it is not at all clear that appraisal is actually an effective means of bringing about organizational unity and conformity. Notwithstanding these observations, it is to the ethos of loyalty and compliance, particularly in public-service organizations, that I turn next to examine how these managerially determined 'virtues' can affect the organization and provision of services.

Loyalty, compliance and the exclusion of truth and dissent

Loyalty, obedience and confidentiality on the part of employees have always been important virtues within private-sector business organizations. They are necessary if firms are to redeem their investments, achieve their objectives and remain competitive. Unfortunately, it is not clear that they always serve the best interests of the wider community. What is commercially advantageous may not be socially desirable. So, for example, it is not clear that those researchers employed by tobacco companies who found out as early as the 1960s that tobacco products were indeed injurious to health were acting in a morally laudable fashion when they witheld this information from the public domain. It is even less clear that this kind of secrecy is defensible in the public sector where it is argued that the citizenry have a right to know what is being done in their name, with their money, ostensibly for their benefit.[38] Without freedom of information, there can be only limited public accountability. Without effective accountability, there is immense scope for irresponsibility.

Unfortunately, the marriage of the tradition of commercial confidentiality with the tradition of state secrecy in Britain appears to have
contributed to the production of a closed culture of intimidation within
many managed public-service organizations.[39] This, the final section of
the chapter, highlights the consequences of having a closed, competitive management culture that has hitherto shown no real sense of
how to develop appropriate norms and methods of ethical responsibility and judgment, either individually or corporately. When
organizational loyalty and obedience become exalted as the most
important moral norms, the consequences are baleful.

The example of whistleblowing
The phenomenon that best illustrates moral closure and narrowness is
that of whistleblowing. Whistleblowers are organizational members,
mostly not at the top of their organizations, who become concerned
about some deficit or harm that is being done within or by the organization and decide that they will draw attention to this. Usually, they start
this process by raising the matter internally. If things do not change or
improve, and they often do not, then they may go public, trying to draw
the attention of MPs, ministers or the media to the iniquity in order to
bring about change. Often whistleblowers have been vindicated in their
protests. Usually, however, this does not stop them from losing their
jobs and suffering intimidation and vilification from colleagues and
employers who may accuse them of bringing the organization into
disrepute.

Although whistleblowing in the public sector is not a new phenomenon – the horrific conditions in long-stay psychiatric hospitals in the
1970s were often first exposed by whistleblowers – it has attained a new
significance in public service since the implementation of the 1990
health and social care reforms when commercial, managerial traits were
given added impetus.[40] Since then, a number of conscientious professionals have felt obliged to draw public attention to matters of
concern. Their efforts have been rewarded with a mixture of contempt,
rejection and attempted dismissal by their organizational superiors.
Geoffrey Hunt, an ethicist and a whistleblower who publicly raised
concerns about standards in higher education, writes:

> Three recent cases in particular have become icons of professional
> dissidence: Graham Pink, a charge nurse, who went public over
> standards of care on a ward in a Stockport hospital, and was dismissed
> . . .; Helen Zeitlin, a doctor who expressed concern about a nursing
> shortage in her Redditch hospital and was made redundant . . .; and
> Chris Chapman, principal biochemist working for Leeds General

Infirmary and Leeds University, made redundant following his claim
that scientific fraud was taking place under commercial pressures ... .[41]

The roots of suppression

Whistleblowing is itself only an extreme instance of a general sense that
people cannot honestly state their opinions and concerns, however
serious, about issues and events in public-service organizations lest
they risk managerial ire and displeasure. An example of this is to be
found in the case of a Family Health Service Authority manager who
wrote to the *Health Service Journal* expressing some dismay at the lack of
anguish and abundance of provision at a National Association of
Health Authorities and Trusts conference.[42] The conference was conducted at considerable expense, in the midst of a recession, on the eve of
public expenditure cuts. This manager, bemused and angered by the
gap between governmental or managerial illusion and self-
congratulation and the experience of life in the NHS, felt so out of step
with officially defined 'reality' that he or she felt unable to publish his or
her name lest it should have adverse personal repercussions.

This suggests an organizational culture of intimidation where those
with sincere criticisms feel unable to share them. More particularly, it is
indicative of a culture which is wilfully self-deceived and wants to
believe in the myth of its own goodness. This judgment is confirmed by
a survey of 50 media health correspondents in 1993 in which it was
found that 'in the two years since the NHS reforms were introduced
staff have increasingly become too frightened to speak out publicly on
standards of patient care, fraud and misconduct in the health service'.[43]

It is not difficult to see how an ethos of intimidation and unquestioning obedience can be imposed upon public-sector workers. Mass
redundancies due to 'downsizing', performance-related pay, increasing job insecurity, individual performance review and short-term
contracts all do much to ensure that individuals and groups feel that
they have no alternative but to maintain a low, uncritical profile within
their organizations. Many professionals are now required to sign contracts with their organizations containing 'gagging clauses' that
actually specifically preclude their venting their concerns, however
serious, in public. Despite this, Hunt notes that 'The whistleblowing has
continued, despite a worsening mood of fear, following on from clo-
sures and mass redundancies, gagging clauses in contracts of
employment ... and, most recently, the bugging of a consultant's office
... .'[44]

The need to preserve organizational 'goodness' and attain the
ordained aims and objectives economically and swiftly contributes to a

requirement for basically uncritical obedience and loyalty from the workforce. Even as organizations talk about being self-critical, welcoming change, empowering workers and nurturing innovation they silence their internal critics.[45]

The need for truthfulness and criticism

There are at least four good reasons for trying to preserve or rehabilitate a culture of open criticism, particularly within public-service management. First, requiring absolute loyalty, obedience and silence from employees imposes huge and harmful demands upon conscientious organizational members. The cognitive dissonance caused by having to keep silent while evil prospers is both personally and organizationally demoralizing. It sets a low moral tone in organizations from which it may be very difficult to ascend. If people are not encouraged to act in good faith, they may take that faith elsewhere, leaving organizations to less scrupulous members. The result is a kind of all-round organizational moral deterioration.

Secondly, if managers collude in their own self-deception, making it clear that they do not wish to know about or address ills and abuses, there is no possibility of their being able to recognize and deal with real problems. The organization will not be an enquiring and learning one which looks towards the actual problems of present and future.[46] It will be essentially a sensorily deprived dinosaur, with no intelligence or adaptive capability.

Thirdly, and following on from this, once people are clear that managers do not want to know the truth about reality, they will tell them only what they want to hear. The incentives to do this in public-service management these days are becoming quite overwhelming.

Fourthly, the resolute avoidance of uncomfortable truths will inevitably induce objective cynicism amongst managers and workforce alike. Once people have become objectively cynical there will be a sense in which they are ironical and distant in their commitments. At a deep level, they will no longer want to know or to care. Thus, the ability of the organization to deliver 'quality' care or 'excellent' service will become little more than a bad joke.

There is a long and dishonourable tradition of killing the messenger who brings bad news. It is understandable that beleagured managers, short of resources and needing to present themselves and their organizations in the best possible light, should want to minimize or disregard the negative aspects of their work.[47] They may well find internal critics a nuisance. But once an organization finds it needs to regard itself as all good and above criticism it enters the realm of fantasy, cut off from reality. This is a kind of fundamentalist, sectarian world, where to question anything is to be perceived to question and threaten every-thing.

Unfortunately, unreal fantasy may well have adverse effects in prac-tice. It is not possible to build an ethical organization on a tissue of lies and misrepresentations, however attractive they may be compared to harsh reality. Producing a culture in which people can be open and honest would represent a considerable step to genuine organizational learning and managerial ethical reflection. According to Drucker, 'Dis-agreement is the most effective stimulus to the imagination that we know.'[48] Whatever the veracity of that idealistic assertion, it is clear that ethics and intimidation do not mix. This is a point which must not be ignored for reasons of short-term managerial expediency.

8

Changes and chances

And I saw a new heaven and a new earth; for the first heaven and the
first earth had gone away .... And I saw the holy city new Jerusalem
coming down out of heaven from God ....

(Revelation 21.1–2)

The would-be fundamentalist ... confronts the proclaimed tradition of
God's supreme sovereign power with a belief and hope, yet is
surrounded by contrary evidence. Inevitably, the problem must be
solved as it usually is for most fundamentalists, either by reference to
eschatological dynamics (which must remain mythic-speculative) or by
resorting to a complex systematic dualism.

   Whilst a certain amount of 'cognitive dissonance' can be tolerated by
a group, too many prophecies passing their 'sell-by date' does create
problems. It necessitates revision and reconstruction and not all
followers will subscribe to reinterpretation: some will leave as a direct
result of promises not being fulfilled.[1]

The Christian religious tradition has an ambivalent relationship with
change. On the one hand, religion is often seen as a comforting resort
and source of certainty during times of chaos and distress. This helps to
account, perhaps, for the growth of fundamentalistic Christian sects in
the present era, approaching the millennium, perceived to be a time of
convulsive change in all parts of society. On the other hand, much of the
Christian religious tradition is itself obsessed with the future and with
change. Believers claim to have an inspired hope that changes, and will
change, the world. Since its inception, enthusiastic Christians, especially
those in sectarian groups, have eagerly looked for the radical change
that will be brought about with the second coming of Christ. The
Kingdom of God is hoped for and looked for as a time when the faithful
will experience the full joys of salvation that rightly belong to them.
Earthly powers will be overthrown, conventions will be upend-
ed, and the saved will sit down together to feast at a divine banquet of
plenty in the new Jerusalem. In the meanwhile, the sectarian's task is to

118

change himself or herself and others by conversion and repentance; fundamental and ongoing lifestyle change in accordance with the divine will is required of those who wish to experience eternal glory and salvation. The prophesied, coming Kingdom demands it.[2]

The sectarian hope of the inestimable benefits of radical, future-oriented change burns brightly in the hearts of many contemporary management theorists and practitioners. Indeed, it is one of the most prominent traits that Christian sectarians and managers share in common. The main difference between the two groups, however, is that while fundamentalist Christians see change as coming through the will and power of God, their managerial counterparts believe in the efficacy of change management theories and techniques to produce a brighter, better future.

The aim of this chapter is to provide a critique of some aspects of change management, a practice that is necessarily metaphysical because the future is both unknowable and uncontrollable. First, the context of contemporary organizational change is outlined. Then I will review the theory and practice of change management as it is found in the literature of Organizational Development. Some of the problems associated with applying this kind of theory to change in the public sector are then considered. Finally, drawing on my own experience of a particular organizational change in the NHS, some principles of how to mismanage change are adumbrated. Frequently, change management is painful, costly and ill-conceived from the oft-ignored perspective of employees and service users. My conclusion is that change management is a difficult and ambivalent process. It is much more difficult to execute successfully and beneficially than its advocates suggest. It has considerable potential to damage and harm individuals and society. In this respect, the ideals that drive change management are not so very different in their effects than the apolcalyptic hopes of the sectarians. Sometimes they may bring hope, empowerment and deliverance; often, they engender the very chaos, misery and disappointment that they purport to alleviate.

The background to change management

One of the deep myths of contemporary society is that we live in the midst of deep, inevitable change. Human beings have always been aware of their own changes which finally culminate in death (though notions of immortality have been advanced to stem the inevitable tide of change and dissolution). Against this personal vulnerability to change, physical, social and metaphysical structures have generally seemed to have a certain solidity and permanence. Now, however, the whole world is perceived as in a constant state of flux. From the atomic level, through human activity, to the heavens above there is no rest. Everything is in ceaseless and often disordered motion from the perspective of late-twentieth-century human beings.

Social institutions and organizations are not excepted from this rule. Great manufacturing industries and companies in the private sector have risen and fallen, leaving nothing behind of all their solidity, pomp and show. In Britain, the pillars of the Welfare State, education, the NHS, housing and the social security system continue to be shaken by ongoing turmoil, re-organization and change. All this against the background of recurring economic recessions, wars and perceived environmental decay. We live upon an unsteady and apocalyptic stage.

There is, of course, nothing new about change in itself. Every individual or institution changes gradually, often imperceptibly, over time. It is the volume, rapidity, radicality and discontinuity of the changes which are presently occurring which is new and which requires managing. In response to rapid techological, competitive and other changes, business organizations are changing shape, changing their fundamental *raison d'être*, changing their ways of doing business, changing patterns of ownership, downsizing and changing their culture.[3] Peters teaches that things are changing so fast that managers must learn to 'love change' and to 'thrive on chaos' if their organizations are to have any kind of future: 'excellent firms of tommorow will cherish impermanence – and thrive on chaos'.[4]

The turbulence affecting privately owned industrial and service organizations has not left British public service untouched. For example, the last decade has seen fundamental change at every level of the NHS, from Whitehall to the local GP's surgery. It seems that permanent, fundamental change is here to stay. Change management has thus become a key matter of the moment. To cope with all these changes, change managers, or 'change masters' have been called into being.[5] Arguably, no manager today can avoid the challenge of change management. Many job descriptions give a central place to change management skills.

It is optimistically argued by the instigators of significant change that what they propose will be for the better. Many of those who have to live with the chaos and uncertainty that accompanies the process, as well as with the final outcomes of change management, would disagree. In principle no-one wants things to remain static, old-fashioned or backward looking. However, the experience of radical change over the last decade in the NHS, for example, has left staff and users very unclear about whether anything of value has really been achieved. By contrast, they are often very clear about the enormous cost in terms of demoralization, loss and uncertainty for individuals and groups that enforced change has brought. Despite the air of Olympian competence exuded by the 'change masters', change management remains a chancy, ambivalent business which often brings as much destruction as creative innovation. Relatively little is known about successful change management generally. Even less is known about it in the public sector; such knowledge as there is stems mainly from *post hoc* learning from painful and unanticipated experience. What is known is difficult to apply proactively and effectively in very different contexts.

The theory of change management

There are a number of works from the Organization Development tradition outlining general principles of change or transition management.[6] Broadly, they all deal with: (a) identifying where one wants one's organization to be; (b) diagnosing where the organization presently is and what will stop it from moving towards the desired goal; then (c) thinking through the process of how the transition from present to desired state can be managed and manipulated.

Organizational Transitions is an authoritative example of this genre. It suggests that the starting point for thinking about change is by looking at the *demands for change*. These will be of various degrees of potency, they may come from different sources and they may be of different natures (so, for example, a demand for change may come from new government legislation or from consumers). Managers have to determine whether there is a need to change, and whether they have any choice about this. In doing so, they must identify the core mission or *raison d'être* of their organization to discriminate between competing priorities and courses of action. The next stage is to *define the future state* towards which the organization should move, formulating a leadership vision of the future desired state, thinking out possible future scenarios and contemplating the consequences of not changing. A complementary activity here is *describing the present state* of the organization. This analysis/diagnosis is essential if change is to be effective and well-informed; without it, there is the danger of proceeding on false assumptions and in ignorance.

Comparison of the present state and the future desired state starts *the transition phase*. Managers must then determine the types of changes which will be required, assess the readiness and capability of the organization to change, identify the forces/people who will resist or facilitate change, devise an activity plan, determine where to intervene and design transition management structures. It is then possible to move into the *transition state*. In this phase, it is necessary to manage any resistance to changes, to facilitate change by, for example, changing reward systems, to model new roles and ways of acting, to ensure that appropriate education and training systems undergird the changes and to ensure collaboration. If these principles are applied, successful change management of complex organizations can be accomplished.

Problematic aspects of change management

It is one thing to outline a simple, linear model for change management like the one described, quite another to conduct successful change management in practice. There are a number of issues and problems here, some theoretical, some practical, some concerning change management in general, some relating to change management in public service in particular. Often these issues have substantial ethical and practical implications. They should be taken seriously before change management is embarked upon. Here I will briefly consider some of the general problems before more intensively scrutinizing a few of the crucial issues that seem to be ignored in the implementation of change management, specifically in the NHS.

General issues and problems

The definition and nature of change
At the level of semantics, it is often not clear what the nature of change is or the degree, level or intentionality of activity that is being envisaged when change management is discussed. Transformatory change that brings into being new organizational forms and different services or products may be different from strategic change or local operational change. Incremental or gradual change is part of everyday life, and much change occurs without anyone consciously planning it. Are, then, the same change management skills and concepts relevant to every kind of change?[7]

The positive moral evaluation of change
Rather than being regarded as morally neutral difference, the very idea of change is often tacitly conflated with notions of progress and development. Change may then be regarded as an unequivocal good in itself, rather than as an ambivalent means to an end. Thus, collusion with change may be uncritical while resistance to it may be seen as morally offensive and therefore heavily proscribed.

Minimizing the size and reality of change

The overwhelming difficulty of achieving major change in a large organization is often minimized by would-be change managers. Many organizations are very conservative. They conform to certain archetypes, that is compositions of structures and systems, which are given coherence or orientation by an underlying set of ideas, values and beliefs.[8] They do not easily alter archetype. Existing organizational design constrains future movement, the benefits of change are not recognized to be greater than the costs, and the vested interests of particular groups are undergirded by present structures. Constraints on change include situational constraints, interpretive schemes of values and interests held by organizational members, interests, dependencies of power and domination, and organizational capacity. The interplay of these five dynamic elements affects whether or not change takes place, and in what way. Often stasis prevails.

Lack of knowledge about change management

Unfortunately, very little is known about effective change managment. The study of change management, especially in the public sector, is in its infancy.[9] Different contexts and complex factors influence the course of change in different organizations. Reliable knowledge and universally appropriate techniques are hard to come by and difficult to replicate. Most problematic of all, outcomes of change are not totally predictable; they may not be what was expected, or they may be negative in their effects.[10] The more radical and numerous the changes introduced at any one time, the more difficult it is to predict or control their effects.[11] If change management was a medical treatment technique many questions might be asked of its known and proven efficacy and beneficence from a moral point of view before it was implemented. Such moral doubts do not often seem to cause the steps of the managerial change masters to falter.

Failure to apply existing knowledge

Many of the principles that might prima facie help to ensure the beneficence of change and to minimize its baleful effects are ignored in organizations like the NHS, together with contra-indicators to change. Kanter suggests that for change to be possible and successful

- there must be enough stability and security for people to learn and work change through;
- teamwork, consensus and communication and a sense of each person's value are important;

- it is important to create the space for people to act and to make available to them the problems of the organization so they can act upon them rather than pretend there are no problems, or that they have all been solved at the top;
- initiative and enterprise should be encouraged, and a culture of pride and change should be built up;
- rewards should take the form of investing in people before they carry out their projects;
- central and local power need to be balanced, as does the flow of information – power must be both available and focused.

The role of managers in relation to innovation is to obtain and use power in a way that mobilizes people and resources to get things done. Problem definition, coalition building and mobilization of resources are integral to corporate innovation, as is the participative/collaborative style which empowers subordinates rather than just controlling them.[12]

Kanter contrasts this approach to that of non-innovating, hierarchical organizations like the traditional NHS. In segmentalist, non-innovating organizations, hierarchies are long and honouring the chain of command is a virtue. There is a lack of lateral co-operation and communication, and information is restricted. Change is initiated only from the top downwards. It may be initiated peremptorily and without participation, creating uncertainty, insecurity and mistrust throughout the organization. Where innovation is allowed to occur, it is undertaken by a special group of people under limited circumstances, not by everyone in the organization. Other innovators are positively discouraged. This critique is pertinent to change management in the public sector and voluntary organizations. The point is that a particular set of attitudes, structures and factors must exist before change management is likely to be successful; it cannot occur in an organizational vacuum by fiat.

Change management or change influence?
In the light of the above, it can intelligibly be asked whether it is, in fact, possible to manage change. It might be pleasant to contemplate the possibility of engineering the future for one's organization. The trouble is that so many factors, rational and irrational, expected and unexpected, intervene that the possibility of proceeding in a coherent and orderly way from A to B seems a vain one. Perhaps, then, it would be more realistic to talk of change influence rather than change management. The future mocks human attempts to control or predict it accurately, as Utilitarian philosophers know to their embarrassment.

Specific issues

When it comes to the public sector, and the NHS in particular, there are a number of vital practical and moral issues that seem to be minimized or ignored by those initiating change.

Significant differences between the private and public sectors

Much of the theory of change management has emerged from the private business sector. There are real differences of socio-political context and accountability between public-sector and private-sector organizations.[13]

Public services are complex. They have multiple, sometimes conflicting, goals, delimited spheres of activity and complex values. While private companies must primarily consider the interests of their shareholders' investments and the bottom line of making a profit, public organizations have to take the public interest into account in many different ways. They must be responsive to politicians and short-term political pressures. Legislation and centralized policy as well as values of equity, consideration and consistency have to be heeded. Managers are accountable to external bodies like parliament, as well as to local communities. They are constrained in their employment policies. The criteria of success of their organization and policies are various and bear little resemblance to those used in the market-place where the disciplines of economy, efficiency, effectiveness, excellence and enterprise provide a basic discipline and framework.

Many of the elements which make change management in the private sector desirable, possible and successful are absent in the public sector. When it comes to a large, non-profit-making organization with a long, socially appreciated tradition of providing services relating directly to the well-being and health of all citizens, it could be said that radical change is contra-indicated. The hierarchical, segmental structure and culture of the NHS, offering valued services with little real competition in a reasonably stable market environment, has not been such as to foster and encourage organizational innovation. Change management is, then, difficult to implement and is substantially resisted, both within the organization itself and amongst 'users' who may legitimately see no need for changes and worry about their possible effects. The onus is, therefore, heavily upon the change managers to demonstrate the need for change, to create the environment and structure in which it is possible, and to ensure that change is not harmful to a plurality of public interests. This is not an easy task.

The politics of change management

Much of the change management literature assumes the right of managers to instigate change and then to ensure that by all means this occurs. This kind of top-down approach ignores the politics of decision-making, possibly to the detriment of interested members of the organization and others such as consumers. The ends and means employed in public services are ultimately determined by, and have to be acceptable to, party politicians. But politics, in the more general sense, also significantly impinges on change management. Organizations themselves can be seen as political coalitions of individuals and groups with their own purposes and objectives.[14] The power structures of organizations shape whose voices, purposes and aims are privileged, who determines the nature of change, and who will benefit from it.

All groups and individuals involved in change in public services can be seen as having their own interests and values. They are engaged in ongoing struggles and alliances to gain power and influence even if this is covert, or hidden beneath a dominant consensus which excludes minority or weak dissenting voices. This is further complicated by the fact that many people outside the service, for example prospective consumers and local politicians, perceive themselves to have legitimate interests and values which should be taken into account by managers. There are potential conflicts of interest and values between service users and managers, local politicians and other interest groups. These conflicts, and the way they are dealt with, cannot be dismissed in thinking about change management.

It is possible to concretize these points in questions like: Who decides what changes there will be? Who will benefit from them? Who instigates change and feels powerful? Who is required to change and feels powerless? Who has the power to make sure that the changes happen? Who can successfully resist change proposals, and to what extent? Whose voices and concerns will not be heard or heeded in the change management process? Who can be safely ignored? Who will bear the cost of change? Frequently these fundamental questions remain unconsidered by self-styled change managers.

The costs of change

Change tends to be regarded as an unequivocal good in contemporary popular managerial perception. This obscures the costs of change. Even the prospect of change can cast a shadow over an organization and disrupt present operations and personnel. There are certainly significant financial costs to change when there is increased staff turnover, but I am mainly concerned here with the human costs of change.

Discontinuous or radical change, or the threat of it, produces stress within individuals who are affected by it. When people's lives and sense of meaning and continuity is disrupted they go through a grief process analogous to that of losing a person.[15] Change represents a real personal and psychological threat and increases individual and organizational defences: 'Unless people have the opportunity to participate in the changes they will not be able to influence the formation of new social systems and the result will be an increase in suspicion, hostility and aggression.'[16]

Change is extraordinarily painful; it often diminishes people's capacity to perform in an optimum way. It may bring increased illness within the workforce and affected communities and so contribute to making society less healthy. All of which is made more poignant and urgent when it is realized that the burden of uncertainty often falls most heavily upon the weakest members of organizations and of society:

> [B]ecause the power to control uncertainty is very unequally
> distributed, the greatest burden of uncertainties tends to fall on the
> weakest, with the fewest resources to withstand it, and in trying to
> retrieve some sense of autonomy and control they often compound and
> confirm their weakness.[17]

Organizations and managers are often unable or unwilling to recognize the need to grieve and mourn the loss of the past order. Instead, they push on towards the future without regard for these important, fundamental feelings, indifferent to this kind of warning given by Harvey-Jones: 'Damage to individuals will not be forgiven and will ensure that further adjustment is not possible.'[18]

Change often leads to discontinuity, disorder and distraction. People are confused, communication becomes haphazard, distracted managers ignore emotional reactions to change, there is energy loss (especially if change is negatively perceived) and key personnel may be lost. Initiative may break down, morale may plummet and management may lose credibility. Internal competition for survival which defeats organizational purposes may break out. This can be managed by gaining commitment from the workforce by helping people mourn the past and become excited about future possibilities, as well as by reducing uncertainties in the present with good communication and honouring promises.[19] Managers do not have to maximize pain by dividing and ruling at the expense of their workers.

It is easy to ignore or minimize the human and financial costs incurred in change management strategies, but it is also possible to take them seriously. This should be done in public services aiming to maximize rather than to destroy well-being amongst the citizenry and the workforce.

How to mismanage organizational change

I want now to broaden my critique of change management by outlining some theses on how to mismanage change. For two years, I was chief officer of a Community Health Council which was trying to represent the general public in responding to radical plans for re-organization of the local NHS in a large English city put forward by the Regional Health Authority (RHA). These plans involved the closure of several hospitals, the merger of some health authorities, the re-deployment of staff and facilities, and so on.

Prima facie, any plans to improve health services should command wide public support, so long as those plans are rational, sensible and well explained. As happens so often in the NHS, the process of consultation produced widespead gloom, cynicism and disillusionment. It was not change as such which was unacceptable, upsetting and demoralizing, so much as the way it was proposed and consulted upon. Much goodwill and commitment to change was never mobilized by the RHA, while much antagonism was. Reflection upon the way in which change came to be so negatively perceived led me to abstract the following theses or commandments for change mismanagement.

Discerning readers will be able to reconstruct the event or practice behind each enunciated thesis below with little difficulty. Adherence to these principles will make change as difficult and as painful as possible. The theses are biassed, idiosyncratic and fragmentary. But then so are the change management theories written from 'above', of which they form a partial critique. These principles or theses illustrate the human and organizational cost of change in a way which I hope is useful and restores balance to a literature which is mostly written from the manager's perspective and often minimizes this cost. Here, then, are some theses on how to mismanage change based on the view from 'below'.

1. Assume that everyone will understand and accept the need for change immediately. Do not admit to any difficulties, ambiguities or negative aspects to your plans; this will nurture distrust and suspicion.
2. Do not explain immediately, openly and clearly what you want to do and why you want to do it. In particular, do not admit that the changes proposed have anything to do with resource distribution or cuts.
3. Allow a time for rumour to prevail to increase anxiety and destabilize the workforce and service users. This precludes the possibility of building real coalitions and a shared vision of desirable change.

4. Appear arbitrary and unyielding in the plans you put forward. Inflexibility makes people feel unheard and powerless and increases their resistance to change.

5. If you change your plans pretend that you have not done so. Deny that you have done so because particular interest groups have influenced you or because there were fundamental problems in the plans you initially proposed. This amplifies the impotence and frustration of 'outside' interested groups such as staff and service users.

6. Do not consult widely on the problems you need to address and the possible solutions to them with interested parties before releasing a definitive plan. This will ensure failure to learn from people who have real, 'coalface' knowledge and so the solutions proposed will be inadequate or irrelevant.

7. Do not recognize the right of other parties to have an interest in your plans. The denial of legitimate interest to members of the public, service users and members of staff simplifies the planning process even if it does mean that services may eventually not meet people's needs and affirms a democratic deficit in the health service.

8. Be surprised and hurt when other groups and people attack or question your intentions and good faith. This helps to create a communication barrier and may prevent awkward questions from the citizenry being asked or taken seriously.

9. Do not base your plans on accurate information and predictions. A broad brush, visionary and approximate approach to actual facts and figures will erode public trust in any proposals, and, indeed, in those who have put them forward. It will help to reduce confidence at all levels.

10. Be visionary without being shackled by tiresome facts and hope people will go along with the force of your personality or the power you have over them. The vague assurance that all will be better in the end will prevent staff and users from being able concretely to envisage their own futures or those of the services they use, depend upon and work in. This removes proposals from the realm of the proximate and realistically conceivable, maximizing alarm and anxiety.

11. Always let the timescale slip for release of plans and the implementation thereof. This ensures lack of impetus and maximizes chronic demoralization, decay, lack of investment and destabilizing uncertainty of a corrosive nature.

12. Do not allow time for effective consultation. This retains the initiative with the change masters and increases pressure and anxiety for groups who might want to respond effectively to any proposals, eroding their good will.

13. If people express concerns about proposed changes which conflict with your own, console yourself with the thought that (a) they are trouble makers and not representative of others; (b) they really do not and cannot understand that what you want to do really is the best thing; and (c) there are Luddites in every age who always dislike change, however necessary or desirable it is.

14. Never answer letters or queries from 'outside' interested parties like service users or deliverers. This makes people feel powerless and unheard and increases the change manager's power – with any luck they will go away. There is no quicker way of making people feel insignificant and angry than by giving them the implicit message that you do not even read their official correspondence. If you have to respond in some way, do so late so they can make no use of any information you might provide.

15. If you have to deal directly with angry interested parties, listen to them indulgently, appear to take their concerns seriously – then get on with the real business of managing change.

16. Reserve all initiatives to yourself – this increases your power while enhancing the powerlessness of others.

17. Leave the futures of your staff vague. This destabilizes people on a personal level. Hopefully, quite a lot of those who might be most effective in opposing or in implementing the proposals will leave, providing an open field for the change you desire.[20]

Conclusion

Change is a sign of life. It is an inevitable part of the lives of all individuals and organizations at some level, to greater or lesser degrees. In the present age of social and organizational instability, the attempt to manage or at least influence change cannot be avoided. However, it has to be recognized that very little is yet known about how to initiate and manage radical change in different kinds of organizations. This means that change is likely to be very traumatic for all of those who become caught up in it. It is particularly difficult and costly for those who have to respond to the initiatives of others rather than initiating and planning change themselves. For those who have to live with change willy-nilly, it can be a heavy and dispiriting burden. Far more consideration needs to be given to the costs of change and those who have to live with them if change management is to be perceived as a positive, progressive activity rather than as a blight on the lives of ordinary employees and service users.

Change can manifest itself as growth, improvement, expansion and learning. It can bring opportunities as well as threats.[21] It can be welcomed gladly and voluntarily rather than be feared and denied. If change management is to have the possibility of producing these positive features, however, it must usually be very carefully planned and implemented. In particular, managers need to be more modest and less 'macho' in advancing and adopting fairly crude ideas and techniques of change management that may very well not work, or not work in the way they are expected to.

Managers, especially in public services, should have massive support in suggesting changes in the service if they propose them in good faith and the changes seem sensible, enhancing ones. Unfortunately, ignoring the critical issues discussed above and applying the theses I have outlined on mismanagement is bound to alienate people and increase their resistance to change. This is tragic, particularly in organizations like the NHS which has enjoyed the kind of support from the public and its own workforce that change managers in the private sector might well look upon with envy. It is not enough for enthusiastic managers to adopt simple schemata for managing change and then to expect other people to obediently pursue the leaders' vision of a better future. Rather, it must be recognized that change, especially in the public sector, has many ramifications and costs which are not necessarily borne by those who see themselves as change managers or initiators. Change and change management are complex, costly matters, not to be lightly or wantonly undertaken.[22]

9

Prophets and sages

Beware of false prophets, which come to you in sheep's clothing, but
inwardly they are ravening wolves. Ye shall know them by their fruits.

(Matthew 7.15–16a AV)

Paul tells the Corinthians to 'Make love your aim and earnestly desire
the spiritual gifts', expecially prophecy (1 Cor. 14.1). Yet as we have
seen, the gifts are pursued as signs of power, not solely for love. This is
true of prophecy and words of knowledge in particular, which may be
used to coerce, shame, alarm and instil a sense of fear in the individual.
All too often, prophecy witnesses not to love, but to the charisma and
power of the prophet, and to the power of the community that
witnesses its action.[1]

A familiar figure in many religious groups is that of the charismatic.
Such figures, who may be called shamans, prophets or wise men (or
women) amongst other titles, are deemed to have privileged and direct
insights into the nature of events and reality by virtue of direct inspiration or visions from the beyond. As individuals they do not have
well-defined organizational roles. Their power does not come from any
kind of formal institutional position. Frequently, they may be peripatetic rather than attached to a local community, and they do not
necessarily conform to social norms. Their utterance has a self-
confirming authority that arises from within their own personality and
their personal experience. Charismatic individuals are agents of change
and newness within religions and other organizations. They often
become prominent at times of great social anxiety and uncertainty
when no-one understands what is going on or what should be done. At
such times, there is scope for the charismatic to be heard and for a new
direction to be identified.[2]

It is not difficult to identify the broad type of the charismatic within
contemporary management, particularly in 'new wave' management
theory. Indeed, the term 'management guru', with its very direct
religious reference to Sikh or Hindu spiritual guides, has been coined in

recognition of the quasi-religious activity of some management theorists and practitioners.[3] These are figures, some of whom travel the world, who make a living from guiding managers and providing them with 'new' myths, metaphors and understandings that will help them to cope with the unpredictable changes and chances of their condition.

I do not propose here to give an account of management gurudom in general; this has already been admirably provided by Andrzej Huczynski.[4] Nor do I propose to give an overall resumé of the life and thought of a representative selection of management gurus.[5] I will not even compare and contrast the methods and messages of different 'gurus' to any great extent. My aim is simply to draw attention to the fact that at least some of these figures may actually have styles and messages that seem to have been directly influenced by religious, particularly Christian, ideas and practices.

To this end, I shall analyse aspects of the thought and style of three management theorists who are also peripatetic performers: Tom Peters, Gerard Egan and Charles Handy. Peters and Egan emanate from the USA, Handy from the UK. Egan is essentially academically based, while Handy and Peters seem to work for themselves. Although I am not aware of Peters having any kind of religious background, he is by far the 'hottest', most overtly 'religious' member of this trio, conforming most closely to the classic type of the charismatic prophet. Charles Handy has a considerable background in the Anglican Church and his work is redolent with Christian religiosity. He is probably the most theological, thoughtful, analytic and critical of the three, being more of a spiritual guide than a revivalist prophet. What is most surprising, perhaps, is that Gerard Egan, a practising Catholic priest, appears to be the least overtly religious and theological of these gurus.

Tom Peters: the prophet

Tom Peters's name has been mentioned many times in this book. He is, perhaps, the doyen of management gurus of the 'new wave', having published a number of highly successful books and travelled the world to promote these with personal appearances and seminars. His first major work, written with the more obscure Robert Waterman, *In Search of Excellence*, was highly influential on both sides of the Atlantic in the 1980s. Hailed as in itself both a sign and cause of the recovery of American business and management, it has had effects throughout the British private and non-profit sectors, not least in making the pursuit of 'excellence' an aspiration to which many organizations adhere. Peters's copious written works, while easily readable, must now rival the Bible in total words – *Liberation Management* alone has 830 pages in its paperback edition. It is not just in terms of literary profusion that Peters rivals holy scripture. Many of the ideas that he uses, together with the style he adopts, have strong resonances with the Judaeo-Christian tradition. Peters bears a striking resemblance to the type of the exemplary prophet or charismatic leader as found within that tradition.

Characteristics of charismatic figures
Martyn Percy outlines the characteristics typical of religious charismatic figures.

In the first place, they have a *charismatic message*. This is usually revolutionary in character. It promises salvation, and requires a rejection of ties to the external order so that 'the *message itself* becomes the only route of escape from a perceived crisis'.[6] The message is necessarily simplistic both in grammar and content. It often creates 'an aura of pertinency, apart from the argument itself'.[7] It has to generate a sense of collective identity between the audience and the charismatic leader, saying 'what people want to hear, but do not know how to say themselves'.[8] The message needs to incoporate 'polarized aggression', being strongly 'for' some things and against others. Charismatic leaders often create powerful 'threats' and contra-powers by their discourse. This throws their message into relief, giving it urgency and credibility.

Secondly, charismatic leaders tend to have certain *personality elements*. These may include: high status of some kind (gained, for example, from the ability to demonstrate miracles); an ability to remain aloof, distant and mysterious; the display of 'conquerable imperfection'; a sense of personal special calling; sexual mystique; and the ability 'to act, and behave in a dramatic, professional way'.[9] Further essential traits may be the ability to work miracles, or at least to be perceived to produce dramatic results, and the ability to provide myths and symbols that provide a meaning framework for constructing reality in the charismatic situation: 'Myths, when properly established, can be a rhetorical means of creating oneness with an audience.'[10]

Finally, there are some *delivery elements* that are typical of charismatic figures. They tend to be extremely eloquent, excellent orators whose style is as important and compelling as the message itself. They will use vocal inflections and changes of volume or pitch to attain vocal force and persuasion. Rapid responses, pauses and repetition help to cast an aural spell. This prevents critical analysis and the construction of other persepctives. Situational, non-verbal cues such as physical attractiveness and touch can also be used to good effect.[11]

Not all these characteristics will be found in all charismatic leaders and situations. However, it is worth bearing them in mind when one turns to Peters's written works which seem to manifest many of them. First, however, some further analytical material on prophets can usefully be added from the sociological work of Max Weber.

Weber understands a prophet to be 'a purely individual bearer of charisma, who by virtue of his mission proclaims a religious doctrine or divine commandment'.[12] A prophetic revelation:

> involves for both the prophet himself and for his followers a unified view of the world derived from a consciously integrated and meaningful attitude towards life .... To this meaning the conduct of mankind must be oriented if it is to bring salvation, for only in relation to this meaning does life obtain a unified and significant pattern.[13]

While the structure of meaning which prophets invoke may take very different forms, the imperative to overarching meaning is always present in prophetic missions. These always contain 'the important religious conception of the world as a cosmos which is challenged to produce somehow a 'meaningful' ordered totality, the particular manifestations of which are to be measured and evaluated according to this requirement'.[14]

Weber distinguishes between ethical and exemplary prophets. The former, like Moses, promulgate codes of instruction and doctrine, while the latter renew or found religions on the basis of their own behaviour and example. Prophets usually stand outside the guild structures of organized religion and they frequently have a circle of followers composed 'of those who support [the prophet] with lodging, money and services and who expect to attain their salvation through his mission'.[15]

Peters as prophet

In the light of the analytic categories put forward by Percy and Weber, Tom Peters seems quite clearly to be a charismatic figure, indeed a prophet. Many of Peters' works are indebted to religious language and style drawn from the Christian tradition. *In Search of Excellence*, for example, uses the concept of the 'faithful remnant' which denotes those in Israel who remain faithful to God in Old Testament prophecy, as the title for its first part.[16] Within his work, there is a strong emphasis on individual faith and corporate values rather than upon cold analytic reason as the focus for management. Perhaps the place where Peters most clearly reveals his charismatic, prophetic nature is in his book, *Thriving on Chaos*, a work full of religious style, insights and language.[17]

Thriving on Chaos

Thriving on Chaos is not a short book. Like most 'best sellers' produced by management gurus, however, its basic argument is easily summarized. Businesses exist in a chaotic, ever-changing environment. If they are to survive and flourish, they need to follow the Peters prescription. This involves creating total customer responsiveness, pursuing fast-paced innovation, achieving flexibility by empowering people, learning to love change and building systems for 'a world turned upside down'. None of these nostrums are unique to Peters. However, it is not so much the content of Peters's thought that is important, original or 'charismatic', but more his style and mode of communication.

Measuring Peters's message in *Thriving on Chaos* against Percy's analytic categories, it is certainly revolutionary. Unless managers accept, even love, chaos and learn to live with it, their organizations will perish. If they do what Peters tells them to, then they stand some chance of surviving, of being saved. The message is blunt and simplistic. He argues, for example, that there are only two ways to respond to the era of sustainable excellence, that 'madness *is* afoot' and that 'nothing is predictable'.[18] The latter claim, which begins a section entitled, 'Predictability is a thing of the past', radically over-simplifies the complex nature of reality and human courses of action; in fact, it is distorting and basically untrue.

Peters's message is highly pertinent in a time of acute anxiety about the future. It creates a sense of identity between himself and his worried readers who can resonate to his clear description and articulation of their precarious predicament. Polarized aggression that adds urgency to the message is provided by raising the spectre of successful foreign companies who will take the place of American companies if they do not change their ways. This gives urgency and credibility to the message.

Several personality elements appear to underwrite Peters's message and to give it credibility. He enjoys high status, being enormously famous and well paid. He also gives the impression of being able to help businesses do rapid turnrounds to succeed – a kind of miracle working. Although he writes in the first person and talks about his own experience, Peters reveals little about himself and his background in his books. He never, for example, talks about any religious influences or background. Thus he can appear a little mysterious and aloof. Judging from the high prices that Peters can raise for a day seminar in the UK (around £500 per person) he must be a good actor and performer. A reading of his books reveals his skill at coining myths and metaphors ('liberation', 'thriving on chaos') that help to build up a credible sense of alternative reality.

I cannot comment upon Peters's oratorical skill and eloquence, nor upon his physical or sexual attractiveness, but there seems enough evidence here to convict him of either consciously or unconsciously cultivating the persona of a charismatic prophet. This becomes more clearly the case if one looks a bit more closely and analyses more theologically the way in which his thinking and argumentation develops in *Thriving on Chaos*.

The theology of Thriving on Chaos

Peters's basic religious system is that of corporate, consumer, competitive capitalism. At no point is the process of exploitation, expansion, profit-making, retailing and consumption challenged. Within this system, the underlying metaphor for contemporary managerial reality is that of chaos. This understanding is undergirding and total, as was the Old Testament prophets' understanding of the nature of God. To depersonify the transcendent by getting rid of any kind of overt deity, as Peters does, is not to dispose of its transcendent nature, though it may make it less obvious. To assert that the world is chaotic is to use a popular scientific idea which functions as an overarching primary meaning and metaphor. Like any kind of profoundly religious assertion, its veracity cannot be questioned or tested by ordinary people; it can only be accepted or rejected. Acceptance of this concept is the acceptance of an overarching moral order within which all events, meanings and experiences can be situated and explained. Thus Peters offers

> a unified view of the world [albeit the unified view is one of
> fragmentation and change rather than solidity and permanence as
> ancient prophets may have preferred] derived from a consciously
> integrated and meaningful attitude towards life . . . . To this meaning
> the conduct of mankind must be oriented if it is to bring salvation, for
> only in relation to this meaning does life obtain a unified and
> significant pattern.[19]

In *Thriving on Chaos*, Peters appears to derive his own personal authority and influence from an implicit assertion that he is closely in contact with and knowledgeable about the destructive and creative chaos which we presently face. He knows the forces of chaos and has mastered them. Like that other charismatic figure, the shaman, he has mastered the spirits which threaten to overwhelm.[20] It is possibly too fanciful to say that Peters regards himself as God who, it will be remembered from Genesis 1, is the other main being in our shared cultural mythology who has mastered, and thrived on, chaos. However, he certainly speaks with authority about the overwhelming forces of change and destruction which comprise a commonsensical view of 'chaos'. He acts as a channel or voice of the transcendent chaos which communicates its nature through him and gives him wisdom, power and authority. Who, but God or perhaps his prophet, can really thrive on chaos, master it and speak intelligibly about it?

Like the exemplary prophets of old, Peters outlines a number of doctrines and commands – 45 to be precise – which will guide his followers to organizational salvation. These culminate in a new love commandment: Learn to love change.[21] This may be compared with Jesus' words in the Gospel of John: 'A new commandment I give unto you, That ye love one another' (John 13.34, AV). A subsidiary command flowing from Peters's first dictum is, 'Evaluate everyone on his or her love of change.'[22] The tone of these commands is direct, didactic and distinctly moral. Like his prophetic predecessors, Peters is never afraid to appeal to the world of morals, visions and values – these, too, must be harnessed to managerial endeavour.

Peters alludes explicitly to religious language and themes drawn from the Judaeo-Christian tradition. The implicit importance of the biblical myth of chaos, mastery and creation in Genesis 1 which sets the tone for the entire book has already been noted. The phrase, 'the world turned upside down' which is incorporated in the title of his first section and so sets the tone and direction for it, 'Prescriptions for a world turned upside down', comes from the biblical book of Acts.[23] Interestingly, this phrase has echoed down the centuries, particularly at times of social disruption and turmoil when prophets flourish. It re-surfaced, for example, during the time of the English Civil War. Not only does Peters use key religious phrases and images to set the tone of *Thriving on Chaos*, he discusses the process of adopting his methods explicitly as 'religious conversion'.[24]

Perhaps the most pertinent aspect of Peters' prophetic activity is the style and process of his exhortation, revelation and evangelization. Here he seems to have learned much from the prophets of old. This becomes apparent if the basic argument of *Thriving on Chaos* is exposed and caricatured a little. It then reads like this.

1. We are living in an era of chaos which is very threatening and anxiety provoking and will destroy businesses and managers. The enemy, in the form of competitors, is at the gate. They are fierce and alien (Japanese) and threaten to destroy the promised land which has been betrayed by the inflexible and complacent giant corporatists. This is the classic way of construing crises for biblical prophets.[25]
2. The old order is passing away – old ways of doing things will not work, there is a need for the radically new. Again, this is a con-sistent theme in the Old Testament prophets as well as in apocalyptic writers.

3. Salvation is at hand! If you turn from your old ways and listen to the prophet then there is some chance that you will be saved. You must do exactly what the prophet tells you to do and follow him with all the zeal you can muster. You must be converted to the new moral order which is clearly spelt out in commandments. You must receive the spirit whereby you, too, become, for example, '*obsessed with listening*'.[26]

4. It is important to decide for Peters's way of doing things now, this minute, or it will all be too late in this chaotic and rapidly changing world.

5. If you do this a great future will open up before you. You, too, will be in tune with ultimate reality and will be able to manipulate the creative and destructive spirits of chaos to your own advantage. You will have chaos actually on your side!

6. The alternative to this is death in an increasingly chaotic, competitive and challenging environment. So you have no choice at all really.

Using this kind of rhetorical strategy, Peters sets up a dynamic of fear, anxiety and discontent amongst his readers. An atmosphere of real, but non-specific, generalized threat is evoked; nothing could be more threatening and less specific than chaos. The legitimacy and permanence of the present order is then problematized. Peters conjures up a dualistic, polarized world in which businesses are either conspicuously successful or conspicuous flops; very few of his examples in the book are about average companies which change a bit, or only gradually, yet still manage to keep afloat. Peters then reveals his easy-to-grasp principles of salvation which people must follow if they are to avoid annihilation. The threatened extinction is not in fact inevitable because Peters has managed to colonize and befriend chaos in such a way that it can become an ally.

This approach creates the symbolic ecology within which Peters can credibly commend his rather pedestrian management principles to his readership, situating them firmly and directly within a religio-emotional dynamic of death/fear – salvation/hope. It is this that helps to make them so compelling and attractive to the contemporary manager struggling amidst the complexities of a real and changing world.

It would be fascinating to explore further the roots of the charismatic religious/prophetic style, dynamic and content in Peters's writing. Is Peters a religious man who uses classic theological resources and styles to directly inform his management discourse? Is he drawing on implicit religious mythology and styles in American culture, such as that of the travelling preacher, to get his message across? Is he simply a shrewd manipulator who realizes that the prophets knew a thing or two about how to get hold of people's attention? Does he actively and consciously seek to use religious and prophetic themes and models of discourse, or is his usage unconscious and merely the reflection of the permeation of such themes through American society anyway? These questions deserve further attention if a full understanding of the nature of 'gurudom' in management theory and practice is to be developed.

Charles Handy: a spiritual guide

Charles Handy, an Irishman, is arguably the most influential religious thinker in Britain today. Handy started his working life as an oil company executive, then became a business school academic and a conference centre director, before becoming a freelance thinker, speaker and writer. He now describes himself as a social philosopher, commuting between his various homes in London, Norfolk and Tuscany. His many books treat of the nature of organizations, schools, voluntary organization, the future of work, middle age and religion. They have now sold over one million copies worldwide. Mostly, these books are aimed at those who work in and manage organizations. Handy is a frequent broadcaster on *Thought for the Day* on BBC Radio 4 and it is probably this medium that has gained him his wide influence and fame.[27]

There is no need to seek covert religious influences and ideas in Handy's thought and writing. He is quite overt about his personal life and religious upbringing. The child of an archdeacon in the (Anglican) Church of Ireland, he was for a number of years the warden of St George's House, Windsor and a committed worshipper in the chapel there. One of his early books, published in 1978, is entitled *Gods of Management*. This does not attempt any kind of Christian theological analysis of managed organizations; indeed, the gods in question are actually the pagan gods of Roman and Greek mythology. However, it does bear witness to an ongoing interest on Handy's part in the 'spirit' and unmanageable aspects of organizations. It also testifies to Handy's keen eclectic eye for arresting myths and metaphors whereby action-guiding thought can be structured.[28]

It is unclear to what extent Handy is now a practising, orthodox Church member of any particular denomination, but he is happy to describe himself as a 'renegade professor of business with theological affinities'.[29] His 'Thoughts for the Day' are replete with insights and rhetorical devices drawn from the Christian religious tradition, as one might expect.[30] The style and content of his recent 'secular' writings (if these can usefully be distinguished) are also much influenced by religious style and content, as will be seen when it comes to the analysis of one of his best-known works, *The Empty Raincoat*.[31] Before proceeding to that analysis, however, it is worth asking the questions, what kind of management guru or religious figure is Handy and what are the ingredients of his considerable success?

Handy as a religious figure

Handy is not a prophetic or charismatic figure in the mould of Tom Peters. He is much less rhetorical and evangelical in terms of his written style and is much less inclined to passion and imperatives in his books. His message is much more loosely woven and multi-stranded, at least on first sight. It is very seldom that this author instructs people on 'how to do it, my way'. Rather, Handy presents himself more as an analyst and thinker than as a leader or preacher. This presumably reflects an academic background, which is also apparent in his wide use of ideas and sources of ideas other than himself.

However, Handy is not without some of the characteristics and skills of more colourful management gurus. The message that he presents in his most recent books, despite its multi-variant analysis, is essentially a very simple 'revolutionary' one: the future is going to be increasingly changeable for society and organizations and we are going to have to change with it, making the most of the opportunities that we can provide for ourselves. Like Peters, Handy examines the threats and challenges posed by the unknown, chaotic future, and then shows how they might be met. Salvation and some kind of personal and social security will be possible – but only if we learn to embrace the possibilities that the future throws up and become intelligent in our lives and working practices. Handy provides a verbal map of the world in which organizations and individuals are forced to live, articulating their fears and predicament (e.g. of short-term employment or no employment at all, of not being valued by their employers and colleagues, of failing to master the possibilities presented by new technologies).

Handy writes clearly, in short sentences, and uses a fund of personal stories. This makes his message easy to assimilate. Insofar as he is strongly 'for' anything it is for the infinite possibilities of human beings to adapt to their environment and make the most of themselves. On the whole, Handy does not create spectres of evil, doom and gloom, being essentially optimistic: 'The hope lies in the unknown, in that second curve, if we can find it. The world is up for reinvention in so many ways. Creativity is born in chaos.'[32]

Handy has the high status attached to gurus that emanates from his wealth and various positions in life. However, far from appearing aloof and mysterious, his life appears to be an open book. He gains affinity and authority with his audience by talking a good deal about his own personal and organizational experience. In many ways the charismatic personality trait that he majors on is that of 'conquerable imperfection'. He freely admits his own mistakes and errors and this allows others to admit theirs, all in the cause of doing a bit better in the all-important future. His very personal, even solipsistic, approach could perhaps be summarized in these words that Handy actually puts in the mouth of the resurrected Jesus in one of his 'Thoughts for the Day':

> Now is your chance to be resurrected, to redeem your life, to be a new you, a true you, and to leave your sleeping past behind. And you can be sure ... that you will be able to do it, because if I can, You [*sic*] can.[33]

While Handy in no way claims to work wonders or to produce results of any kind with his thinking, he is a master of the guiding myth, metaphor and image. The image of a sculpture called 'the empty raincoat', that conjures up a vision of modern human life without the human beings being contained within it, is just one example of his dexterity with words, narratives and stories that are easily assimilable to the reader.[34] Perhaps this facility with words, together with his propensity to expound clearly, to repeat a narrow range of themes succinctly and in different ways, and to yield to moral concern and some gentle exhortation is a product of watching sermon technique in action for many years. As Handy's radio performances demonstrate, he is an accomplished and moving orator.

Handy can lay claim to many of the characteristics of a successful charismatic figure. However, the absence of certain characteristics like aggressive dualism, personal aloofness, simple solutions for gaining salvation, faith in his own personal authority and the desire to make disciples in any obvious way makes me reluctant to place him in the prophetic category. With his story-telling, myth-making and analytic mode of fairly reflective discourse, it seems more appropriate to desig-nate Handy as a kind of spiritual guide – a 'guru' in the original sense of the word. Handy does not seem so much to want to save individuals and organizations from a wicked world, as Peters does, but to help them gain the inner wisdom or spirituality that will enable them to continue to live in and colonize the world. In this respect, *The Empty Raincoat* represents his most profound spiritual work.

The Empty Raincoat
The Empty Raincoat, like its predecessor, *The Age of Unreason*, is not just a book about managers and organizations. It is really about the fundamental meanings with which people surround their lives in a

rapidly changing world. Handy's width of perspective and reflective style confer dignity and seriousness upon the managerial function. He considers global and social changes, as well as organizational issues. It is this breadth and focus on meaning and a sense of higher purpose and morality that give the book a sort of 'spirituality'. Sometimes, indeed, the quest to develop a quasi-religious spirituality is explicit; Handy approvingly cites Vaclav Havel who 'has argued that we will only avoid "mega-suicide" in our time if we rediscover a respect for something otherworldly, something beyond ourselves'.[35]

In the first part of *The Empty Raincoat*, Handy discusses the paradoxes facing the modern world. For example, there is the paradox that work is needed to create wealth, but fewer and fewer people have jobs; or the paradox that people live longer but if they are in work they have less time to do what they want than they used to have. Next, Handy suggests three principles for helping to keep these paradoxes in equilibrium. These are the principles of the 'sigmoid curve' which enables people to start to develop new thinking and prospects into the future; the 'doughnut principle', whereby people and organizations need to distinguish what is essential and to distinguish this from other peripheral activities; and the 'Chinese contract' whereby people learn to compromise and create 'win-win' agreements instead of trying to do others down for their own benefit. The third part, significantly entitled 'Practising the preaching', aims to help people manage paradoxes in reality. Here Handy outlines the need for federalism in organizations and societies, examines the meaning of business, argues for the need to redesign life and the way time is spent, and advocates the need to engineer a situation of social justice. The final part is about the quest for meaning and an ultimate rationale for doing things. Here Handy becomes overtly theological, advocating the need for some kind of faith (not necessarily in a particular god) based on a sense of continuity, connection and direction. Arguments are made for seeing present endeavours in continuity with future generations and thinking long-term, re-creating a sense of community and belonging, and gaining a sense of direction and purpose that is beyond oneself.

One does not need to be a theologian, or to notice Handy's overt references to thinkers like Saint Augustine, who warns that the greatest sin is to be turned in on oneself, to detect much religious influence in *The Empty Raincoat*.[36] From Handy's use of stories, images and myths, to his argument for the need for ultimate purpose and communities based on trust that can extend into the future, the book is shot through with faith elements. Even the fact that Handy believes that 'hope lies in the unknown' bespeaks a kind of optimism based on ultimate hope in the future. Handy seems to propound a kind of secularized Christianity where morality and hopes for a better, beneficent future are retained, but there is no need for any particular kind of God. It is perhaps just as well that the Judaeo-Christian God is not present in Handy's thought, for such a God might have problems with Handy's relative lack of concern about the rights and wrongs of capitalism and the realities of the exclusion and exploitation of the poor in the brave new world that is to come. In common with most of the management gurus, Handy ultimately sells optimism, faith and ideas for solutions to the worried wealthy rather than hard-headed analysis to the poor.

Gerard Egan: a secularized priest?

On the face of it, the fact that a Catholic priest, Gerard Egan, appears in my list of management gurus might appear to provide almost con- clusive evidence that management and religion are integrally enmeshed. One might also expect that a religious believer and 'insider' like Egan would be the most overtly 'religious' of the gurus considered in terms of style, message and personal traits, demonstrating ease and facility with powerful myths and metaphors and drawing upon the skills of the charismatic preacher. Nothing could be further from the reality of Egan's written work.

Egan started his adult life as a Jesuit priest and he continues to teach at a Jesuit university. Although he remains a priest, this is not apparent from the extensive bibliographical details that appear in his books. What is emphasized is his academic career and the very considerable contribution that he has made to counselling and human relations training since he took his doctorate in clinical psychology. Egan is presently a professor of organization studies and psychology, and programme director for the Centre for Organizational Development at Loyola University of Chicago. In recent years, he has broadened his interests from counselling and helping individual relationships to look- ing at organizational issues, while acting as a management consultant to senior managers in many large companies worldwide. He has published books on counselling, human relations and change manage- ment.[37] His most comprehensive work on management is *Adding Value*, published in 1993. It is this volume that is analysed here for evidence of religious or theological style traits and influence.

Adding Value
Adding Value aims to present a system of comprehensive, integrated management that draws on and integrates three models of manage- ment, designated A, B and C. Model A, Managing Business and

Organizational Processes, is concerned with questions of the design, facilitation and assessment of organizations and deals with matters of business, organizational, managerial and leadership effectiveness. Model B, Initiating and Managing Change, provides a framework for 'instituting and managing innovation and change'.[38] Model C, Managing the Shadow Side of the Organization, is a model for coping with the non-rational or arational aspects of organizational life such as everyday messiness, the needs and idiosyncracies of employees, organizational politics and organizational culture. Egan does not reckon to provide a panacea or 'quick fix' with his integrated model schema. He seeks to point up the areas that may need attention in any organization and to provide broad principles for working on these. In any particular context, the models will need to be differently interpreted and applied.

Egan's writing shares some characteristics with that of other 'gurus' like Handy and Peters. He is, for example, optimistic about the future, sure that his methods will work, clear in his presentation which follows the style of 'thought by bullet point' and is very repetitive and vague about the actual outcomes that following his advice will produce. Like the others, he is quick to use stories and examples that demonstrate his points well. Similarly, most of what he has to say draws upon the common well of management ideas including those of the 'new wave' that focus upon excellence, innovation, being close to the customer and organizational culture.

There are, however, also significant differences. Apart from the fact that Egan tends to be more instructional than inspirational, more analytical than rhetorical, it appears that he makes little or no use of religious styles, insights or techniques in putting his message across. There are one or two moments in *Adding Value* where it just might be possible to detect his drawing upon insight gained from his own religious experience and commitment. For example, he describes the point of satisfying a customer's needs and wants as the 'sacred moment' in operations, and the process whereby managers are appointed without training as 'ordination'.[39] His ABC model is, of course, triangular in shape, perhaps providing a resonance with trinitarian theology. However, for the most part, religious inspiration, style or analysis is lacking, even when Egan explores the 'shadow side' of organizations which might be thought to offer much scope for theological insight and reflection. For Egan, the shadow side of the organization does not really include the harm that organizations do. It simply refers to the culture of the organization:

The shadow side of a company or institution includes the factors that affect, either positively or negatively, organizational productivity and quality of work life in substantive and systematic ways but are not found on organizational charts or in organizational manuals and are not discussed in the formal or official forums of the institution.[40]

Egan has many useful things to say about managing the arational or shadow side of organizations, amongst other things. However, I suspect that it would be impossible from reading *Added Value* to deduce that Egan had any theological training or religious commitment. Religious sensibility and analysis has been entirely, and perhaps deliberately, excluded.

Egan as a religious figure

A consequence of this exclusion is that, far from appearing to be any kind of religious figure like a preacher or prophet, Egan seems to be completely converted to secular managerialism. Although there is something to be said for this in that the use of religious ideas and methods can be deceptive and highly manipulative, there is also a loss here. First, Egan fails to analyse religious elements within management theory and practice. Secondly, Egan the priest fails to provide any religious or ethical critique of managerialism. Like any other management theorist or consultant, and more so than someone like the secular Peter Drucker, Egan does not question the prevalent economic order, the maximization of wealth, the unrestricted exploitation of human and natural resources, and so forth. While many Catholic priests are applying their talents to the liberation of the poor in South America, in North America Egan is teaching big business how to be more effectively exploitative! Maybe such criticism would arrest a promising consultancy career with big business, but it seems a little surprising that he should be so faint-hearted – especially when managers seem increasingly self-critical and open to insights and ideas from almost any quarter, including that of religion.

Earlier, I speculated upon the reasons for Tom Peters's charismatic religious style and method, given that he does not claim to adhere to any religion. It is equally tempting to speculate why a religiously committed figure like Gerard Egan should exclude his faith from his work with managers. Perhaps as an academic in a 'secular' discipline he feels that it would be inappropriate to allow religious insight and style to inform his work. Possibly, having to adhere to the standards of the secular academy, he thinks that using religious ideas and methods would invalidate his work. Maybe as a theologian, he has a sophisticated understanding of religion that prevents him from resorting to the ideas and techniques with which figures like Handy and Peters feel so comfortable. Fundamentalist and charismatic figures often tend to resist gaining a critical perspective upon their faith systems and avoid dialogue with those who have a different kind of faith, seeing such endeavour as a self-subverting waste of time. There is no cause to think that Egan is in any way a fundamentalist. However, theological scepticism may disable him from effectively using religious and theological ideas. Whatever the reason, it seems likely that, unless Egan learns to draw more directly upon the religious tradition, styles and words that are shot through the work of many management gurus, his own career prospects within this genre are likely to be severely limited!

Conclusion

In this analysis of three management 'gurus' I hope that I have successfully demonstrated that there is often a substantial and perceptible religious influence upon the thought, teaching and style of management theorists. Tom Peters and Charles Handy provide evidence that religious ideas and styles often pervade management theories in their presentation if not always in their actual content. Gerard Egan provides evidence of a connection between organized Christianity and managerialism, demonstrating that they may be highly compatible in significant ways. Interestingly, however, it seems that Egan has become effectively 'converted' to management ideas and theories within the context of his consultancy work. He eschews the religious insights, styles and methods that other management theorists find so congenial.

The whole relationship between different religious groups, ideas, styles and practices and those of management theorists and practitioners deserves a much more detailed analysis than has been possible here. It is clearly a complicated one. However, it is important to recognize the apparently direct influence of religious ideas and styles upon contemporary popularizers or 'prophets' of management theory. The success of religious ideas and styles in management theory, demonstrated by Peters and Handy, provides some supporting evidence that management is indeed a significantly religious activity. Managers amongst others appear to resonate to the kind of religious style and language used by gurus like these. This might prompt further enquiry into the broadly 'religious' needs of managers and the kinds of theories and styles that speak to their condition. At one level, it seems that the kind of religious thought and practice that managers find useful and will pay for is actually fairly naive, uncritical and basic. Peters and his like sell a kind of religion, even a kind of ecstatic religion of faith and hope. This cheers and enlightens the anxious lives of managers at a time of great social change and uncertainty.

It is important that managers and others should realize that implicitly religious styles, ideas and methods are being put across by popular management theorists. If religio-emotional dynamics, methods and themes are used to commend principles, it is as well to be aware that one's assent to them is being gained in this way. Managers might well be sceptical of Jehovah's Witnesses telling them how to run their companies, perceiving them to be somewhat ideologically confined. Perhaps they should extend a similar wariness to the thought of popular gurus and try to become clear about the nature of the total ideological package that they are being offered.

Following on from this, managers might pay a great deal more attention specifically to the ideological framing of popular managerial thought. Its religious and theological infrastructure would benefit from closer and more conscious inspection and critical examination. Thus, in connection with Peters's thought, fundamental questions might be asked of his undergirding myths and metaphors. Is the world chaotic? Is it unpredictable? Is there no choice but to follow Peters's ideas that everything must move faster and that the past and present are of little value? These apparently abstract questions form the horizons of practical managerial activity. They deserve serious attention if managers are not to risk falling into a blinkered religious worldview which distorts reality.

Religious and theological ideas and dynamics often gain popularity when the social order is under threat. At such times, prophets with answers based on certain revelation and personal charisma are sought and found to fill gaps in the superstructure of meaning and action, as well as to provide energy and encouragement. Sometimes, these prophets turn out to have accurate and valuable perceptions and lead people through difficulty to a place of real promise. But, as people in biblical times knew well, there are more false prophets than true. They are often difficult to distinguish from the real thing at the time. Wandering prophets can come and go with no responsibility for what is done in the name of the message they proclaim. Others have to live with the consequences of this message, which may be quite devastating.

In a world where human beings really need to take responsibility for their own judgments, plans, anxieties and uncertainties, it is dispiriting to see managers flocking to follow prophets with monolithic visions. If managers must follow the prophets, however, perhaps there is no better advice that can be offered than that contained in the New Testament, written at a time when there were more prophetic types around and people were perhaps a little more wary of them: 'Beware of false prophets, which come to you in sheep's clothing, but inwardly they are ravening wolves. Ye shall know them by their fruits' (Matthew 7.15–16a, AV). Better to test the fruit before swallowing the rhetoric. Or, to put it in more pragmatic terms, better to assess the real outcomes and effects of prophetic ministries before signing up for the expensive day seminar.

Conclusion

I began this book by suggesting that management could be seen as a mysterious phenomenon in that it was not widely understood and, like a mystery cult, it functioned as a kind of religion. Having described the nature and evolution of management theory and practice, the latter claim was developed to show that there was a prima facie case for regarding modern management as religious in a number of its aspects and functions. Indeed, I suggested that in many ways, particularly some types of 'new wave'-influenced management theory and practice had many of the characteristics of Christian fundamentalist sectarianism. After speculating upon the possible reasons for, and origins of, the religious nature of management in the contemporary world, I argued that rather than denying the religious nature and characteristics of management, its practitioners and theorists might more usefully aim to become critical 'theologians' of their activity.

I then began to outline a critique of some aspects of management theory and practice from a religio-ethical perspective, paying particular attention to the 'worm's eye' view which is frequently ignored and neglected, and exemplifying mostly from the practice of management within the public sector. Within this broad horizon, first, the importance of words for constructing and maintaining a view of reality was considered. Some common metaphors and myths in managerial discourse were examined and their limits and implications were exposed. The idealizing, perfectionist tendencies of much contemporary management theory, manifested in techniques such as Total Quality Management, were then assayed. Following this, dualistic and exclusivist aspects of management were scrutinized to show that the very clarity of direction of managerial activity throws up problems of its own. A sense of purpose, optimism and 'organizational goodness' is bought at a considerable price. This perception was developed further by surveying issues of ethics, virtues and values within organizations that need to exert control over their members. Next, change management, with its implications and costs were considered. Finally, the thought and practice of three 'gurus' who mediate and disseminate meanings for managers were described and evaluated.

I stated at the outset of this work that my analysis and coverage of management theory and practice would be suggestive and partial. It has made no attempt to be comprehensive in any way and it has probably raised more questions that it has answered. So, for example, if there is any value in looking at management, or at least some kinds of management, as religion, then there is clearly great scope for exploring the nature of managerial religion further and in greater depth. The historical links between management and mainstream religion need to be excavated much more thoroughly, as do the contemporary circumstances that might cause a 'religion' like management to flourish and managers to seek the reassurance of a particular kind of faith system. All the topics that have been considered could have been considered at greater length and with the benefit of different sources and perspectives. I can only hope that the analysis that I have tentatively offered will encourage others to become engaged in the kind of detailed work that might amplify or refute the perceptions outlined here.

Notwithstanding the limitations of a book like this, I hope I have achieved a number of useful things.

In the first place, I have tried to show that there is value in regarding management as a religion and using a broadly religio-ethical perspective to analyse it. This throws into relief certain aspects of its theory and practice which might otherwise go unnoticed. That management is in many important respects a faith system that depends upon myths, symbols and rituals is not something to be ashamed of or to deny. If this is in any way the case, however, it is important to understand and analyse the content of this particular faith system. This might enable its beneficent effects to be enhanced and developed while its less admirable aspects can be questioned and possibly extinguished.

Secondly, the analysis that has been undertaken shows that management, like religion, has effects that may be unintended and can be harmful. While managers are mostly people of goodwill who genuinely seek the welfare of their organizations, and even of society, the theories and practices of management are in themselves value-laden. They embody assumptions and ways of looking at the world, that may inadvertently help to prevent good intentions from being realized and well-being from being promoted. Thus, for example, the language of warfare may prevent trusting relationships being created, while the uncritical use of certain strategies of Individual Performance Review might actually help to stifle creativity, dissent and ethical behaviour amongst organizational members.

Thirdly, the use of examples from the public sector has shown that while management techniques and ideas can be transported into this sector from the private sector, this can have strange, unpredictable and even negative effects. It therefore needs to be recognized that management ideas and techniques are not neutral or culture-free. The introduction of 'new wave' management thinking from the US private sector into the British public sector may have provided a shot in the arm for the latter, galvanizing it into activity and change on a wide scale. However, the uncritical, rapid importation of ideas from the culture of American business has had a downside, too. It is not at all clear what the short- and long-term benefits of managerialism will prove to be, while it is very clear that the cost of introducing management has been very considerable for organizations and individuals. The prevalence of the rhetoric of 'downsizing', 'excellence', and so on is sometimes comic. Sometimes, however, the blanket implementation of ill-understood, unadapted theories to a completely different culture and context is very damaging in its effects. If managerial theories emanating from the US private sector can be seen as a grain of corn contained within a husk, it seems that when they are transported across the Atlantic and adopted in the British public sector the grain (e.g. training, development, empowerment) is often thrown away and the husk (e.g. performance-related pay, short-term contracts, uncritical loyalty) is kept. The only defence against this kind of maladaptive response is to try and become more critical of ideas and techniques and to learn from the experience of others before those practices and theories are actually introduced.

One substantive issue still requires a little discussion. At the beginning of this book, I suggested that management could be seen not just as religious in general terms, but specifically as a kind of Christian heresy, or as a kind of fundamentalist Christian sect. I need to discuss these assertions a little more here in the light of the foregoing analysis.

The roots of heresy and sectarianism in the Christian tradition lie in individuals or groups adopting and exaggerating the importance of one set of perceptions and beliefs at the expense of abandoning equally important counter-balancing beliefs. So, for example, in the early Church much dispute centred round whether Jesus was just God, just human, or in fact a perfect mixture of both, the latter perception being regarded as orthodox. Throughout the history of the Church, there has been a tendency for people to develop to an extreme some insights while abandoning others. Sometimes, this has led to groups hiving themselves off in the name of achieving greater purity or adhering closely to the truth. Readers will be aware of all kinds of Christian religious groups in the modern world who have decided to pursue just such a course. Often, these sectarian groups pursue a strategy of cutting themselves off from wider society, taking a literal view of the Bible, believing themselves and their members alone to be saved, and looking foward with eager anticipation to the coming judgment of God when they will be vindicated and their opponents will be damned.

Clearly and rightly, most managers and management theorists would not recognize themselves as members of a millennarian Christian sect like those that litter the 'Bible Belt' of Mid-West America. However, as we have seen, many of the ideological features typical of such groups can be seen in modern management. In this book, I have pointed up the militaristic, perfectionistic, dualistic, moralistic, exclusivist aspects that seem to inhere in much managerial theory and practice, particularly that which has been influenced by 'new wave' management thinking. This is not surprising given the fairly overtly evangelical style of this kind of thinking, represented by the writing of luminaries such as Tom Peters.

In one important respect, however, the concept of a sect is perhaps not applicable. Sectarians traditionally have tended to meet often and to stick together in well-defined groups. This is not necessarily the case with the great class of people called managers. Although they may adopt the same ideas and practices, with the implicit theologies and worldviews that accompany them, they would not regard themselves as self-conscious members of a close-knit, quasi-religious group. Despite the sectarian ideologies surrounding some kinds of management, then, it might be more accurate to see these religious aspects as more of a kind of New Age religious cult focused upon the individual believer as consumer rather than upon overt membership of a definite religious group. Steve Bruce distinguishes 'client cults' which are structured round the individual relationship between a consumer and a purveyor, and 'audience cults' which are structured round the mass distribution of the spoken and printed word.[1] Neither kind of cult has a fixed, definite membership. It is probably more accurate, therefore, to say that while managerialism has taken on much of the content of traditional Christian sectarian ideas, and although it sometimes has the character of an organized sect (especially from the point of view of 'outsiders'), its exact relationship to sociological typologies of religious groups needs further exploration and definition.

This does not prevent me from adhering to the idea that much managerial theory and practice has the characteristics of a Christian heresy. As has been apparent throughout this book, managers tend to have a very optimistic view of the future, enormous faith in their own capacities to change things for the better, and a poor sense of the limitations and harmful effects that their actions and those of their organizations may have. Each of these ideas has roots that lie deep within our culture generally, but which ultimately have a good part of their origins within the Judaeo-Christian tradition.

Forward-looking optimism emanates partly from the Christian hope that God will redeem humanity in the future. Belief in the human capacity to change things for the better has some of its origins in the religious ideology that humans are made in the image of God and so are co-creators with the divinity. Blindness to the limitations and harmful effects of human activity may come from a sense that human beings have been saved by God and specially chosen to do his will. These ideas and beliefs are valuable in many ways. However, within the orthodox Christian theological tradition, they are balanced and implicitly criticized by other perceptions and ideas.

The Christian tradition does not just value the future, it also values the present; much of the New Testament in taken up with encouraging Christians to value this life and love their neighbours in the present rather than gazing foward and upward into heaven. While the theological tradition does indeed affirm the importance of being co-creators with God, it also contains the corrective notion that the divine is different from the human and has its own plans for the future. Humans may help to make the world better, but they do this under the judgment of God and their efforts are not guaranteed to succeed, however well-intentioned they may be. Finally, the Christian tradition affirms the sinfulness and limitations of humanity, the need for forgiveness and the shadow side of human endeavour.

These counter-balancing ideas help to keep human activity in proportion. Without the tension between them, there is a loss of realistic perception and responsibility. It is because management is so one-sided in its adoption and promulgation of some powerful ideas that come from the Western religious tradition that I am inclined to regard it as, at least in part, a Christian heresy. Part of the task of making the religion of management more self-critical and responsible would, therefore, be to re-insert the counter-balancing notions that have been briefly discussed here. This does not mean that management theorists and practitioners have to become theists or Christians. It just means that it might be helpful to learn from dialogue with the religious tradition how to redress certain emphases in management which may be partly religiously derived and which therefore need some kind of theological critique if they are to be seen in their correct proportion.

Managers in the modern world carry enormous responsibilities and bear the weight of huge, often unrealistic expectations. They deserve to be critically supported within their important work. The tenor of this book has been to suggest that managers and management theorists need to acquire a more ironic, balanced view of their activities. This is where a religio-ethical critique from a worm's eye perspective may be significant. Management needs to stop being a kind of fundamentalism that has a set of theories that have little or nothing to do with what actually eventuates in practice. There is, therefore, a need to develop some sort of critical theology that asks sharp, basic questions and goes beyond simply affirming the status quo. The theory and practice of management, seen as analogous to the enacted theologies of religious faith communities, could learn much from the experience of such communities and their theologians, both in terms of the methods they employ to consider issues and of the questions and answers that they pose. Becoming articulate and critical about one's faith and belief assumptions does not necessarily entail becoming uncommitted to action or to belief. It does, however, allow the possibility of escaping from the kind of unrealistic, over-optimistic, one-sided naive belief that characterizes much managment thinking and practice. There is some chance that believers who are self-aware and critical of their faith may be more judicious about their practice, less belligerent in their claims and attitudes and, just possibly, less destructive in their effects upon the world.

Managers are busy, practical people who may be aware that they are somehow involved in activity with value and ethical connotations but are not necessarily very articulate about what this actually means. Often ethical and value issues are ignored, possibly with unfortunate if unintended consequences for those involved in or affected by practice. It seems important, therefore, that managers should become much more aware and articulate in an integrated way about their basic moral philosophies and assumptions, and in such a way that these become applied to practice, not just encapsulated in idealized moral codes. Only thus can managers really begin to enter into meaningful, responsive ethical dialogue about directions and actions with 'customers' and critics.

Finally, it is important for managers to begin to appreciate the perspective of those that they manage, to see their activity from a worm's eye perspective. There is plenty of inarticulate resentment about the follies of 'the management' in many organizations. Articulate, constructive criticism is, however, seldom sought, elicited or valued if it comes from 'below'. It is not suprising, therefore, that there is often a gap between what managers think and hope they are doing and perceptions of this amongst the managed. This cannot be helpful if management is to be truly effective and enabling for organizations and those that they serve. It is vital that some kind of dialogue begins between the managers and the managed (perhaps even between the managed and managing parts of individual managers) and that management theories and practices should be seen for what they are from below. This would make management a more facilitative activity that commands support rather than bemused resentment.

Much of what I have said in this book has been sharply critical of managerial orthodoxies in theory and practice. If managerial practitioners and theorists are willing to hear and accept a critique of their activity from broadly religious, ethical and worm's eye perspectives, there is every hope that they might become more realistic, articulate and confident about what they can actually offer and perform. This would help them to enter more confidently into dialogue with the managed and non-managers without having to resort to the jargon or unrealistic self-delusion which has often brought management into disrepute in wider society. To live without illusion and in contact with a complex view of reality is essential for such an important and influential group of people in contemporary society.

Management is too universal and too important an activity to be left simply to managers. All members of society, managers and non-managers, have some responsibility to enter into dialogue about the kind of management and managers that are appropriate in different settings and institutions. If this book contributes to the process of getting management in proportion, assaying its strengths and weaknesses, and helping the managed and managers to talk to each other more openly and honestly then its purpose will have been achieved.

Coda: *An essay on management to its religious admirers*

In the last century, Judge Fitzgerald reported the following incident to the author George Eliot. While attending

> the beginning of the Dublin Exhibition he was struck with the attention of the Archbishop of Dublin to the interior of his hat, which at first he took for devout listening to the speeches, but on close examination saw he was reading something, and as this was so intent he was prompted to look into the hat, and found the Archbishop had *Middlemarch* there laid open.[1]

I was reminded of this story by the words of the *Church Times* reporter who went to interview another Archbishop, David Hope, just before his enthronement in York in 1995. This time, the reading matter was not concealed:

> He is reading Charles Handy at the moment, and at the end of our interview got up from his hands and knees [he had been helping to find his interviewer's contact lens] to read a piece out. It describes, for him, the right approach to the National or, as we must now call it, the Archbishops' Council. It was a lesson from Silicon Valley.[2]

Setting aside the respective literary and other merits of Eliot and Handy, the juxtaposition of these two vignettes may reveal just how far management thinking has entered and gained authority within established religious groups. When Handy rather than Eliot sets the tone for a religious organization and its leadership the world really has changed. John Drury, who wrote the original article in which the incident of the Archbishop's hat is recounted, sees this event as 'a glimpse of the subterranean springs which supply believing in the corporate individual', the Archbishop of Dublin being 'the doubter turned corporate, ecclesiastical believer' while George Eliot was 'the Evangelical turned individual believer outside the walls'.[3] Some of the subterranean springs of belief now supplying the Church of England

157

and other religious organizations from outside are those of management theory and practice.

The British churches have been slow to take up managerial theories
and practices. Of course, as organized bodies for centuries, from parish
to national level, management and administration of some kind has
been a feature of church life. But it is only lately that the main denominations have come to see themselves as being in need of formal
management using generic management practices and theories.[4]

A key symbolic moment for the advent of full-blown management in
the Church of England was the accession of George Carey to the
Archbishopric of Canterbury. In a pre-enthronement interview in 1991
with the *Reader's Digest*, the new Archbishop stated that he believed
that his Church should be run more like a business, arguing that, after
all, Jesus himself was a management expert. Behind this symbolic
acceptance of management by the Church's chief executive lies a
complex of factors that have made it appear indispensable.

One factor is probably that of fashion. The Church, particularly the
established Church of England, tends to follow the world in adopting
its methods and practices, but at some distance. Closely related to the
structures of national government in its order, it is not surprising that
when Whitehall adopted managerial practices and theories, the Church
of England would follow.

A second factor is the financial and manpower crisis facing the
Church of England amongst other denominations. With falling numbers of members and ministers, increasing expenses and an economic
crisis caused by financial ineptitude the methods of management with
their emphasis on clarity, effectiveness, efficiency and economy seemed
an obvious balm to apply to organizational wounds.

Thirdly, the Church of England has seen its social and political
influence wane over recent years together with a weakening of the
bonds of establishment with the state. This has been accompanied by
the growth of a sectarian mentality which has been much more concerned to affirm the importance of the active membership of a
committed minority of the population, rather than the inclusion of all
citizens of the country.[5] Although disestablishment is not imminent,
this, together with the factors mentioned and others, has meant that the
Church has had to enter the religious market-place for more members
and resources much more directly and vigorously. Business and marketing methods such as advertising and using the mass media are in the
ascendant together with an evangelical theology oriented towards
bringing new people into church. Management theories and techniques
are complementary, even integral to this approach.

While the churches may have been slow to begin to assimilate management theories and methods, there is now an accelerated pace of adoption. The Church of England is now replete with new corporate logos, diocesan mission statements, parochial aims and objectives, an annual individual performance review of clergy, short-term contracts and the whole paraphernalia of management. It is not just new arch-bishops who ponder the words of Charles Handy. Many clergy are keen to acquire MBAs and other kinds of management education. Organiza-tions suitably acronymed like MODEM (Managerial and Organization Disciplines for the Enhancement of Ministry) have been set up to ensure that 'by the year AD 2000 the values and disciplines of those engaged in the management of secular and Christian organisations will be mutu-ally recognised and respected'.[6]

A number of books have also appeared which apply management principles to the church.[7] Perhaps most significantly, in practical terms, the Church of England has instituted organizational managerial reform at the highest level, based on 'a dialogue between Christian theology and organizational theory'.[8]

The rise of managerialism in the Churches is inevitable, unstoppable and, in many ways, desirable. It would be hard, for example, to justify a continuing, irresponsible waste of limited resources or to be in favour of an organization just blindly meandering along with no sense of direction or purpose. The impulse to introduce management theories and practices that appear to meet the needs of religious communities is, therefore, entirely understandable. However, there are issues involved in this introduction that need a good deal more critical attention if the advent of management is to have a good chance of being beneficent rather than baleful. I will list and briefly discuss these issues here.

Management as a religion

A recent report published by the Church of England deplores the kind of postmodern casualization of faith whereby traditional Christianity is discarded in favour of a kind of à la carte, individually chosen mixture of beliefs and practices drawn from all religious systems and none.[9] It may seem ironic, therefore, that the Churches themselves are appar-ently unconcerned about importing ideas and practices from management, which can itself be seen as a kind of religion. Manage-ment is a collection of beliefs, symbols, myths, rituals, understandings and practices that together make up a total worldview within which individuals can situate themselves and act meaningfully. There is a strong case for evaluating it directly as, at least in some respects, a religious movement.

The main problem here may be one of recognition. Although all religions have their roots in the symbolic and irrational, since the time of the Enlightenment mainstream denominations have spent much of their time trying to persuade themselves and others that their beliefs and practices are rational and 'respectable'.[10] This means that they are prone to import techniques and implicit faith systems almost without criticism in order to appear as rational as any other 'secular' organization. The quest for apparent rationality and social conformity appears to have blinded religious believers to irrationality in apparently 'secular' quarters. While they may be highly sensitive to and suspicious of overtly religious enthusiasm, for example in evangelical sects, ideas and techniques that have wide acceptance in the 'secular' realm are not subjected to religious critique. They should be, for there are often substantial religious and irrational aspects to even the most scientific-looking kinds of activities such as management. Insofar as management can be seen as a religious movement, indeed a world religious movement, it should be scrutinized and recognized as such.

The problem of recognition and perception is deepened, perhaps, by the fact that many people regard management as simply a set of 'neutral' techniques that, like money or nuclear power, can be selectively used as a means to an end. This, too, needs to be problematized within the religious community. As we have seen in the case of the introduction of management into the public sector, managerial techniques and methods actually shape and change organizations and groups.[11] Particular ways of doing and thinking about things are value-laden. They render some things visible and possible, other things insignificant. Techniques for gaining clarity of purpose and vision may push religious groups to exclude width of concern and different interests. Up-to-date accounting techniques may encourage them to become even more preoccupied with what can be counted and measured and less able to deal with the value of the intangible.

The latter example is well illustrated by the work of Richard Laughlin who has made a particular study of accountancy techniques traditionally used within the Church of England. Laughlin argues that 'the lifeworld values of the Church have been largely preserved because, he suggests, in this context the corrosive potential of an accounting mentality has, to date, been successfully resisted'. By contrast, Laughlin found that the lifeworld values of railwaymen and women in European railways had been severely damaged by the techniques and procedures of accounting:

> established accounting disciplines did not act neutrally to facilitate the reproduction or survival of the existing lifeworld by enabling its practices to become more efficient or effective. Rather, their introduction tended to be corrosive of established lifeworld values.[12]

Management techniques are world-, community-, individual- and action-shaping forces like the Christian religion itself. It is important that their potential to shape, influence and control is critically evaluated before they are unthinkingly deployed within the religious community because they will have a direct and decisive influence on the nature of that community. Management techniques are not religiously innocent or neutral. It is very important, therefore, that care should be taken in the techniques and practices that are selected.

The implicit theology of management

Managerial techniques are value and theory laden. They carry implicit meanings and worldviews within them. Theologian Don Browning, writing about practices of all kinds, but particularly about those adopted by religious communities, states:

> These practices are theory-laden. By using the phrase *theory-laden*, I mean to rule out in advance the widely held assumption that theory is distinct from practice. All our practices, even our religious practices, have theories behind and within them. We may not notice the theories in our practices. We are so embedded in our practices, take them so much for granted, and view them as so natural and self-evident that we never take time to abstract the theory from the practice and look at it as something in itself.[13]

It is for this reason that the adoption of particular techniques and practices is enormously important, for they help to shape a particular worldview.

It would be good to see much more careful theological analysis of the beliefs, metaphors, myths theories and assumptions implicit within managerial techniques and made explicit in managerial theory. Here are just a few of the fundamental beliefs and doctrines that seem to lie within much managerial practice:

- the world and other people exist for the benefit of organizational survival, exploitation and expansion;
- human beings can control the world and create a better future if they use the right techniques;
- individuals must be subordinate to greater goals decided by their superiors;
- relationships are fundamentally hierarchical and require clear lines of upward accountability and downward responsibility;
- the nature and condition of work should be such as to extract the maximum from the employee;

- everything worth doing can in some way be measured;
- the future can be planned and colonized.

All these 'doctrines', assumptions or underpinning myths are highly problematic from the point of view of Christian theology. In general terms the implicit 'theology' of management is wildly over-optimistic, narrow, Pelagian and utopian in a way which puts Marx to shame. It is trivializing and unrealistic about the nature and pluriformity of human beings and human endeavour as well as about the chaotic nature of the world.

Religious communities should be able to recognize faith systems when they see them. Management is a faith system with its own implicit theologies which are incarnated in techniques and practices. These theologies need to be identified and challenged before they are unwittingly assimilated through the mediation of supposedly neutral techniques.[14]

The unintended, negative effects of management

All human endeavours and activities have harmful, negative effects. Management is no exception to this rule. Within the public sector, the introduction of management has produced many unintended harmful effects, as this book has shown. Similar results may eventuate within the religious community unless people are critical and careful.

Unfortunately, just as people in many organizations are beginning to see very clearly what the drawbacks of the wholesale implementation of managerialism are, the churches are falling into the same errors and mistakes. In the Church of England, for example, many clergy are now not only poorly paid, they are on short-term contracts that deprive them of security in the name of organizational flexibility and responsiveness. The vicar who could stay in one place for years and say exactly what he thinks in response to faith or conscience is now a thing of the past. Clergy are regularly appraised and if they do not seem to be going along with the organizational mission they can be increasingly easily removed.

Ecclesiastical hierarchy and the rights of employing churches are powerfully reinforced by the introduction of management techniques and theories. There is little evidence so far that the introduction of managerialism is empowering the workforce or making it freer to act in faith, though there is evidence of demoralization, intimidation, the need to conform and a move towards unionization on the part of parish clergy. The net result of this process is likely to be remarkably similar to the introduction of managerialism in the public sector. A few people

will feel more powerful and freer, while many will not. Whether or not
the Church will be more efficient, effective or economical due to the use
of management techniques is unknown as yet. Probably, as in the NHS,
no-one will have taken any base measurements that would allow the
effects of management to be evaluated.

As with any other religious movement, the theories and practices of
management can produce negative as well as positive effects. It
behoves a community of faith that is interested in promoting human
well-being, indeed in proclaiming in word and practice a vision of full
humanity within and outside itself, to become aware of the possible
harmful effects of the implementation of management and to try and
minimize these.

Dialogue or cultural assimilation?

Christianity has always lived in a state of tension with other religions
and with its surrounding culture. Sometimes, it has tried to isolate itself
from cultural trends. At other times it has been keen to assimilate and
adapt to them. Often, mainstream religious denominations like to
adopt a critical but sympathetic stance towards important social movements and thought systems, engaging in dialogue with them. This, as
we have seen, is the stance of many of those who want to introduce
management into the Churches. It will be recalled that the mission of
MODEM is to ensure that 'by the year ad [*sic*] 2000 the values and
disciplines of those engaged in the management of secular and Christian organisations will be mutually recognised and respected'.[15]

The impulse to dialogue and mutual learning is an admirable one.
However, there is always the danger in this kind of situation that
partners in dialogue will be unevenly matched and have differing
amounts of commitment to, and interest in, the process. In recent years,
Christian attempts at dialogue with movements like the counselling
movement have ended up with Christians importing a lot from 'secular' techniques and worldviews and showing great respect for their
proponents and practitioners, while the latter show scant interest in
learning from religious practitioners. Instead of respectful, two-way
dialogue and learning occuring, a process of one-way assimilation takes
place, with distinctively religious insights and practices being ignored
or abandoned. The wholesale importation of counselling techniques
and understandings into pastoral ministry has pulled it in a very
particular direction which has jeopardized its rooting within the Christian tradition. It would be very unfortunate if the same thing were to
happen in relation to management theories and practices.[16] The last
thing that is needed is for the popular counselling paperbacks that have
informed much ministry for the last few decades to be replaced by

popular management best sellers as the *vade mecum* of the religious minister.

Management is not in itself bad or evil, but its theories and techniques should not be allowed to form religious identity. Some measure of cultural assimilation is necessary for religious groups to relate effectively to their surrounding context and culture. However, this should not occur at the expense of those groups developing their own norms, ideas, practices and beliefs that spring from a particular faith. Religious believers will need to be vigilant if they are not to be net importers of a very powerful ideology that may in some respects be inimical to Christian belief and identity.

An end to prophecy and social criticism?

Perhaps the most worrying aspect of the uncritical adoption of popular managerial ideas and techniques within religious groups is that it may be a symptom of the kind of overall assimilation that will leave churches unable and unwilling to stand out against problematic cultural norms and values. The model of the market and all that goes with it, including management, is a very clear and simple way of understanding the world and relationships – that is why it is so powerful. However, once individuals and groups are committed to this model, to the values that support competition in it (such as the need to be profitable, effective, efficient and economical) and to the techniques of management, accounting, marketing and so on that support it, there may be little scope for presenting a different vision or creating different kinds of community and relationship.

This position is similar to that which American denominations created in the last century. These groups needed to recruit a substantial voluntary membership. To do this, they had to compete in a kind of spiritual market-place, using the techniques of business and management. The result was that they successfully perpetuated their existence. However, they also lost the capacity to be critical of the mores of American business and society, so assimilated were they into the culture of the market-place and business.

Analysing this successful *rapprochement* between religious and social norms and practices, historian Charles Moore concedes that without it mainstream Christianity would have died in the USA. Moore is, however, critical of a tendency that has ended up with churches being more concerned with profits than prophets. He observes:

> What was wrong with the liberal Social Gospelers was not that they were blind to business corruption, or that they lacked ideas for social legislation, or even that they imagined that social perfection was easy and lay just around the corner. The problem was that they had

exchanged the emotional fervor of Christianity, its deep and moving feeling for the terrible burden of human depravity, for a breezy faith in efficiency.[17]

He concludes his book, *Selling God*, with the following remarks on the state of religion in the USA today:

'normal' religion is alive and well in American life. The downside of that statement is that wellness does not carry with it transformative power. The paradigm-busters are nowhere in view. Those people who wait in these times for the numerically impressive organizations of American religion to coalesce into a powerful redemptive force are bound to find the present circumstances profoundly unsatisfying. Where are the real religious prophets? Can there be any in a country whose self-image rests on fast, friendly, and guiltless consumption? . . . Would-be religious prophets have to learn the ways of Disneyland in order to find their audience, but even that popular touch cannot give them the capacity to reach the many Americans who would feel comfortable at a prayer breakfast held under McDonald's generous golden arches. How can the prophets among us terrify those people with an apocalyptic vision of a planet left desolate by careless stewards who have used up its fields, wasted its energy, and blackened its air and waters? . . . Probably they cannot. So we are left with nothing new under an unforgiving sun whose burning rays carry cancer and God knows what else through an ozone-depleted atmosphere.[18]

There is no need to ascend to Moore's global and apocalyptic heights to make the point that if Christianity becomes too assimilated to business culture, importing its techniques and implicitly also its ideology, then its capacity to be prophetic and critical in society is likely to be diminished. This is significant not just in the sense of protesting against exploitation and ecological despoilation, but also at a more mundane level. Many individuals in contemporary society have been crushed and oppressed by managerialism and its negative effects. It is not unreasonable to hope that Christian groups might offer them critical support and a vision of something different, even something better, instead of more of the same.

Conclusion

In the Gospel of Matthew, Jesus is recorded as saying:

You are the salt of the earth; but if the salt has lost its taste, how shall its saltness be restored? It is no longer good for anything except to be thrown out and trodden underfoot by men. (Matthew 5.13, RSV)

The message of this brief essay is that one of the threats to Christian 'saltiness', that is to its identity and distinctiveness, could be its uncritical acceptance of managerial theories and methods. If management is a kind of religion, with its own powerful ideologies and assumptions about the world embodied in particular techniques, it demands proper theological examination and critique before it is adopted in whole or in part. The effects of management can be baleful. Its assimilation may threaten the exploration of an identity more adequately based on Christian religious tradition. It is essential, then, that those who look to management as a solution to the practical problems of churches should engage in rigorous critical examination of its theories and practices, preferably before they begin decisively to shape groups and individuals.[19]

It is worth religious communities taking the time critically to examine the implicit and explicit values and theologies of management. This should lead to some definite, conscious decisions about which aspects of management should be adopted, bearing in mind that this is to adopt particular worldviews and practices that will shape the Christian community and its capacity to think and act in particular ways. By the same token, religious groups should try and clarify which aspects of their life, identity and ministry they regard as essential. They need to ensure that these are not sacrificed to, or distorted by, the need to introduce managerial methods. It would also be good to see religious groups having some confidence in their own insights and methods and using these to enrich management instead of just importing management neat. Christianity has remained a living religion for nearly two millennia. It would be a tragedy if it were to sell its wisdom and heritage for a mess of managerialism, particularly since it is not at all clear that management theories and techniques will actually deliver the benefits and outcomes that are claimed for them.

Much that is useful and productive will probably emerge from the introduction of some managerial methods into religious communities. My own stance is not a Luddite one, and I hope it does not appear negative or alarmist. I am, nonetheless, very concerned that an insufficiently critical approach is being taken towards the introduction of the mantras of management into the overtly religious sphere. Part of the challenge of Christianity/religion to society is to promote a vision of human possibility, transcendence and mystery that stands over and against the closure and control represented by much management theory and practice. It will be sad, to say the least, if religious groups become unable to witness to anything other than the virtues of the managed, consumer-centred, market-place ostensibly focused on the perceived needs of religious 'customers'.

Notes

Introduction

1. For more on the practical use of the academic, analytic functions of theology outside churches and faith communities, see Stephen Pattison, 'Can we speak of God in the secular academy?', in Frances Young (ed.), *Dare We Speak of God in Public*? London: Mowbray, 1995.
2. 'Many top managers feel miserable and unloved at work and increasingly isolated from others in the workplace as they climb the managerial tree' (Barbara Miller, 'Devil of a job: hell of an image', *Health Service Journal*, 24 October 1996, pp. 24–6).

Chapter 1

1. Graeme Salaman, *Managing*. Buckingham: Open University Press, 1995, p. 2.
2. Christopher Pollitt, *Managerialism in the Public Sector*. Oxford: Blackwell, 2nd edn, 1993, p. 5.
3. Peter Drucker, *Management: Tasks, Responsibilities, Practices*. Oxford: Butterworth Heinemann, 1974, pp. 20–1.
4. Ibid., p. 22.
5. D. S. Pugh and D. J. Hickson, *Writers on Organizations*. London: Penguin, 4th edn, 1989, p. 86. This kind of rather abstract description or prescription for the managerial role has been amplified and earthed in more recent studies. Salaman, for example, summarizes the roles, skills and competences needed for managers who have an overall vision of improving the performance of their subordinates in the setting of a 'learning organization'. See Salaman, *Managing*.
6. Henry Mintzberg, *Mintzberg on Management*. New York: The Free Press, 1989, p. 10.
7. Ibid., p. 14.
8. Keith Grint, *Management: A Sociological Introduction*. Cambridge: Polity Press, 1995, ch. 3.
9. Ibid., p. 48.
10. Ibid., p. 47.
11. Cf. Salaman, *Managing*, p. 3.
12. See further, Salaman, *Managing*.

13. Gerard Egan, *Adding Value: A Systematic Guide to Business-Driven Management and Leadership*. San Francisco: Jossey-Bass Inc., 1993, p. 4.

14. Quoted in Pollitt, *Managerialism*, p. 25.

15. Quoted in ibid., p. vi.

16. Grint, *Management*, pp. 17ff.

17. Andrzej Huczynski, *Management Gurus*. London: International Thomson Business Press, 1996, ch. 4.

18. Ibid., p. 118.

19. Carol Kennedy, *Guide to the Management Gurus*. London: Century Business, 1991, pp. 160–1. For a critique of Taylorism see, e.g. Bernard Doray, *From Taylorism to Fordism: A Rational Madness*. London: Free Association Books, 1988.

20. Adapted from Huczynski, *Management Gurus*, p. 17.

21. Ibid., p. 19.

22. See Janet Newman and John Clarke, 'Going about our business? The managerialization of public services', in John Clarke, Allan Cochrane and Eugene McLaughlin (eds), *Managing Social Policy*. London: Sage, 1994, p. 15; Pollitt, *Managerialism*, p. 23.

23. Tom Peters and Robert Waterman, *In Search of Excellence*. London: Harper and Row, 1982.

24. Huczynski, *Managment Gurus*, p. 35.

25. Ibid., pp. 35–8.

26. See ibid., p. 38. A good sense of this kind of managerial ethos can be obtained from reading almost any book by Charles Handy or Tom Peters. A fundamental critique of some of the assumptions underlying these visionary ideas can be found in Francis Fukuyama, *Trust*. London: Penguin, 1996, ch. 2.

27. See Pollitt, *Managerialism*, p. 24.

28. Huczynski, *Management Gurus*, p. 58. Stanford University has actually run a course called 'Business as a Spiritual Discipline' and 'spiritual' and religious thinking seeps into much managerial thought in the USA. For an account and critique of this see Stephen Pattison and Rob Paton, 'The religious dimensions of management beliefs', *Iconoclastic Papers*, Vol. 1(1), 1996. (Published electronically.)

29. MBO revolves around the precept that in order to survive and perform optimally, corporate goals should be divided into objectives and assigned to particular units and individuals. See further, Kennedy, *Guide*, ch. 9.

30. Noting the lack of real dispute and theoretical disagreement amidst management theorists compared to other academics and writers, Huczynski comments: 'It would be difficult to find another field of educational activity in which intellegent and sometimes educated minds were so harmoniously disposed. There may be an occasional disgreement about eductional methods in managment education but rarely about basic doctrine' (Huczynski, *Management Gurus*, p. 270). For further discussion of this remarkable sense of harmony, synthesis and longevity in basic management theory, see ibid., esp. ch. 8.

31. See further, Charles Handy, *Understanding Organizations*. London: Penguin, 3rd edn, 1985, pp. 190ff.

32. Drucker, *Management*, p. 134ff.

33. This account of the rise of managerialism in public services draws mainly on Pollitt, *Managerialism*, chs 2 and 3. I take 'managerialism' to be the consistent application of a reasonably coherent set of ideas and practices that together form an ideology. This contrasts with the more episodic or casual use of some management ideas and techniques which had always been of some interest within public administration.

34. Ewan Ferlie, Lynn Ashburner, Louise Fitzgerald and Andrew Pettigrew, *The New Public Management in Action*. Oxford: Oxford University Press, 1996, p. 31.

35. Roy Griffiths, *NHS Management Enquiry*. London: DHSS, 1983, p. 12.

36. This list is adapted from Stewart Ranson and John Stewart, *Management for the Public Domain: Enabling the Learning Society*. Basingstoke: Macmillan, 1994, p. 15.

37. See Pollitt, *Managerialism*, p. 56.

38. See Kennedy, *Guide*, p. 42.

39. For more on the Public Service Orientation, see Ranson and Stewart, *Management for the Public Domain*; Ferlie *et al.*, *The New Public Management*, p. 15.

40. For human resource management approaches see Salaman, *Managing*, ch. 2.

41. John Clarke, Allan Cochrane and Eugene McLaughlin, 'Why management matters', in Clarke *et al.* (eds), *Managing Social Policy*, p. 4.

42. See Ferlie *et al.*, *The New Public Management*, pp. 216ff.

43. Newman and Clarke, 'Going about our business?', p. 16.

44. Pollitt, *Managerialism*, p. 84.

45. For surveys of the impact of managerialism see, e.g. Ferlie *et al.*, *The New Public Management*; Stephen Harrison, David Hunter and Christopher Pollitt, *The Dynamics of British Health Policy*. London: Unwin Hyman, 1990; Ray Robinson and Julian Le Grand (eds), *Evaluating the NHS Reforms*. London: King's Fund Institute, 1993.

46. Ferlie *et al.*, *The New Public Management*, p. 244.

47. Newman and Clarke, 'Going about our business?', p. 23.

48. Ranson and Stewart, *Management for the Public Domain*, p. 4.

Chapter 2

1. John Hick, *An Interpretation of Religion*. Basingstoke: Macmillan, 1989, ch. 1. For description and discussion of various theories of religion from different disciplinary perspectives see, e.g., Daniel Pals, *Seven Theories of Religion*. New York: Oxford University Press, 1996.

2. For a discussion of these difficulties from a sociological perspective see, e.g., Steve Bruce, *Religion in the Modern World*. Oxford: Oxford University Press, 1996, pp. 6–7. For general sociological discussions of the nature of religion, see, e.g., Michael Hill, *A Sociology of Religion*. London: Heinemann, 1973, ch. 1; Betty Scharf, *The Sociological Study of Religion*. London: Hutchinson, 1970, ch. 2.

3. Alasdair MacIntyre, *After Virtue*. London: Duckworth, 1981, p. 73. For further assessment of MacIntyre's significance for management, see the symposium, 'The manager and morality', in *Organization*, vol. 2(2), 1995.

4. Clifford Geertz, *The Interpretation of Cultures*. London: Fontana, 1993, p. 90. It is useful to compare this definition with a cultural-linguistic definition of religion used by a Christian theologian, George Lindbeck. Lindbeck suggests that religions should be 'seen as comprehensive interpretive schemes, usually embodied in myths or narratives and heavily ritualized, which structure human experience and understanding of self and world'. 'Stated more technically, a religion can be viewed as a kind of cultural and/or linguistic framework or medium that shapes the entirety of life and thought. ... Its doctrines, cosmic stories or myths, and ethical directives are integrally related to the rituals it practices, the sentiments or experiences it evokes, the actions it recommends, and the institutional forms it develops.' See George Lindbeck, *The Nature of Doctrine*. London: SPCK, 1984, pp. 32 and 33.

5. Roger Cooter, *The Cultural Meaning of Popular Science*. Cambridge: Cambridge University Press, 1984, p. 190.

6. See, e.g., Graham Cleverly, *Managers and Magic*. London: Longman, 1971, ch. 5.

7. Yiannis Gabriel and Tim Lang, *The Unmanageable Consumer*. London: Sage, 1995.

8. Cleverly, *Managers and Magic*, ch. 5, discusses the ritual aspects of market research which he likens to the Roman ritual of slaying birds and inspecting their entrails to predict the future; the more anxious the situation was, the more birds were slain.

9. Ibid., p. 91.

10. For a critique of the use of strategic planning as a tool of domination that is more about political controversy and subjective judgment rather than objective reality, see Mats Alvesson and Hugh Willmott, *Making Sense of Management*. London: Sage, 1996, pp. 129ff. Mintzberg argues that planning is a craft involving subjectivity, learning and judgment. See Henry Mintzberg, *Mintzberg on Management*. New York: The Free Press, 1989, ch. 2.

11. Rosemary Stewart, *Leading in the NHS*. Basingstoke: Macmillan, 2nd edn, 1996, p. xii; emphasis in original. For an interesting feminist critique of this kind of 'heroic' management in the NHS, see Celia Davies, *Gender and the Professional Predicament in Nursing*. Buckingham: Open University Press, 1995, especially Chapters 3 and 8.

12. Ibid., p. 3; emphasis in original.

13. Ibid.; emphasis omitted.

14. Keith Grint, *Management: A Sociological Introduction*. Cambridge: Polity Press, 1995, p. 124. Grint's chapter, 'The alchemy of management', gives an excellent critical account of the vagaries of leadership.

15. For more on what constitues leadership, see Rosemary Stewart, 'Studies of management jobs and behaviour; the ways forward', *Journal of Management Studies*, vol. 26, 1989, pp. 1–9.

16. For more on the subjectivity and potential for distortion that may enter into accountancy, see Alvesson and Willmott, *Making Sense of Management*, pp. 139ff.

17. Francis Fukuyama, *Trust*. London: Penguin, 1996, ch. 1.

18. Peter Drucker, *Management: Tasks, Responsibilities, Practices*. Oxford: Butterworth Heinemann, 1974, pp. 225ff.

19. Alvesson and Willmott, *Making Sense of Management,* p. 20.

20. MacIntyre, *After Virtue,* p. 73.

21. Philip Strong and Jane Robinson, *The NHS Under New Management.* Buckingham: Open University Press, 1990, p. 3; emphasis added.

22. Ibid., p. 165; emphasis added.

23. Ibid., p. 187; emphasis added.

24. For a characterization of sectarian views and attitudes, see, e.g., Hill, *A Sociology of Religion,* chs 3 and 4, esp. pp. 77f. See also, Bryan Wilson, *Religion in Secular Society.* Harmondsworth: Penguin, 1969, ch. 11. For a discussion of the nature of fundamentalism especially as a response to the modern world, see Ernest Gellner, *Postmodernism, Reason and Religion.* London: Routledge, 1992.

25. Academic training, in particular, might even be seen to be a disadvantage in this context! See Mintzberg, *Mintzberg on Management,* ch. 5.

26. For such tracts see, e.g., John Harvey-Jones, *Making It Happen.* London: Collins, 1987.

27. Tom Peters and Robert Waterman, *In Search of Excellence.* London: Harper and Row, 1982, ch. 2.

28. Ibid., p. 37.

29. Ibid., pp. xxv and 29

30. Ibid., p. 74.

31. Walter Principe, quoted in Ursula King, *Women and Spirituality.* London: Macmillan, 1989, p. 6.

32. Grace Davie, a sociologist of religion, cites this linguistic usage as evidence that the sacred is being 'plundered by the secular' as it starts to find ways of spilling over into everyday thinking. See Grace Davie, *Religion in Britain since 1945.* Oxford: Blackwell, 1994, p. 41.

33. Geertz, *The Interpretation of Cultures,* p. 90.

34. Cooter, *Cultural Meaning,* p. 190.

Chapter 3

1. For more on modern believing, New Age religion, etc. see Grace Davie, *Religion in Britain since 1945.* Oxford: Blackwell, 1994 and esp. Steve Bruce, *Religion in the Modern World.* Oxford: Oxford University Press, 1996, chs 7 and 8. Gellner argues that while the rational-technological paradigm of knowledge is dominant in the modern world, this is characterized by 'emotional thinness'. Satisfactory individual and social existence requires the additional support of rituals, symbols, etc. if it is to be sustained and flourish. See Ernest Gellner, *Postmodernism, Reason and Religion.* London: Routledge, 1992, pp. 80ff.

2. For a discussion of religion as a response to anxiety, see Paul Tillich, *The Courage to Be.* London: Fontana, 1962.

3. Anthony Giddens, *Modernity and Self-Identity.* Cambridge: Polity Press, 1991, p. 16; emphasis in original.

4. For 'pre-millennial tension', see further, Martyn Percy, *Words, Wonders and Power.* London: SPCK, 1996, p. 190, n. 18.

5. For the descriptive collage of the managerial condition that follows, I draw upon diverse sources including Keith Grint, *Management: A Sociological Introduction.* Cambridge: Polity Press, 1995; Andrzej Huczynski, *Management*

Gurus. London: International Thomson Business Press, 1996; Mats Alvesson and Hugh Willmott, *Making Sense of Management*. London: Sage, 1996, ch. 1.

6. Grint, *Management*, p. 62.

7. Ibid., p. 61.

8. For symbols and rituals as a defence against uncertainty, see Graham Cleverly, *Managers and Magic*. London: Longman, 1971, ch. 5.

9. For critiques of the limits of rationality in management generally see Alvesson and Willmott, *Making Sense of Management*; Grint, *Management*, ch. 1. For rationality in the modern world generally, see Gellner, *Postmodernism*.

10. As far as I know, a comprehensive history of the interaction between Christianity and management has yet to be written.

11. Grint, *Management*, p. 17. Other critics are less impressed by the importance of ecclesiastical managerial precedents. Pollitt quotes an NHS manager from 1986: 'Management? As far as I'm concerned it's a bad habit left over from the Army and the Church' (Christopher Pollitt, *Managerialism in the Public Sector*, Oxford: Blackwell, 2nd edn, 1993, p. vi). For the influence of religious ideas of time on contemporary social and organizational structures see, for example, Richard Fever, *The Penitence of Purgatory*. Cambridge, Cambridge University Press, 1995.

12. Henry Mintzberg, *Mintzberg on Management*. New York: The Free Press, 1989, p. 5.

13. David Forrest, 'Self-destructive HRD'. *Training and Development Journal*, December 1984, pp. 53–7, pp. 55–6. For an account of religion in contemporary America, see Bruce, *Religion in the Modern World*, ch. 6.

14. Laurence Moore, *Selling God: American Religion in the Market-place of Culture*. New York: Oxford University Press, 1994.

15. Ibid., p. 119.

16. See ibid., ch. 8 for the Social Gospel movement and its implications.

17. Ibid., p. 10.

18. See ibid., chs 2, 3 and 7.

19. Huczynski, *Management Gurus*, ch. 7.

20. Moore, *Selling God*, p. 218.

21. For analytic work in these areas see, e.g., Stephen Linstead, Robert Grafton Small and Paul Jeffcutt (eds), *Understanding Management*. London: Sage, 1996; Stephen Fineman (ed.), *Emotion in Organizations*. London: Sage, 1993.

22. Alvesson and Willmott, *Making Sense of Management*, pp. 31ff.

23. See ibid., ch. 1, for a critique of the limits of managerial rationality, neutrality, etc. The rationality of management is arraigned as a falsifying myth in Linda Putnam and Dennis Mumby, 'Organizations, emotion and the myth of rationality', in Stephen Fineman (ed.), *Emotion in Organizations*.

24. Peter Hodgson, *Winds of the Spirit: A Constructive Christian Theology*. London: SCM Press, 1994, p. 5.

25. See, e.g., Sallie McFague, *Metaphorical Theology*. London: SCM Press, 1983.

26. Quoted in Alvesson and Willmott, *Making Sense of Management*, p. 182.

27. Ibid., pp. 182–3.

28. A critical, creative text about the limits and implications of metaphors in management is Gareth Morgan, *Images of Organization*. London: Sage, 1986.

29. For more on how language shapes and determines the nature of reality and

fundamental orientations to it see, e.g., Richard Rorty, *Contingency, Irony and Solidarity*. Cambridge: Cambridge University Press, 1989; Don Cupitt, *The Long-Legged Fly*. London: SCM Press, 1987.

30. For more on the creative use of narrative and story, see Don Cupitt, *What is a Story?* London: SCM Press, 1991.

31. John Patton, *From Ministry to Theology*. Nashville: Abingdon, 1990, p. 70. For more on transformational knowledge, soft knowledge and knowledge that arises from talking back to experience, see Donald Schön, *The Reflective Practitioner*. Aldershot: Avebury, 1991.

32. For more on the 'spirit' of organizations see, e.g., Walter Wink, *Unmasking the Powers*. Philadelphia: Fortress Press, 1986.

33. For more on this kind of critical theological perspective, see Don Browning, *A Fundamental Practical Theology*. Minneapolis: Fortress, 1991; Don Browning (ed.), *Practical Theology*. San Francisco: Harper and Row, 1983.

34. For more on religous and ethical activity as artistic performance see Cupitt, *The Long-Legged Fly*.

35. Percy, *Words, Wonders and Power*.

Chapter 4

1. Martyn Percy, *Words, Wonders and Power*. London: SPCK, 1996, p. 23; emphasis in original. John Wimber is a charismatic religious figure who is the leading figure in a fundamentalist Christian sect called the Vineyard movement. This movement has significant numbers of adherents in the USA and is also influential in the UK.

2. Henry Mintzberg, *Mintzberg on Management*. New York: The Free Press, 1989, p. 12.

3. Mangham notes that 'language is the currency of interaction at all levels of encounter and its manipulation is a key feature of persuasion .... organizations are created, maintained and changed through talk' (Iain Mangham, *Power and Performance in Organizations*. Oxford: Blackwell, 1986, p. 82).

4. Tom Peters, *Liberation Management*. London: Pan Books, 1993.

5. Huczynski observes that 'Popular managment ideas possess clarity of communication while, at the same time, avoiding obviousness'. This means that the concepts have to be explained and unpacked, giving managers a sense of achievement, participation and ownership when they have grasped their content. See Andrzej Huczynski, *Management Gurus*. London: International Thomson Business Press, 1996, p. 60.

6. See, e.g., Colin Morgan and Stephen Murgatroyd, *Total Quality Management in the Public Sector*. Buckingham: Open University Press, 1994, ch. 1, esp. pp. 20ff. With reference to acronyms and abbreviations, Huczynksi observes: 'Acronyms are popular in management .... They give a pseudo-scientific precision to commonplace observations and make them appear at once sociologically profound and wittily dismissive' (Huczynski, *Management Gurus*, p. 60).

7. In psychodynamic terms the concept of total customer satisfaction is underwritten by an appeal to the basic paradise myth whereby all babies drink happily and to their hearts' content from their mothers' breasts and everyone

gets what they want when they want it. Have the TQM theorists never heard of shortage of resources, sibling rivalry and the mother who walks away despite her child's frustrated cries?

8. Neil Postman, *Amusing Ourselves to Death*. London: Methuen, 1987.

9. Huczynski observes that most popular management ideas make an appeal to the manager as an individual, they tend to be psychological rather than sociological in origin and to enhance the individual manager's sense of control and self-esteem. See Huczynski, *Managment Gurus*, pp. 67ff.

10. For a good analysis of psychoanalytic language, upon which Huczynski draws extensively, see Ernest Gellner, *The Psychoanalytic Movement*. London: Paladin, 1985.

11. The language of 'donwsizing' provides a good cautionary example of the real and sometimes destructive power of neat, easy concepts and words to shape reality. The concept's originator, Stephen Roach recently repented of its use and popular deployment, but not before many organizations had disposed of large numbers of their employees. See 'Downsizing: picking up the pieces', *MSF At Work*, November 1996, pp. 10–11. For HRM, see Graeme Salaman, *Managing*. Buckingham: Open University Press, 1995, ch. 2.

12. George Lakoff and Mark Johnson, *Metaphors We Live By*. Chicago: University of Chicago Press, 1980, p. 3.

13. Ibid., p. 5. For general and comprehensive background to the nature and use of metaphors, see, e.g., Andrew Ortony (ed.), *Metaphor and Thought*. Cambridge: Cambridge University Press, 2nd edn, 1993.

14. Robert Solomon, *Ethics and Excellence*. New York: Oxford University Press, 1993.

15. Ibid., p. 19. Solomon tends to conflate 'myth' and 'metaphor' in his usage. Actually they are different and function differently, but are often closely related and associated within religious systems. For the nature and importance of myths as opposed to metaphors see, e.g., Rollo May, *The Cry for Myth*. New York: W. W. Norton, 1991; Joseph Campbell, *The Masks of God: Creative Mythology*. London: Penguin, 1976, ch. 9. Campbell notes four main functions for myths. These are the awakening and maintenance in the individual of a sense of awe; the rendering of a cosmology that makes the world intelligible; the validation and maintenance of the social order; and the centring and harmonization of the individual. Myths are, thus, omnipervasive in all parts of human life. For a study of organizational myths, see Yiannis Gabriel, 'On organizational stories and myths: why it is easier to slay a dragon than to kill a myth', *International Sociology*, vol. 6(4), 1991, pp. 427–42.

16. Solomon, *Ethics and Excellence*, p. 25.

17. Ibid.

18. Ibid., p. 24.

19. Ibid.

20. Ibid., pp. 37–8.

21. Ibid., p. 44.

22. Ibid., p. 46.

23. Ibid., ch. 5.

24. Ibid., p. 65.

25. See, e.g., Jeffrey Abrahams, *The Mission Statement Book*. Ten Speed Press, 1995.

26. Charles Dickens, *Bleak House*. Glasgow: Collins, 1953, p. 388.

27. For the use of metaphor in religious language see Sallie McFague, *Metaphorical Theology*. London: SCM Press, 1983; Janet Martin Soskice, *Metaphor and Religious Language*. Oxford: Clarendon Press, 1985.

28. For more on how language shapes and determines the world and fundamental orientation to life see, e.g., Richard Rorty, *Contingency, Irony and Solidarity*. Cambridge: Cambridge University Press, 1989; Don Cupitt, *The Long-Legged Fly*. London: SCM Press, 1987; Gareth Morgan, *Images of Organization*. London: Sage, 1986.

29. For more on postmodernism, see David Harvey, *The Condition of Postmodernity*. Oxford: Blackwell, 1989.

30. See, e.g., Gareth Morgan, *Imaginization*. London: Sage, 1993.

31. Umberto Eco, *The Island of the Day Before*. London: Minerva, 1996, p. 207. For the vital importance of narratives and stories for human life of all kinds see Don Cupitt, *What is a Story?* London: SCM Press, 1991.

Chapter 5

1. Martyn Percy, *Words, Wonders and Power*. London: SPCK, 1996, p. 5.

2. For more on the origins and ambivalent effects of idealism in Christianity see Stephen Pattison, 'The shadow side of Jesus', *Studies in Christian Ethics*, vol. 8(2), 1995, pp. 54–67.

3. Tom Peters and Robert Waterman, *In Search of Excellence*. London: Harper and Row, 1982, ch. 6.

4. Tom Peters, *The Pursuit of WOW!* London: Macmillan, 1995, p. vii.

5. Colin Morgan and Stephen Murgatroyd, *Total Quality Management in the Public Sector*. Buckingham: Open University Press, 1994, p. 3. Cf. Steven Fleming, Kenneth Bopp and Kirk Anderson, 'Spreading the "good news" of quality management', *Health Care Management Review*, vol. 18(4), 1993, pp. 29–33, which argues that TQM is an evangelical faith system, devoted, like Christianity, to rooting out flaws so that not one customer is lost!

6. Morgan and Murgatroyd, *Total Quality Management*, p. 5.

7. Ibid., p. 8; emphasis in original.

8. Ibid., p. 46.

9. For a good critical discussion of the difficulty and value-laden nature of defining quality in public services, see Kieron Walsh, 'Quality and public services', *Public Administration*, vol. 69, 1991, pp. 503–14.

10. Morgan and Murgatroyd, *Total Quality Management*, pp. 14–15.

11. Ibid., p. 22.

12. Ibid., pp. 28–9.

13. Fleming *et al.* compare this putting the customer first with the altruistic service of others within the Christian fellowship. See Fleming *et al.*, 'Spreading the "good news" ', p. 32.

14. Morgan and Murgatroyd, *Total Quality Management*, p. 21; emphasis added.

15. Ibid., p. 6.

16. For another set of idealized 'counsels of perfection' for quality, see Peters's twelve attributes of a quality revolution; in Tom Peters, *Thriving on Chaos*. London: Pan Books, 1989, pp. 70ff. For an interesting, even devastating, critique of the concept of quality as used in public services, see David Seedhouse, *Fortress NHS*. Chichester: John Wiley and Sons, 1994, pp. 51ff.

17. Morgan and Murgatroyd, *Total Quality Management*, p. 70.

18. Some years ago, I formulated a 'law of gloss'. This states that 'The acreage of glossy paper lauding the achievements and virtues of a public-service organization and advertising its services increases in inverse proportion to the amount and quality of service that can be provided'. See Stephen Pattison, 'Glossing over the facts', *Health Service Journal*, 10 September 1992, p. 19.

19. For a good critical review of the limits of commercial consumerism and, indeed, the ways that it can actually limit rather than extend choice in the market-place, see Yiannis Gabriel and Tim Lang, *The Unmanageable Consumer*. London: Sage, 1995, ch. 2.

20. See Ellen Annandale, *Working on the Front Line: Risk Culture and Clinical Decision-Making in the New NHS*. York: ESRC Risk and Human Behaviour Programme, n. d., for a consideration of patients as the locus of risk and threat of litigation or complaint to nursing staff who, therefore, adopt a distant and defensive posture towards them.

21. Donald Winnicott, *The Maturational Process and the Facilitating Environment*. London: Karnac Books, 1990, p. 145.

22. Commenting upon what we know of the effects of psychotherapy, Carl Rogers observes that in a helpful therapeutic relationship that produces useful change clients actually narrow the gap between ideal and reality: 'The client changes and reorganizes his concept of himself. He moves away from perceiving himself as unacceptable to himself, as unworthy of respect, as having to live by the standards of others. He moves towards a conception of himself as a person of worth, as a self-directing person, able to form his standards and values upon the basis of his own experience . . . . His aims and ideals for himself change so that they are more achievable. The initial discrepancy between the self that he is and the self that he wants to be is diminished' (Carl Rogers, *On Becoming a Person*. London: Constable, 1967, p. 65).

23. For more on the importance and mechanisms of involving the public more directly in determining the nature and standards of public service see, e.g., Ranson and Stewart, *Management for the Public Domain: Enabling the Learning Society*. Basingstoke: Macmillan, 1994.

Chapter 6

1. Martyn Percy, *Words, Wonders and Power*. London: SPCK, 1996, p. 91.

2. For more on the nature and history of Christian dualism, exclusion of heretics (the 'enemy within') and demonization of the world and those 'outside' see, e.g., Elaine Pagels, *The Gnostic Gospels*. London: Penguin, 1989; *The Origin of Satan*. London: Allen Lane, 1995, esp. the last two chs. See Norman Cohn, *Chaos and the World to Come*. New Haven: Yale University Press, 1993, for the origins of dualism within an apocalyptic world view.

3. For more on the paradox of religious destructiveness, see John Bowker,

Licensed Insanities. London: Darton, Longman and Todd, 1987. For the relationship of this to aggressive dualism see, e.g., Walter Wink, *Engaging the Powers*. Minneapolis: Fortress Press, 1992. For interesting evidence of the connection between militarism, dualism and religion in early Christianity and which might be detected in some forms of contemporary managerialism, see Robert Lane Fox, *Pagans and Christians*. London: Penguin Books, 1988. Lane Fox notes: '*Pagani* were civilians who had not enlisted through baptism as soldiers of Christ against the powers of Satan. By its word for non-believers, Christian slang bore witness to the heavenly battle which coloured Christians' view of life' (ibid., pp. 30–1).

4. Mary Midgley, *Wickedness*. London: Routledge and Kegan Paul, 1986.

5. See Mats Alvesson and Hugh Willmott, *Making Sense of Management*. London: Sage, 1996, p. 37. For interesting psychodynamic perspectives on organizational dualisms and splitting see, e.g., Anton Obholzer and Vega Zagier Roberts, *The Unconscious at Work*. London: Routledge, 1994.

6. When I was a child, we were told that the reason that the local cathedral had doors exactly opposite each other at opposite ends of each transept was that when the monks carried in a body for funeral rites, they would enter by one door then turn at a sharp right angle up to the altar. If the devil was following the procession to get the dead monk's soul he would have to continue straight ahead, exiting via the door on the other side of the cathedral which would be shut after him.

7. See Peter Drucker, *Management: Tasks, Responsibilities, Practices*. Oxford: Butterworth Heinemann, 1974.

8. Ibid., p. 84, discusses the importance of 'planned abandonment'.

9. Charles Handy, *The Empty Raincoat*. London: Arrow Books, 1995, ch. 3.

10. For interesting reflections on the significance of the past and memories for organizations and individuals, see Mary Douglas, *How Organisations Think*. London: Routledge and Kegan Paul, 1987, esp. ch. 6; Charles Elliott, *Memory and Salvation*. London: Darton, Longman and Todd, 1985.

11. Interestingly, however, sometimes politicians of various hues try to wrap themselves in the tradition to claim that they are the inheritors and defenders of past values even as they encourage managers to press on with future-oriented change that has nothing do with the past.

12. For an interesting consideration of organizational nostalgia as a comfort against an uncomfortable present, see Yiannis Gabriel, 'Organizational nostalgia – reflections on the "golden age" ', in Stephen Fineman (ed.), *Emotions in Organizations*. London: Sage, 1993.

13. Rosemary Stewart, *Leading in the NHS*. Basingstoke: Macmillan, 2nd edn, 1996, p. 13.

14. For an extended treatment of failure in practice, see Stephen Pattison, *A Critique of Pastoral Care*. London: SCM Press, 2nd edn, 1993, ch. 7.

15. See further, e.g., Charles Handy, *Understanding Voluntary Organizations*. London: Penguin, 1990.

16. For more on the importance of taking seriously plurality of interest and the proper political context of management in the public sector, see Stewart Ranson and John Stewart, *Management for the Public Domain: Enabling the Learning Society*. Basingstoke; Macmillan, 1994, part 2.

17. See Drucker, *Management*, part 4, for a management theorist's view of the social impacts and social responsibilities of managed organizations.

18. See, e.g., Alvesson and Willmott, *Making Sense of Management*, for a critique of this myopia. They write: 'As the political quality of managment practice is denied or trivialized, consideration of the personal, social and ecological costs of the managerial methods of enhancing growth, productivity, quality and profit is largely ignored. Scant attention is paid to the increase in stress, the loss of autonomy in work and leisure or the degradation of the environment – all of which are associated with the drive for "efficient management" ' (p. 37).

19. For an anguished protest against the effects of managerialism on nursing and the growth of what he calls a 'hate culture' see Michael Wilkinson, 'Love is not a marketable commodity: new public management in the British National Health Service', *Journal of Advanced Nursing*, vol. 21, 1995, pp. 980–7.

20. Burgoyne, quoted by Alvesson and Willmott, *Making Sense of Management*, p. 28.

21. Ibid.

22. Ronald Barnett, *The Limits of Competence*. Buckingham: Open University Press, 1994, p. 74.

23. Handy admits to having been brought up in industry on the principle, 'If you can't count it, it doesn't count'. Charles Handy, *Beyond Certainty*. London: Arrow Books, 1996, p. 137.

24. Barnett, *Limits of Competence*, pp. 81–2.

25. I describe the phenomenon of the process of measurement disturbing everything so that nothing can actually be seen properly as the 'panoptic paradox'. It is analogous to trying to see the mud at the bottom of a still pool of water clearly by putting a stick into it and stirring it up. Significantly, Drucker notes, 'Complicated controls do not work. They confuse. They mis-direct attention away from what is to be controlled, and towards the mechanics and methodology of control. But if the user has to know how the control works before he can apply it, he has no control at all. And if he has to ... figure out what a measurement means, he has no control either' (Drucker, *Management*, pp. 409–10).

26. The early Christian theologian Tertullian argued that the best way to stamp out heresy and thus preserve group unity was to stop people asking questions, because it is 'questions that make people heretics'! See Pagels, *The Origins of Satan*, p. 164.

27. Alvesson and Willmott, *Making Sense of Management*, p. 198; emphasis added. For an interesting, tangential, historical commentary on the creation of insiders as 'heretics' and the urge to purify the world by disposing of those who come to be seen as embodying evil and corruption see Norman Cohn, *Europe's Inner Demons*. London: Pimilico, rev. edn, 1993.

Chapter 7

1. Martyn Percy, *Words, Wonders and Power*. London: SPCK, 1996, pp. 112 and 113.

2. Carol Kennedy, *Guide to the Management Gurus*. London: Century Business, 1991, p. 48.

3. Peter Drucker, *Management: Tasks, Responsibilities, Practices*. Oxford: Butterworth Heinemann, 1974, p. 432.

4. Ibid., p. 67.

5. Ibid., p. 261.

6. Ibid., ch. 26.

7. Ibid., p. 370.

8. Ibid., p. 371.

9. Ibid., p. 303.

10. For a more value-driven but less ethically reflective approach to organizations, see, e.g., the various works of Tom Peters. For a comprehensive overview of business ethics generally, see Tom Beauchamp and Norman Bowie (eds), *Ethical Theory and Business*. Englewood Cliffs, NJ: Prentice Hall, 4th edn, 1993. For a richer, more philosophical vision of ethics and management see Robert Solomon, *Ethics and Excellence*. New York: Oxford University Press, 1993.

11. See further, e.g., Rudolph Klein, *The Politics of the NHS*. London: Longman, 2nd edn, 1989.

12. This list has been adapted from Andrew Wall, *Ethics and the Health Services Manager*. London: The King's Fund, 1989. For a more recent discussion of the difficulties of relating ethics and management in public service see Andrew Wall, 'Ethics and management – oil and water?', in Souzy Dracopoulou, *Ethics and Values in Health Care Management*. London: Routledge, forthcoming.

13. Department of Health, *Report of Corporate Governance Task Force*. London: Department of Health, 1994.

14. Institute of Health Services Management, *Statement of Primary Values*. London: Institute of Health Services Management, 1994.

15. For a description and swingeing critique of QALYs, see David Seedhouse, *Fortress NHS*. Chichester: John Wiley and Sons, 1994, pp. 86ff.

16. Hugh Flanagan and Peter Spurgeon, *Public Sector Managerial Effectiveness*. Buckingham: Open University Press, 1996, p. 67.

17. For the benefits and uses of appraisal, see ibid., ch. 6; and Valerie Stewart and Andrew Stewart, *Practical Performance Appraisal*. London: Gower, 1977, ch. 1.

18. Flanagan and Spurgeon, *Public Sector Managerial Effectiveness*, pp. 69–70.

19. Hugh Flanagan, 'On stage for a successful performance review', *Health Services Manpower Review*, March 1988, pp. 10–11.

20. Flanagan and Spurgeon, *Public Sector Managerial Effectiveness*, p. 73.

21. All the foregoing critical points are made in ibid., ch. 6.

22. Flanagan, 'On stage', p. 10.

23. Keith Grint, *Management: A Sociological Introduction*. Cambridge, Polity Press, 1995, p. 71.

24. See further, ibid., pp. 73ff., for these criticisms.

25. Ibid., p. 81.

26. Ibid., p. 72.

27. Ibid., p. 88.

28. Ibid., p. 75.

29. For panopticism, see Michel Foucault, *Discipline and Punish*. London: Penguin, 1979, pp. 195ff.

30. For more on technologies of control that have encroached ever further into the individual person in the interests of social control and governance, see, e.g., Nikolas Rose, *Governing the Soul*. London: Routledge, 1989; Arlie Russell Hochschild, *The Managed Heart*. London: University of California Press, 1983; Stephen Fineman (ed.), *Emotion in Organizations*. London: Sage, 1993.

31. Drucker, *Management*, pp. 348–9; emphasis added.

32. P. D. Anthony, *The Ideology of Work*. London: Tavistock Books, 1977, p. 258.

33. For more on the 'inner' self as a key locus of control see, e.g., Anthony Giddens, *Modernity and Self-Identity*. Cambridge: Polity Press, 1991; Christopher Lasch, *The Culture of Narcissism*. New York: W. W. Norton, 1991. Robert Jackall, *Moral Mazes*, New York: Oxford University Press, 1988, provides a sobering portrait of conformity and obedience as the primary individual and corporate 'virtues' in US big business.

34. Mike Hepworth and Bryan Turner, *Confession*. London: Routledge and Kegan Paul, 1982, p. 23.

35. Tom Douglas, *Scapegoats*. London: Routledge, 1995, p. 19.

36. For instructive material on how individuals 'hide' themselves and 'live between the lines' in panoptic organizations and total institutions, cf. Erving Goffman, *Ayslums*. Harmondsworth: Penguin, 1969.

37. For alternatives to top-down appraisal, e.g., consultancy, peer review, see, e.g., Michael Jacobs, *Holding in Trust*. London: SPCK, 1989.

38. See further, Clive Ponting, *Secrecy in Britain*. Oxford: Basil Blackwell, 1990; Sissela Bok, *Secrets*. Oxford: Oxford University Press, 1986; Sissela Bok, *Lying*. London: Quartet Books, 1980.

39. For an intriguing discussion of the perils and pitfalls of trying to integrate commercial and political values, see Jane Jacobs, *Systems of Survival*. London: Hodder and Stoughton, 1992.

40. For early whistleblowers in the public sector, see Virginia Beardshaw, *Conscientious Objectors at Work*. London: Social Audit, 1991.

41. Geoffrey Hunt (ed.), *Whistleblowing in the Health Service*. London: Edward Arnold, 1995, p. xv.

42. Anon., 'Dangerous deceptions', *Health Service Journal*, 23 July 1992, p. 19.

43. Hunt, *Whistleblowing*, p. xv.

44. Ibid.

45. 'Managers want employees to develop and employ initiative. But managers also want employee initiative and discretion to be exercised in managerially acceptable and disciplined ways.' (Mats Alvesson and Hugh Willmott, *Making Sense of Management*. London: Sage, 1996, p. 29.)

46. For more on the 'learning organization', see, e.g., Chris Agyris and Donald Schön, *Organizational Learning II*. Reading, MA.: Addison-Wesley, 1996.

47. For a psychological account of why people need to think of themselves and their organizations as good, see, e.g., C. R. Snyder, Raymond Higgins and Rita Stucky, *Excuses*. New York: John Wiley and Sons, 1983.

48. Drucker, *Management*, p. 382.

Chapter 8

1. Martyn Percy, *Words, Signs and Wonders*. London: SPCK, 1996, pp. 34 and 146.

2. Maybe the ambivalence about change within the Christian tradition can be accounted for by the notion of control. Change is perhaps acceptable if one is either in control or is likely to be the beneficiary of it. Knowing what is going to happen and being close to the ultimate source of change is, of course, actually very reassuring and comforting. The sectarian vision of change is of change to end all change which thus brings about absolute security and certainty. For more on fascination with the future and millennial hopes, see, e.g., Norman Cohn, *The Pursuit of the Millennium*. London: Paladin, 1970; Malcolm Bull (ed.), *Apocalypse Theory and the Ends of the World*. Oxford: Blackwell, 1995.

3. See Richard Beckhard and Reuben Harris, *Organizational Transitions*. Reading, MA: Addison-Wesley, 2nd edn, 1987, pp. 2–3.

4. Tom Peters, *Thriving on Chaos*. London: Pan Books, 1989, p. 4. See David Harvey, *The Condition of Postmodernity*. Oxford: Blackwell, 1989, for a good discussion of the increasing speed of life and change in the contemporary world.

5. Rosabeth Moss Kanter, *The Change Masters*. London: Unwin Hyman, 1985.

6. See, e.g., Beckhard and Harris, *Organizational Transitions*; Andrew Leigh, *Effective Change*. London: Institute of Personnel Management, 1988; Roger Plant, *Managing Change and Making It Stick*. London: Fontana, 1987; Cynthia Scott and Dennis Jaffe, *Managing Organizational Change*. London: Kogan Page, 1990. A good selection of papers on all aspects of organizational change is to be found in Christopher Mabey and Bill Mayon-White (eds), *Managing Change*. London: Paul Chapman Publishing, 2nd edn, 1993.

7. There is a good discussion of the nascent and emergent typology of different kinds of change in Ewan Ferlie *et al.*, *The New Public Management in Action*. Oxford: Oxford University Press, 1996, ch. 4, which demonstrates the kind of definitional confusion surrounding this topic.

8. C. R. Hinings and Royston Greenwood, *The Dynamics of Strategic Change*. Oxford: Blackwell, 1988.

9. See, however, e.g., Hinings and Greenwood, *Dynamics*; Andrew Pettigrew, *The Awakening Giant*. Oxford: Blackwell 1985; Andrew Pettigrew (ed.), *The Management of Strategic Change*. Oxford: Blackwell, 1988; Andrew Pettigrew, Ewan Ferlie and Lorna McKee, *Shaping Strategic Change*. London: Sage, 1992.

10. Max Dublin, *Futurehype: the Tyranny of Prophecy*. Markham: Viking, 1989.

11. Ferlie *et al.*, *The New Public Management*, p. 52.

12. Kanter, *The Change Masters*, 1985. Kanter develops these principles further in *When Giants Learn to Dance*. London: Hyman Unwin, 1990. This kind of inclusive, positive, motivation-based, gradualist approach to change management is challenged by Ferlie *et al.* who argue (reluctantly?) that in the case of the reforms in British public service over the last few years, powerful top-down political will and the imposition of multiple radical reforms all at the same time has actually been very effective in producing fundamental transformation. See Ferlie *et al*, *The New Public Management*, chs 1–4. Perhaps this diagnosis is more intelligible in the light of economic recession which reduces employee resistance to change: 'the "new working practices" that are

becoming more common in the West, and the spread of corporate cultures that go with them are premised upon the "dull economic compulsion" of mass unemployment or the threat of it' (Keith Grint, *Management: A Sociological Introduction*. Cambridge: Polity Press, 1995, p. 178).

13. See Christopher Pollitt, *Managerialism in the Public Sector*. Oxford: Blackwell, 2nd edn, 1995; Stewart Ranson and John Stewart, *Management for the Public Domain Enabling the Learning Society*. Basingstoke: Macmillan, 1994.

14. See, e.g., Robert Lee and Peter Lawrence, *Organizational Behaviour: Politics at Work*. London: Hutchinson, 1985.

15. Peter Marris, *Loss and Change*. London: Routledge and Kegan Paul, rev. edn, 1986.

16. Robert de Board, *The Psychoanalysis of Organisations*. London: Tavistock, 1978, p. 143.

17. Peter Marris, *The Politics of Uncertainty*. London: Routledge, 1996, p. 1.

18. John Harvey-Jones, *Making It Happen*. Glasgow: Fontana, 1989, p. 141.

19. Kanter, *When Giants Learn to Dance*, esp. ch. 3.

20. Managers who are really interested in effective ways of implementing autocratic, radical, top-down change could learn much from Niccolo Machiavelli, *The Prince*. London: Oxford University Press, 1935.

21. See Marris, *Loss and Change*.

22. In an appraisal training session I found myself formulating the following epigram: 'Stability is a universal aspiration, an individual virtue, an ecological necessity – and an organizational sin.'

Chapter 9

1. Martyn Percy, *Words, Wonders and Signs*. London: SPCK, 1996, p. 135.

2. For more on charismatic figures, charisma and prophecy, see, e.g., Robin Gill, *Prophecy and Practice*. London: Marshall Morgan and Scott, 1981; Charles Lindblom, *Charisma*. Oxford: Blackwell, 1990.

3. Andrzej Huczynksi, *Management Gurus*. London: International Thomson Business Press, 1996, p. 42. Huczynski has his own threefold typology of 'gurudom': academic gurus, consultant gurus and hero-managers. See ibid., pp. 40ff.

4. See ibid. Disappointingly, Huczynski is only superficially interested in the religious characteristics of the gurus.

5. This kind of resume can be found in Carol Kennedy, *Guide to the Management Gurus*. London: Century Business, 1991.

6. Percy, *Words, Wonders and Signs*, p. 53; emphasis in original.

7. Ibid., p. 54.

8. Martin Spencer, quoted in ibid.

9. Ibid., p. 57.

10. Ibid.

11. See ibid., pp. 57–9.

12. Max Weber, *The Sociology of Religion*. Boston: Beacon Press, 1964, p. 46.

13. Ibid., pp. 58–9.

14. Ibid., p. 59.

15. Ibid., p. 60.

16. Compare, e.g., Isaiah 37.31–32, RSV: 'And the surviving remnant of the house of Judah shall again take root downward, and bear fruit upward; for out of Jerusalem shall go forth a remnant, and of Mount Sion a band of survivors.'

17. Tom Peters, *Thriving on Chaos*. London: Pan Books, 1989.

18. See ibid., pp. 3, 7 and 9; emphasis in orginal.

19. Weber, *Sociology*, p. 59.

20. For more on shamanism, see, e.g., I. M. Lewis, *Ecstatic Religion*. Harmondsworth: Penguin, 1971

21. Peters, *Thriving*, pp. 387ff.

22. Ibid., p. 465.

23. Referring to the mission of Paul and Silas, themselves inspired evangelists in the early Church, some of their opponents go to the rulers of the city of Thessalonika 'crying, These that have turned *the world upside down* are come hither also' (Acts 17.6, AV; emphasis mine). For more on the significance of chaos in religion see Peter Berger, *The Social Reality of Religion*. Harmondsworth: Penguin, 1973: 'The sacred cosmos emerges out of chaos and continues to confront the latter as its terrible contrary' (p. 36).

24. Peters, *Thriving*, p. 149.

25. In the Old Testament, prophets constantly point out that the ills of Israel have been brought about by the misdoings of the ruling classes who are now going to be punished by foreign invaders as the prophets foretell. Now they must face an imminent day of judgement. See, e.g., Amos 5.18.

26. Peters, *Thriving*, pp. 145ff; my emphasis.

27. This information is put together from the author's note in Charles Handy, *Waiting for the Mountain to Move*. London: Arrow Books, 1995, and from Charles Handy, *The Age of Unreason*. London: Business Books, 1989, p. vii.

28. Charles Handy, *Gods of Management*. London: Arrow Books, 1995.

29. Handy, *Waiting*, p. 1.

30. Some of Handy's 'Thoughts' are collected in Handy, *Waiting*.

31. Charles Handy, *The Empty Raincoat*. London: Arrow Books, 1995. Handy's most recent book is *Beyond Certainty*. London: Arrow Books, 1996. This mainly recapitulates points and arguments made in *The Age of Unreason* and *The Empty Raincoat*.

32. Handy, *Empty Raincoat*, p. 270.

33. Handy, *Waiting for the Mountain to Move*, p. 57.

34. Handy, *Empty Raincoat*, pp. 1–2. Other metaphors with which Handy plays creatively include the 'doughnut organization', the 'shamrock organization' and the 'triple "I" organization'. See Handy, *Age of Uncertainty*; *Empty Raincoat*. These metaphors are just complex enough to be a little obscure and require some work on the part of the reader, but simple and intriguing enough to engage that reader's interest, essential aspects of successful guru communication.

35. Handy, *Empty Raincoat*, pp. 3–4.

36. Ibid., p. 264.

37. For more on Egan's work and background, see Adrian Coles, 'From priesthood to management consultancy', *Counselling*, vol. 7(3), 1996, pp. 194–7.

38. Gerard Egan, *Adding Value: A Systematic Guide to Business-Driven Management and Leadership*. San Francisco: Jossey-Bass Inc. 1993, p. 13.
39. Ibid., pp. 42 and 3–4.
40. Ibid., p. 91.

Conclusion

1. Steve Bruce, *Religion in the Modern World*. Oxford: Oxford University Press, 1996, ch. 8.

Coda

1. John Drury, 'The Archbishop's hat', in Doctrine Commission of the Church of England, *Believing in the Church*. London: SPCK, 1981, p. 192.
2. Paul Handley, 'Holder of the ring', *Church Times*, 8 December 1995, p. 11.
3. Drury, 'The Archbishop's hat', pp. 199ff.
4. Before 1990 the only two substantial books that had been written about Church management in a British context were Peter Rudge, *Ministry and Management*. London: Tavistock, 1968; and *Management in the Church*. London: McGraw-Hill, 1976.
5. For evidence of this growing sectarian outlook consider policies of restrictive baptism that mean that only the children of active Christians are allowed to be baptised in a parish church.
6. John Nelson (ed.), *Management and Ministry*. Norwich: The Canterbury Press, 1996, p. 226.
7. See, e.g., ibid.; Robin Gill and Derek Burke, *Strategic Church Leadership*. London: SPCK, 1996.
8. Archbishops' Commission on the Organisation of the Church of England, *Working as One Body*. London: Church House, 1995, p. 1.
9. Church of England Board of Mission, *The Search for Faith and the Witness of the Church*. London: Church House, 1996.
10. For the roots of religion, see Peter Hodgson, *Winds of the Spirit: A Constructive Christian Theology*. London: SCM Press, 1994, ch. 1. For non-rationality in secular organizations, see, e.g., Stephen Fineman (ed.), *Emotion in Organizations*. London: Sage, 1983; Stephen Linstead *et al.* (eds), *Understanding Management*. London: Sage, 1996; Nils Brunsson, 'The irrationality of action and action irrationality', *Journal of Management Studies*, vol. 19(1), 1982, pp. 29–44.
11. For cautionary material on this note in the context of a non-profit organization, see the sad tale of how the uncritical introduction of managerial assumptions and techniques into a therapeutic, professional-led culture in RELATE caused considerable alienation and disruption that is still unresolved. See, e.g., Jane Lewis, David Clark and David Morgan, *Whom God Hath Joined Together*. London: Routledge, 1992, esp. ch. 5; Jane Lewis, 'Management consultants and voluntary organisations', *Non Profit Studies*, vol. 1(1), 1996, pp. 18–26.
12. Mats Alvesson and Hugh Willmott, *Making Sense of Management*. London: Sage, 1996, p. 145.
13. Don Browning, *A Fundamental Practical Theology*. Minneapolis: Fortress Press, 1991, p. 6; emphasis in original.

14. For some suggestions for theological critique, see Stephen Pattison, 'Should pastoral care have aims and objectives?', *Contact*, vol. 120, 1996, pp. 24–34.

15. Nelson (ed.), *Management*, p. 226.

16. This cautionary comparison between counselling and management has been made in Bryan Pettifer, 'Human resource management', in Nelson (ed.), *Management*, p. 190.

17. Laurence Moore, *Selling God: American Religion in the Market-place of Culture*. New York: Oxford University Press, 1994, p. 220.

18. Ibid., p. 276.

19. There is some critical material on management and managerialism in Nelson (ed.), *Management*; Richard Higginson, *Transforming Leadership*. London: SPCK, 1996; Gill and Burke, *Strategic Church Leadership*. However, in all these books the level of critique is very basic and they are overwhelmingly positive about the usefulness and appropriateness of managerial ideas within the religious context. As has happened in the past, practices are first being introduced on the basis of perceived necessity and uncritical enthusiasm and only subsequently criticized and evaluated. Gill and Burke commend the kind of strategic thinking techniques used to reshape universities as suitable for use in the Churches. Can British universities really be seen to count as positive evidence for the usefulness and beneficence of managerial ideas? I doubt if there are many people working at grass roots level who would say their experience of being managed in higher education has been an overwhelmingly positive one. Perhaps there is scope for managers to learn from the Christian community about respect, mutual accountability, inclusiveness and the imperfect results of human endeavour that might be usefully supplemented by some attempt to enact a doctrine of corporate forgiveness.

Index